HISTORIC MAGNOLIA HOUSE

VOLUME ONE

CELEBRITY & THE IRONIES OF FAME

THE FIRST IN A SERIES OF MEMOIRS ABOUT
TRAVEL GUIDES, TABLOID *EXPOSÉS*, & THE
LANDMARK WHERE THEY WERE PRODUCED

DARWIN PORTER & DANFORTH PRINCE

The interior of Magnolia House has been used by at least eight filmmakers as the photogenic locale for their screen adventures and fashion layouts.

PREVIOUS WORKS BY DARWIN PORTER
PRODUCED IN COLLABORATION WITH BLOOD MOON

BIOGRAPHIES

Playboy's Hugh Hefner
Empire of Skin

Carrie Fisher & Debbie Reynolds
Princess Leia & Unsinkable Tammy in Hell

Rock Hudson Erotic Fire

Lana Turner, Hearts & Diamonds Take All

Donald Trump, The Man Who Would Be King

James Dean, Tomorrow Never Comes

Bill and Hillary, So This Is That Thing Called Love

Peter O'Toole, Hellraiser, Sexual Outlaw, Irish Rebel

Love Triangle, Ronald Reagan, Jane Wyman, & Nancy Davis

Jacqueline Kennedy Onassis, A Life Beyond Her Wildest Dreams

Pink Triangle, The Feuds and Private Lives of Tennessee Williams, Gore Vidal, Truman Capote, and Famous Members of their Entourages.

Those Glamorous Gabors, Bombshells from Budapest

Inside Linda Lovelace's Deep Throat, Degradation, Porno Chic, and the Rise of Feminism

Elizabeth Taylor, There is Nothing Like a Dame

Marilyn at Rainbow's End, Sex, Lies, Murder, and the Great Cover-up

J. Edgar Hoover and Clyde Tolson
Investigating the Sexual Secrets of America's Most Famous Men and Women

Frank Sinatra, The Boudoir Singer. All the Gossip Unfit to Print

The Kennedys, All the Gossip Unfit to Print

Humphrey Bogart, The Making of a Legend (2010), *and*
The Secret Life of Humphrey Bogart (2003)

Howard Hughes, Hell's Angel

Steve McQueen, King of Cool, Tales of a Lurid Life

Paul Newman, The Man Behind the Baby Blues

Merv Griffin, A Life in the Closet

Brando Unzipped

Katharine the Great, Hepburn, Secrets of a Lifetime Revealed

Jacko, His Rise and Fall, The Social and Sexual History of Michael Jackson

Damn You, Scarlett O'Hara, The Private Lives of Vivien Leigh and Laurence Olivier (co-authored with Roy Moseley)

FILM CRITICISM
Blood Moon's 2005 Guide to the Glitter Awards
Blood Moon's 2006 Guide to Film
Blood Moon's 2007 Guide to Film, and
50 Years of Queer Cinema, 500 of the Best GLBTQ Films Ever Made

NON-FICTION
Hollywood Babylon, It's Back! and Hollywood Babylon Strikes Again!

NOVELS
Blood Moon,
Hollywood's Silent Closet,
Rhinestone Country,
Razzle Dazzle
Midnight in Savannah

OTHER PUBLICATIONS BY DARWIN PORTER
NOT DIRECTLY ASSOCIATED WITH BLOOD MOON

NOVELS

The Delinquent Heart
The Taste of Steak Tartare
Butterflies in Heat
Marika (a roman à clef based on the life of Marlene Dietrich)
Venus (a roman à clef based on the life of Anaïs Nin)
Bitter Orange
Sister Rose

TRAVEL GUIDES

Many Editions and Many Variations of *The Frommer Guides*, *The American Express Guides*, *and/or TWA Guides, et alia* to:

Andalusia, Andorra, Anguilla, Aruba, Atlanta, Austria, the Azores, The Bahamas, Barbados, the Bavarian Alps, Berlin, Bermuda, Bonaire and Curaçao, Boston, the British Virgin Islands, Budapest, Bulgaria, California, the Canary Islands, the Caribbean and its "Ports of Call," the Cayman Islands, Ceuta, the Channel Islands (UK), Charleston (SC), Corsica, Costa del Sol (Spain), Denmark, Dominica, the Dominican Republic, Edinburgh, England, Estonia, Europe, "Europe by Rail," the Faroe Islands, Finland, Florence, France, Frankfurt, the French Riviera, Geneva, Georgia (USA), Germany, Gibraltar, Glasgow, Granada (Spain), Great Britain, Greenland, Grenada (West Indies), Haiti, Hungary, Iceland, Ireland, Isle of Man, Italy, Jamaica, Key West & the Florida Keys, Las Vegas, Liechtenstein, Lisbon, London, Los Angeles, Madrid, Maine, Malta, Martinique & Guadeloupe, Massachusetts, Melilla, Morocco, Munich, New England, New Orleans, North Carolina, Norway, Paris, Poland, Portugal, Provence, Puerto Rico, Romania, Rome, Salzburg, San Diego, San Francisco, San Marino, Sardinia, Savannah, Scandinavia, Scotland, Seville, the Shetland Islands, Sicily, St. Martin & Sint Maarten, St. Vincent & the Grenadines, South Carolina, Spain, St. Kitts & Nevis, Sweden, Switzerland, the Turks & Caicos, the U.S.A., the U.S. Virgin Islands, Venice, Vienna and the Danube, Wales, and Zurich.

Biographies

From Diaghilev to Balanchine, The Saga of Ballerina Tamara Geva

Lucille Lortel, The Queen of Off-Broadway

Greta Keller, Germany's Other Lili Marlene

Sophie Tucker, The Last of the Red Hot Mamas

Anne Bancroft, Where Have You Gone, Mrs. Robinson?
(co-authored with Stanley Mills Haggart)

Veronica Lake, The Peek-a-Boo Girl

Running Wild in Babylon, Confessions of a Hollywood Press Agent

Histories

Thurlow Weed, Whig Kingpin

Chester A. Arthur, Gilded Age Coxcomb in the White House

Discover Old America, What's Left of It

Cuisine

Food For Love, Hussar Recipes from the Austro-Hungarian Empire, with collaboration from the cabaret chanteuse, Greta Keller

And Coming Next From Blood Moon
Kirk Douglas: More Is Never Enough

WE EXTEND SPECIAL THANKS TO BILL NALWASKY

and dedicate this memoir of a grand old house to anyone who ever stumbled, fell, failed, or died during the pursuit of his or her hopes and dreams.

REST IN PEACE

THE SPIRIT OF MAGNOLIA HOUSE

IF SHE WERE HUMAN, WHAT WOULD SHE LOOK LIKE?

According to some of the many psychics who have articulated the "presences" they encountered at Magnolia House, the "essence" of the place takes many forms. Most agree that it's a feminine presence, and two of them sensed that she was deeply affected by the publication, on site, in October of 2018, of Blood Moon's biography of **Playboy's Hugh Hefner, Empire of Skin,** and that if she ever manifested herself physically, she'd look something like this.

So, enquiring minds REALLY want to know: **The Spirit of Magnolia House…Is she really a bunny?**

CONTENTS

PART ONE
THE ORIGINS AND EARLY INTRIGUES OF MAGNOLIA HOUSE

PROLOGUE — PAGE 1

CHAPTER ONE — PAGE 3
GROWTH OF ST. GEORGE & STYLISH NEW BRIGHTON, FASHIONABLE CELEBRITIES, A CONSTRUCTION BOOM, HOWARD BAYNE ("MR STATEN ISLAND,") CIVIC BOOSTERISM, SILENT FILMS, & NEW KINDS OF CELEBRITIES INVADE MAGNOLIA HOUSE..

CHAPTER TWO — PAGE 27
THE MAGNOLIA-AND-BLOOD-SCENTED SAGA OF JULIA GARDINER TYLER, FIRST LADY OF THE UNITED STATES.

PART TWO
HOW TRAVEL WRITING FOR THE FROMMER GUIDES AT MAGNOLIA HOUSE MORPHED INTO A SERIES OF CELEBRITY-CHASING ADVENTURES

CHAPTER THREE — PAGE 39
INTRODUCTION TO PART TWO
As Europe struggles to regain its economic footing after the ravages of World War II, prices are cheap and enthusiasm is high among Americans eager to "discover" the cultural wealth of "the old world." Arthur Frommer and his associates, one of whom is Darwin Porter, help to reconfigure its touristic landscapes and travel patterns. Magnolia House plays an essential role as "Europe on $$ a Day" evolves into a travel empire.

CHAPTER FOUR — PAGE 49
ROYAL INTRIGUE ON THE PORTUGUESE RIVIERA.
How Darwin, a former Bureau Chief for *The Miami Herald,* on assignment for the Frommer Guides, recognized it as a gossip-infested beehive of royal intrigue, the site to which crowned heads fled after they'd lost their thrones. His encounters with the pretenders to the thrones of France, Spain, and Italy.

CHAPTER FIVE   **PAGE 59**
　IT'S THE 60S AND LONDON IS SWINGING, CARNABY STREET IS HOT, AND DARWIN IS ON SITE FOR *FROMMER'S ENGLAND*. UNEXPECTEDLY, IN EARLS COURT, OVER TEA, HE DEVELOPS A FRIENDSHIP WITH **MARGARET RUTHERFORD**.
　OF COURSE the English have always been eccentric. No other British actress celebrated it as self-satirically as Margaret Rutherford, the (deliberately) dowdy actress who played Miss Marple. Here's what England's then-most-beloved actress was really like.

CHAPTER SIX   **PAGE 63**
　THE IDLE RICH, THE LITERARY COUNTER-CULTURE, AND WHAT'S LEFT OF THE BEAT GENERATION ARE FLOCKING TO **MOROCCO!** IN MARRAKECH, ON ASSIGNMENT FOR THE FROMMER GUIDES, MAGNOLIA HOUSE DEVELOPS AN INFERIORITY COMPLEX AFTER ITS EMISSARIES, PORTER AND PRINCE, SPEND A WEEK AT THE VERY POSH AND HISTORICALLY SPECTACULAR **VILLA TAYLOR**.
　Name any newsworthy celebrity from Europe's *Haute Monde* in the 70s who wasn't aware of what was happening in Marrakech? Check out what happened when Magnolia House got Magical with *"Mme la Comtesse"* Boul de Breteuil at the most secretive hotel in Africa.

CHAPTER SEVEN   **PAGE 69**
　MEETING THE 20TH CENTURY'S MOST FAMOUS INCARNATION OF A VIKING. THE ASSIGNMENT WAS **NORWAY**. DARWIN WAS RESEARCHING SCANDINAVIA FOR THE FIRST EDITION OF A FROMMER GUIDE.
　Drinks and dialogue soon ensued with THOR HEYERDAHL, developer and pilot of the KON-TIKI, the balsa wood raft that disproved the theories of generations of ethnographers who had previously denied that Polynesia could ever have been populated by "drifters" from Peru. An argument ensued. Read about it here.

CHAPTER EIGHT   **PAGE 73**
　WHO WAS **REALLY** HANGING OUT BACK THEN IN MAJORCA? THE ASSIGNMENT WAS THE BALEARIC ISLANDS, A VITAL SUB-SECTION OF *FROMMER'S SPAIN*. EN ROUTE THERE FROM MADRID, DARWIN MET A MOVIE STAR, TOOK HIM UNDER HIS WING, AND ENDED UP AT DINNER WITH "THE FIRST LADY OF TELEVISION"; ZSA ZSA GABOR'S EX-HUSBAND; A FRENCH MATINEE IDOL; AND THE OSCAR-NOMINATED ACTOR WHO PORTRAYED THE CORRUP GOVERNOR OF LOUISIANA, HUEY LONG.
　Hint?: Faye Emerson, George Sanders, Charles Boyer, & Broderick Crawford

CHAPTER NINE   **PAGE 79**
　TEMPERATURES ARE STIFLING, *THE FROMMER GUIDES* ARE IN SEVILLE, AND DARWIN IS DOCUMENTING HOTELS, RESTAURANTS, AND *LAWRENCE OF ARABIA'S* AFFAIR WITH THE DUCHESS OF ALBA.
　How everything Darwin learned about Peter O'Toole and his romantic association with the most-titled woman in Europe (*Cayetana Fitz-James Stuart*) eventually appeared in one of his award-winning show-biz biographies, published in 2015.

Chapter Ten   Page 83
"Ich bin ein Berliner!" Why the crowds went wild when the U.S. President said it that afternoon in Berlin.
Darwin was on site that day, wrapping up field work for *Frommer's Germany* and recalls the raw, searing emotions.

Chapter Eleven   Page 87
Frommer's Italy. Darwin is in Portofino. So are Elizabeth Taylor, Richard Burton, and Rex Harrison. Here's the lowdown on what really happened when the stars of Cleopatra got gossipy for four or five drunken hours as Darwin listened in.
Till then, it was one of the most expensive movies ever made, with marital politics that were the #1 most-watched in the world. Cleopatra, the regal queen herself, would have been either horrified or amused. Decide for yourself.

Chapter Twelve   Page 95
Sweden gave the world two of the greatest Female Stars in the history of cinema, Greta Garbo and Ingrid Bergman.
When Darwin heard that Miss Bergman was "hiding out" at a vacation retreat near Stockholm, he asked Sweden's director of tourism to arrange a private rendezvous with the luminous movie icon. Here's what happened over lunch with the enigmatic superstar of the classic film, *Casablanca*.

Chapter Thirteen   Page 105
Chasing Iguanas and Sex: On location in Mexico with Tennessee Williams during the filming of *The Night of the Iguana*.
Darwin had been on friendly terms with Tennessee Williams since his days as Bureau Chief of the Key West branch of *The Miami Herald*. The shocking secrets he learned during tequila-soaked nights in Puerto Vallarta later got incorporated into Blood Moon's triple biography of the three most important show-biz writers of the 20th Century.

Chapter Fourteen   Page 117
When Divas Clash: Jackie-Oh Vs. Grace Kelly, Her Serene Highness, the Princess of Monaco.
Darwin, multi-tasking as a Frommer researcher and Celebrity Journalist, describes the origins of a feud that became obvious to everyone during dinner with the Duke of Medinaceli after a horse show in Seville. Read about it here.

Chapter Fifteen   Page 125
CALIGULA. It was conceived and (disastrously) financed by Bob Guccione (publisher of *Penthouse*) and hailed as the most decadent movie ever made. Darwin was in Rome during and after its filming. What he learned was later reconfigured into two of his biographies. Read about it here.

CHAPTER SIXTEEN   PAGE 141
BETRAYAL AND DEATH OF A PRINCESS: REPORTS FROM LONDON, PARIS, & MARBELLA
The world went numb after the grisly death of Princess Diana. Darwin reviews how one of her lovers (James Hewitt) profited from her humiliation. It's a sad tale of deceit and despair, but it's all part of a day's work at Magnolia House.

CHAPTER SEVENTEEN   PAGE 149
HOW THE WICKEDEST CITY ON EARTH (TANGIER) BECAME THE DARLING OF THE IDLE BOHEMIAN RICH:
It attracted celebrities of all persuasions and all degrees of depravity. From the exposure gleaned by the team from Magnolia House emerged information later included in books sired by both The Frommer Guides and Blood Moon Productions. Read about it here.

EPILOGUE: MEDIA BUZZ   PAGE 177
RIPPED FROM DARWIN'S DIARIES ARE TALES OF HIS DAYS AS A REPORTER: ENCOUNTERS WITH ELEANOR ROOSEVELT ON MIAMI BEACH; WITH HARRY S TRUMAN AND TENNESSEE WILLIAMS IN KEY WEST; AND WITH JFK THROUGH THE SENATOR'S CLOSE FRIEND, FLORIDA SENATOR GEORGE SMATHERS. THERE ARE EARLY ENCOUNTERS WITH ELVIS, AND WITH JUDY (GARLAND) SINGING "OVER THE RAINBOW."
Did You Know? That Darwin spent part of his childhood with Sophie Tucker, "The Last of the Red-Hot Mammas," and that his attractive (widowed) mother dated movie stars who included Frank Sinatra and Victor Mature?

POSTSCRIPTS FROM THE EDGE: PAGE 189
MEET ONE OF FLORIDA'S LEADING GERONTOLOGISTS, ANITA FINLEY, PUBLISHER OF *BOOMER TIMES & SENIOR LIFE*, A PUBLICATION DISTRIBUTED BY *THE MIAMI HERALD*.
News items that she and Darwin revealed in her magazine and on her radio show have generated headlines in bigger news outlets nationwide.

SCRIBES, SCRIVENERS, & MESSENGERS (AUTHORS' BIOS)   PAGE 205

Magnolia House is a proud, architecturally protected landmark within the St. George, Staten Island, Historical District. It's depicted here in a photo snapped by NYC's Department of Finance as part of its 1940 Real Estate Tax Census.

PROLOGUE

WELCOME TO MAGNOLIA HOUSE

A Historic Home with a Knack for Celebrity & an Appreciation for the Ironies of Fame

This book was conceived as a memoir and celebration of Magnolia House, a historic home long associated with show biz, politics, art, the travel industry, celebrity publishing, and the book trades.

Begun in 1830, it has been deeply connected to the emergence of New York City as a creative player on every level of the world stage. Its owners have maneuvered it through historic cycles that included America's Civil War, the growth of the Silent Film Industry, and the emergence of travel and world tourism as reflections of "the Good Life."

Partly because of its association with a controversial independent publishing venue (Blood Moon Productions) it has also hosted many notorious, infamous, or "merely famous" guests, many of whom became household names. Their links to Magnolia House are documented in this book.

Though departed, they've left their mark and aura. Perhaps they continue to rage, to mourn, and to love here, operating on a timeline that's different (and invisible) from the one we're used to.

I now present to you, MAGNOLIA HOUSE, a cultural landmark with a controversial past.

With best wishes to all of you, and with thanks for your interest, let the magic begin.

Danforth Prince
Innkeeper & Director of Development at Magnolia House,
& President/Founder of Blood Moon Productions,

Magnolia House is fully operational as the site of a two-hour "Pop Culture and Conversational Experience" which AirBnb is marketing as

"CELEBRITY & THE IRONIES OF FAME"

www.AirBnb.com

Chapter One

MAGNOLIA MUSCLE

Social Ambitions, The Civil War, & Frantic Campaigns to Steer Staten Island's Progress by the Building's 19th-Century Owners

75 ST. MARKS PLACE: ITS EARLY DAYS

Magnolia House lies on the north shore of Staten Island, at the point nearest to Manhattan, and across the deepwater channel from Bayonne, New Jersey. Some people refer to the location of St. George, the neighborhood that contains it, as "the crossroads of the world" since ships from most nations pass along the channel it overlooks. Named by the original Dutch settler as the Kill van Kull, it connects the Atlantic Ocean through the Verrazano Narrows to key Ports within New York and New Jersey.

The famous Staten Island ferries depart from a terminal a few blocks from Magnolia House. They pass close beside the Statue of Liberty before arriving, 26 minutes later, near Wall Street at the lower tip of Manhattan.

***

In the 1700s, a stream (it flowed along the course of nearby Jersey Street) was known for its soft, pure water, an essential ingredient in the rum produced by the distillery it fed.

In 1748, a local entrepreneur named Salmon Comes inaugurated a ferryboat service to Manhattan from the base of St. Peter's Place, a two-minute downhill walk from the present-day site of Magnolia House. And in 1835, Thomas Davis, a wealthy Manhattan real estate developer, poured investment funds into the streets and retaining walls of the panoramic neighborhood and marketed it as a fashionable residential community whose name (New Brighton) was inspired by the English resort favored by Britain's Prince Regent.

Magnolia House's 19th Century character originated in the the 1830s. Between 1840 and 1860, the island's population doubled as just-arrived immigrants arrived to work at the newly established factories.

By the 1840s, the subdivision of St. George had become a fashionable summer resort, drawing the elite of Manhattan, including such notorious figures as former Vice President Aaron Burr, who died nearby, humiliated and in obscurity, at the age of 90 in 1834. Around that time, St. George, as a summer resort, was visited by some of the America's most prominent writers, politicians, business tycoons, stage actors, and socialites.

Unlike most American cities, St. George prospered during the Civil War, primarily because of shipping from New York Harbor to points along the Eastern Seaboard and Europe. Many elegant homes were built around here then, mostly in the Queen Anne style with aspects of colonial revival.

It was Saint George, the mythical hero noted for slaying his dragon, who "donated" his name and perhaps his symbolism to the emerging neighborhood that contained Magnolia House.

St. George as a genteel summer resort. Depicted above is a garden scene by Alice Austen, from the late 1880s. Austen, a photographer who snapped more than 8,000 photos during a career that spanned many decades on Staten Island, captured both the social pretentions and unguarded moments of the haute bourgeoisie and the working classes with the eye of a sociologist and the aesthetic sensibilities of an avant-garde feminist.

The end of the war brought a decline in the price of building supplies, encouraging even more growth in a neighborhood quickly providing housing for year-round, rather than summer-only, residents.

Cornelius ("The Commodore") Vanderbilt, for a while the single richest man in America, was one of the most fabled robber barons of America's Gilded Age, having amassed one of the world's largest fortunes through his railways, steamboats, and ferryboat lines, some of which serviced the growing volume of maritime traffice into Staten Island. [One of Vanderbilt's most memorable quotes?: "You have undertaken to cheat me. I won't sue you, for the law is too slow. I'll ruin you."] The Commodore, whose family origins lay deep in colonial Staten Island, later donated his historic ferry service to the public, thereby opening access in and out of Staten Island to the world, and assuring that it would never charge passengers a fare.

Staten Island, circa 1888, children, perhaps from affluent families of St Marks Place, being exposed to the social graces. Photograph by Alice Austen.

[The Vanderbilt family mausoleum, an elaborate replica of a Romanesque Church in Arles, France, and built as a testimony to that family's influence over many aspects of the development of St. George and New Brighton, is a fascinating destination within Staten Island's Moravian Cemetery.]

In 1863, midway through the Civil War, 75 Saint Marks Place was purchased by Augustus Prentice, the richest, best-known attorney in Staten Island.

Prentice was born in 1826 in Connecti-

The Vanderbilt family mausoleum in 1882

cut, his parents having emigrated from England in 1792. Other members of the Prentice family also helped settle New England, though many of their homes were destroyed by British cannonballs during the Revolutionary War.

During an early part of his life, Augustus moved to Florida, still an underdeveloped outback. But after his marriage to socially prominent Catherine Browning, the couple moved to Staten Island, where Prentice became one of its leading citizens, practicing law. Eventually, Augustus called for a meeting of local dignitaries at the now defunct St. Marks Hotel. They issued a charter, and by 1866, about a year after the Civil War, Staten Island had its first formalized municipal government.

Super lawyer Augustus Prentice was photographed at around the time he was enlarging and embellishing Magnolia House as a showcase of his personal wealth.

Established in this house, Prentice became one of the richest and most successful businessmen on Staten Island, investing in banks and railroads and buying up real estate here and in Manhattan. In later years, he'd be compared to another real estate developer, Fred Trump, the father of the present president who was responsible for his son's money and his family's financial success.

It was under Prentice's ownership of this house that one of the least known events in American presi-

Perhaps the most imposing mansion in St. George at the time was the lavishly ornamental home of Anson Phelps Stokes, sited at the time of its construction in the 1870s directly across St. Marks Place from what is now Magnolia House.

Stokes (1838-1913) was a Gilded-Age multimillionaire. The majestic home, which raised the fame, fortune, and celebrity quotient of St. Marks Place to spectacular levels, was demolished in 1920, too expensive to maintain, to make room for an apartment complex.

The black basalt retaining walls that its developers installed at the time to raise its elevations to greater heights for better views have been ferociously preserved and defended by later generations of neighborhood residents.

dential history occurred on these premises. For reasons associated with her involvement in some lawsuits he was handling, Prentice moved in Julia Gardiner Tyler, the flamboyant widow of John Tyler, tenth president of the United States. During her short, controversial reign in Washington, beginning in 1844, she had been politely defined as "the most vivacious First Lady to occupy the White House," and as "An American Marie Antoinette."

At the time, because of her widely publicized sympathies for the Confederacy, her life and the lives of her children were being threatened by Union Army veterans

As the most famous historical figure to ever live at 75 St. Marks Place, a separate, illustrated section on her will follow these remarks about the history of this house.

It was Augustus Prentice who completely transformed the look, dimensions, and layout of 75 Saint Marks Place. He did this by hiring Edward Alfred Sargent (1842-1914), one of the leading architects of 19th-Century America. Born in Hastings, England, Sargent settled into

And this is Magnolia House, the residence that Prentice crafted, as designed by one of the then-two-most-fashionable architects in NYC, Edward Alfred Sargent.

Sargent became so enamored with the neighborhood, that he eventually built a house for himself nearby.

Staten Island at the dawn of the Civil War and embarked on a mission to glamourize its skyline.

Hired for a radical enlargement of 75 St. Marks Place, he more than doubled its size and completely transformed it through the addition of projected bays, a front porch, and rear verandahs which sloped down to the edge of a carriage road running beside the water's edge. Occupants had (and have) views not only of New York Harbor and its access to Newark, but of Brooklyn, Lower Manhattan, and Bayonne. You can stand on its uppermost verandah at night for dramatic views of Manhattan and the New Jersey coast. Until 9/11, one could see the lights of the Twin Towers.

The sloping and terraced rear gardens—frequently used for film and fashion shoots—feature sinuously curved stone retaining walls inspired by an Art Nouveau design and vine-covered pergolas installed by what the American Institute of Architects describe as "the present owners."

In October of 1892, the vastly restored, much-embellished property was purchased by Mary Moore, the widow of the Surgeon General of the Confederate States of America, Dr. Samuel Preston Moore. If you ever saw Clark Gable and Vivien Leigh before the burning of Atlanta in *Gone With the Wind,* you can imagine that he had the hardest and most gruesome job of any doctor in American history. *[The movie depicted almost half a mile of wounded or dying Confederate soldiers, laid out on the ground in fly-covered rows, suffering from battle casualties inflicted by the invading Yankee armies.]*

***

In Respectful Memory, RIP
This Entry is Dedicated to a Daughter of the South and Resident Owner of Magnolia House

MARY MOORE

for Her Role as a Nurse to Wounded and Dying Soldiers During America's Civil War.

The illustration at the top of the next page shows an "angel of mercy" ministering to sick or wounded soldiers during the Civil War. It accompanied a "sketch" by Louisa May Alcott that was published in *The Saturday Evening Post* about her work in a (Union) military hospital during the Civil War. Later, in happier times, Alcott went on to write *Little Women*.

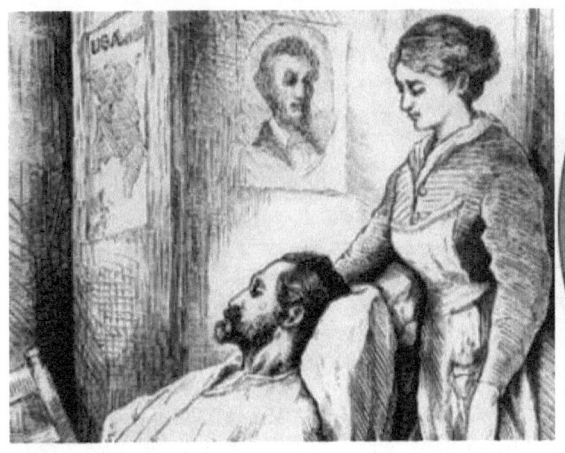 

In her "sketch," Alcott echoed the sentiments of thousands of woman (including Mary Moore) from both sides of the armed conflict. Horrified by the carnage, they reshaped their worlds and broke social boundaries to minister to the human misery of a grisley and memorably brutal war whose bitter sorrows had been previously unimaginable.

According to legend, it was Mary Moore, perhaps in honor of her Southern roots, who named her new home for the Magnolias she planted around the property.

Here follows an excerpt from the "sketch" that Alcott composed about her duties as a wartime nurse during the Civil War:.

***

"They've come! They've come! Hurry up, ladies—you're wanted."
"Who have come? the rebels?"

This sudden summons in the gray dawn was somewhat startling to a three days' nurse like myself, and, as the thundering knock came at our door, I sprang up in my bed, prepared

The photo above depicts the care-worn face of Mary Moore's husband, Dr. Samuel Preston Moore. As Surgeon-General of the Confederate States of America, he died after years of medical horror tending to and cleaning up after what some historians consider more filled with carnage than anything the then-divided United States had seen before and perhaps after.

In the aftermath of his death, his widow, Mary, left the south and emigrated to the mercantile dynamo of New York City, Desperate to forget the bloody medical theater in which her husband had labored, she bought and moved into the newly glamourized, radically enlarged Magnolia House, eventually deeding it to her daughter, Elizabeth, and her new husband, Howard Bayne.

Whereas we couldn't find any photos of the Mary Moore, it's likely that she'd have been actively involved in whatever nursing and first-aid proceedings had been endorsed by her overworked husband, the widely respected and in many ways tragic Surgeon General of the Confederacy.

In the Beginning.....

*"To gird my woman's form,
And on the ramparts die,"*

if necessary; but my roommate took it more coolly, and, as she began a rapid toilet, answered my bewildered question,—("Bless you, no child; it's the wounded from Fredericksburg; forty ambulances are at the door, and we shall have our hands full in fifteen minutes.")

Arrival of the Wounded

The sight of several stretchers, each with its legless, armless, or desperately wounded occupant, entering my ward, admonished me that I was there to work, not to wonder or weep; so I corked up my feelings, and returned to the path of duty, which was rather "a hard road to travel" just then. I pitied them so much, I dared not speak to them, though, remembering all they had been through since the route at Fredericksburg, I yearned to serve the dreariest of them all. Presently, Miss Blank tore me from my refuge behind piles of one-sleeved shirts, odd socks, bandages and lint; put basin, sponge, towels, and a block of brown soap into my hands, with these appalling directions:

"Come, my dear, begin to wash as fast as you can. Tell them to take off socks, coats and shirts, scrub them well, put on clean shirts, and the attendants will finish them off, and lay them in bed."

If she had requested me to shave them all, or dance a hornpipe on the stove funnel, I should have been less staggered; but to scrub some dozen lords of creation at a moment's notice, was really–really–. However, there was no time for nonsense, and, having resolved when I came to do everything I was bid, I drowned my scruples in my wash-bowl, clutched my soap manfully, and, assuming a business-like air, made a dab at the first dirty specimen I saw, bent on performing my task vi et armis (by force of arms) if necessary."

—**Louisa May Alcott,**
reflecting on her duties as a nurse in a military hospital during the Civil War

***

Mrs. Moore's home, by now known as "Magnolia House," and duly registered as that in the official Borough records of Staten Island, was later taken over by her daughter, Elizabeth Moore, and her new husband, Howard R. Bayne.

Born in 1851 in Winchester, Virginia, and a true son of the South, Bayne became an attorney in 1879, and moved to Staten Island in 1882. Bayne was the direct descendant of two U.S. presidents, James Madison and Zachory Taylor. Another ancestor was the explorer Meriwether Lewis, best known for his role as the leader of the Lewis & Clark Expedition that set out to explore the Louisiana Purchase and to claim Oregon and the Pacific Northwest for the burgeoning new United States of America.

Bayne's status as a politician and dealmaker became especially visible in 1909, when he was elected to the New York State Senate in Albany, serving a four-year term and eventually emerging as one of the most visible and outgoing senators in Albany, representing Staten Island. He passed the Workman's Compensation Act in his first year, which made him very popular locally among blue collar workers. During the wrenching upheavals that followed the Civil War, he always retained a public persona as a force for reconciliation between North and South, drawing comparisons to the similarity of names between his birth in Richmond (Virginia) and his present home in Richmond (County), Staten Island. He also retained memberships in, among others, the Colonnade Club of the University of Virginia, the Society of Colonial Wars, the Sons of the Revolution, the Virginia Historical Society, The Virginians of New York, and the New York Southern Society.

Significantly for Magnolia House, he also became President of the Association of Staten Island Arts & Sciences, serving as a kind of host and welcoming committee for filmmakers, socialites, business tycoons, politicians, and the early film crews who descended on the island for location shooting, as they still do today. [*Key scenes from Marlon Brando's* The Godfather *(1972) were shot here.*]

Bayne was known for his parties, often on the lawn at the rear of this house. Many visitors arrived in their yachts. Today, 75 Saint Marks Place is sometimes identified (and featured) in architectural guides and in NYC archives as the "Howard R. Bayne House."

Among the hundreds of people he welcomed were two of America's most celebrated novelists, Henry James and Theodore Dreiser, who on occasion came to St. George to relax and pen novels in the summer months. Bayne forged friendships with both of them.

[**Henry James** *(1843-1916), was a key figure in the transition between literary realism and literary modernism. One of the great novelists of the English language, he's famous for such works as* The Wings of the Dove, The Ambassadors, The Portrait of a Lady, *and the highly popular* Daisy Miller.

None of his novels is as famous as Washington Square, *which was adapted into the 1949 film,* The Heiress, *which brought Olivia de Havilland a Best Actress Academy Award. A young Montgomery Clift played her fortune-hunting suitor, trying to marry her despite the objections of her father, British actor Ralph Richardson.*

During the Gilded Age, Howard Bayne, a native Virginian, moved adroitly between opposing forces. He flourished after the Civil War in the rough-and tumble politics of New York City and State, and became one of Staten Island's most vocal publicists, a one-man chamber of commerce who was comfortable in Commerce, Science, and the Arts.

From his headquarters at Magnolia House, he tirelessly promoted Staten Island as an investment opportunity for the film industry. A member of the New York State Senate, he was instrumental in the development of Worker's Compensation, and developed Magnolia House (where he died in 1933) into a glittering social center for magnificent parties.

Adding luster to the list of artists and writers associated with St. George, Staten Island, James was nominated for the Nobel Prize for Literature in 1911, 1912, and 1916, the year he died in London.

Another famous novelist, **Theodore Dreiser**, often visited Bayne in the summer. A son of Indiana with a German immigrant father, he interviewed and wrote feature articles about, among others, Marshall Field, Thomas Edison, and Andrew

Guess Who's Coming to Dinner?

(Left) **Henry James**. Defined as among the greatest novelists in the English language, he was the respected author of *The Portrait of a Lady*;

and (right) **Theodore Dreiser**. whose characters usually succeeded at their objectives despite their lack of a firm moral code. Each was perhaps searching for "*A PLACE IN THE SUN*" in St. George.

The Presidential Antecedents of
Howard Bayne,
A Son of the South Transplanted to Staten Island and Living at Magnolia House

MADISON

No man had more to do with the writing of the U.S. constitution than Bayne's ancestor, James Madison, president from 1809 to 1817. At 5'4", he had the distinction of being the shortest president in U.S. history. Washington was sacked and burned during his watch. His wife, Dolley Madison, was the White House's first fashion diva and a devout user of snuff.

James & Dolley Madison:

Modern historians define them as "America's first power couple," having drastically affected the course of American politics and history.

Another of Bayne's ancestors was Zachory Taylor (lower right photo), a member of the long-defunct Whig Party. Taylor was president for only a short time, from 1849 to 1850. Nicknamed "Old Rough & Ready," he had made a name for himself during the War of 1812 and also inflicted Mexico with a series of stunning defeats with huge implications for the future United States.

Taylor attended the July 4 festivities in Washington in 1850, one of the hottest days on record. Cholera had broken out and locals were warned not to eat raw fruit or drink water without knowing where it came from.

Back at the White House, Taylor drank a gallon of water and wolfed down a bowl of raw cherries.

Two days later, he became deathly ill, with constant diarrhea and vomiting. He died on July 9, turning the presidency over to Millard Fillmore, whom Queen Victoria called the handsomest man she'd ever seen.

U.S. President Zachory Taylor:

"It would be judicious to act with magnanimity toward a prostrate foe."

In the Beginning.....   13

Carnegie. Among his best-known novels is Sister Carrie (1900), which critics today hail as the greatest of America's urban novels. His An American Tragedy (1925) was adapted into a movie, A Place in the Sun (1951), starring Elizabeth Taylor at her most beautiful, along with her doomed suitor, Montgomery Clift and a dumpy Shelley Winters, whom Clift murders in the film.

Dreiser became somewhat notorious for his affairs, but he bonded with Bayne, and he often visited him at 75 Saint Marks Place with his belle du jour, a changing array of beauties from Manhattan.

He married Sara Osborne White in 1898, but they split up in 1909 when he fell in love with Thelma Cudlipp, the 15-year-old daughter of a colleague. By 1913, he'd fallen for the beautiful actress and painter, Kyra Markham, many years younger than he was.

Dreiser's serial seductions continued—nothing serious until 1919 when he met his cousin, Helen Patges Richardson, born in 1894. He fell madly in love, beginning an affair. He called her "my kissin' cousin."

As the decades went by, she remained Dreiser's constant lover and somehow tolerated his many affairs, since he always came back to her. He finally married her in June of 1944, a year before he died.]

***

HOWARD BAYNE, MAGNOLIA HOUSE & THE DEBUT OF SILENT FILMS

Long before Hollywood evolved into Tinseltown, Staten Island emerged as one of filmdom's early capitals along with Fort Lee, New Jersey. The greenest of New York's boroughs, with miles of wetlands, sandy beaches, hills, and plains, it provided endless backdrops for filmmakers.

It wasn't Texas, Utah, Nevada, Montana, Arizona, or New Mexico, that became the "mother and fatherland" of the film genre known as "the silent Western." It was this verdant, fertile, historic, outer borough of New York City. It's estimated that around a hundred silent Westerns were shot here on Staten Island before the end of 1914. Locals called them "shoot-em-ups." Most were shot on South Beach, with its sprawling lowlands and miles of sand. Of course, the fact these sands bordered the Atlantic Ocean was never depicted. A fake cactus appeared here and there in those early "flickers."

Westerns were produced on the East Coast, including on Staten Island, until 1910, when most producers had relocated to California, although a few remained behind, not wanting to leave the "civilized world of New York for the wilds of California."

Of course, in Staten Island and in New Jersey, there was no scenery to suggest the wide open spaces of the West, but filmmakers didn't seem to mind. Although they did their best to disguise their fashionable city clothing, they paid little attention to cowboy garb.

One so-called cowboy had never seen a live cow. In 1906, he appeared in a western drama set in 1850, wearing motoring togs. The villain was always accessorized with a Mexican *sombrero*, sporting a mustache and entirely dressed in black. The Cowboy vs. Indian conflicts had not been invented yet. Indians, now called Native Americans, were depicted in early movies as "noble savages."

As a spokesman touting Staten Island as a film location and a boon to investors, Senator Bayne befriended the film pioneer, Edwin S. Porter, who began his involvement in motion pictures in 1896, the first year that movies were projected onto a large screen in the United States. He eventually became the most influential filmmaker in America.

For a while, he worked for Thomas Edison, who positioned him as the executive in charge of motion picture production for his studios.

Porter's first film was *Terrible Teddy, the Grizzly King*, a satire on the bearish-looking Theodore Roosevelt. It was shot in 1901, during Roosevelt's tenure as vice president.

Recognizing his importance as a seminal figure in what would evolve into a burgeoning new industry, Bayne wined and dined Porter at 75 Saint Marks Place, lobbying him to use Staten Island for at least some of the location shooting for his *The Great Train Robbery*, filmed in 1903. Running for only 12 minutes, it's hailed today as a landmark in the development of American cinema and was said to have been based on a 1900 train robbery by the outlaw Butch Cassidy,

Today, it's defined as the first American "action-adventure" movie and the first "western" with a recognizable form. By 1905, it was the premier attraction at the first Nickelodeon, and its success firmly established motion pictures as a key component of commercial entertainment in the United States.

According to Bayne, "My friend Edwin (Porter) was essentially a cameraman and a brilliant technician. He became the first recognized director in film history but seemed unhappy at the fame thrust on him."

Porter never recognized the oncoming star system, and basically directed groups of men, with certain solo shots of a sheriff or an outlaw. He saw a film only for plot, not as a showcase for any individual actor, preferring to focus on a band of outlaws, not a single individual. That would come later, when directors often made just one outlaw the focus of their film.

[A famous example of that was Howard Hughes' The Outlaw *(1943), which starred Jane Russell in her debut film as the sultry sagebrush vixen, the camera focusing on her ample bosom. Also making his film debut was Jack Buetel as Billy the Kid. Critics called him "a walking streak of sex blazing across the screen." Contrary to legend, the bisexual aviator and Hollywood producer seduced Buetel, not Russell. These revelations have come out*

Films of Edwin S. Porter

Edwin S. Porter (top photo) is a key player in the early days of silent filmmaking.

The lower photo displays an image from one of his most iconic films, *The Great Train Robbery* (1903).

Reviewed by film historians as the first American action-adventure film, and the first Western, it was directed by Howard Bayne's friend, Edwin S. Porter; had a running length of 12 minutes; cost $150 to make; and was entirely filmed 30 miles south of Magnolia House, in Milltown, New Jersey.

in several newspapers, including the Daily Mail, the New York Daily News, and Blood Moon's bio, Howard Hughes, Hell's Angel, *written at Magnolia House and published in 2005.*]

"Ironically, Porter directed D.W. Griffith, an actor in *Rescued from an Eagle's Nest* in 1907," Bayne said. "It would be Griffith who would go on to become filmdom's most acclaimed director of his day." At least part of

his fame derived from Griffith's oversight of the controversial *Birth of a Nation* in 1915 that glorified the KKK.

Through Porter, Bayne met what might be called the first cowboy star. He was G.M. Anderson, a New York model, later known as "Bronco Billy." Payne had given Anderson a role in *The Great Train Robbery*.

Bayne and Anderson formed a friendship, and he entertained him at his home, having been warned in advance to have a good stash of whiskey on hand.

He followed Anderson's career in the movies, especially after the release of *Bronco Billy and the Baby* in 1908. "Bronco Billy, my buddy, was never given his place in the history of the movies," Bayne said. "He established the western hero as a wanderer, riding off into the sunset to root out evil in the next frontier town. He always had to confront the badman with either his gun or his fists. Fearless on the battlefield, he was shy with the ladies, melting into a bashful grin when confronted with the heroine in a gown. Billy introduced the trick of a cowboy fumbling with his hat, trying to think of what to say to a lady."

Bayne was ever so right in his assessment of Broncho Billy. Long before

Segments of Edwin Porter's 1906 version of the silent film *Kathleen Mavourneen* have been lost forever, including the parts which depicted St. Marks Place, reconfigured in the film as a verdant, leafy street in late 19th century Ireland. This photo of St. Marks Place, snapped in 1894, shows how it looked.

The house in the near foreground, the one with the conical "witches cap" roof, was owned by Mabel Normand, the silent film star befriended by Howard Bayne, owner of Magnolia House. Its outline appears as the most distant of the houses along this row.

Hopalong Cassidy rode in, along with William S. Hart and Tom Mix, Anderson was the first western action hero. Gary Cooper later perfected his technique, and John Wayne dominated the western, but that would come later. Along the way came other heroes: Lash, Tex, Rocky, Crash, Wild Bill, Hoot, Roy Rogers, and Gene Autry, but Broncho Billy was the daddy of all of them.

Magnolia House, today a locale for photographers and filmmakers, was featured as a setting in Edwin Porter's 1906 silent film, *Kathleen Mavourneen*. He based it on an Irish ballad, and he needed to depict a leafy street that evoked Ireland during the 19th Century. He agreed with Senator Bayne that St. Marks Place would be ideal. When the movie opened, Staten Islanders flocked to see it.

Senator Bayne later attended the premier, in 1913, of Edwin Porter's *The Prisoner of Zenda*. [*A second adaptation of Anthony Hope's swashbuckling novel, starring Ronald Colman and Douglas Fairbanks, Jr., was released in 1937. Fifteen years later, in 1952, a second, even more popular reprise of Porter's original silent film was made, this one starring the dashing Stewart Granger.*]

***

Right before his death in 1933, Senator Bayne admitted, "Some dreams are not meant to be." Yet despite that bitter truth, he continued in his relentless pursuit to make Staten Island the film capital of the world.

He became deeply involved in the shooting of *The Perils of Pauline*, an ongoing series of films. Launched in 1914 and released in weekly installments, they featured Pearl White as a damsel in distress in the title role. In each of the short silent films that comprise the series, she's consistently menaced by villains who include Indians, pirates, and other blackguards whom damsels—in distress or not—should probably avoid.

When not facing a lion in a cage, she was thrown to the crocodiles, or else lashed to a whirring buzz saw.

Cue magazine named her "The Original Blonde Bombshell of the Flickers." Some of her episodes were shot on Staten Island, others at Fort Lee. Bayne often drove her to New Jersey. On the way, she told him she was not a true blonde. "Actually, I wear a wig. I don't know the true color of my hair because I've dyed it so many times."

She also claimed that she was the youngest of nine children born in Greenridge, Missouri. Each of the White brood was named for a precious stone like Ruby, Sapphire, or Diamond.

In 1914, virtually everyone in America was singing:

"Poor Pauline, I pity poor Pauline!
One night, she's drifting out to sea,
They tie her to a tree,
I wonder what the end will be.
The suspense is awful!
Bing! Bang! Biff! They throw her o'er a cliff!"

In her early serials, she insisted on doing her own stunts. As might have been anticipated, something would go wrong. She was tied to a hot air balloon that was mistakenly cut from its moorings, sending the hysterical star into a high-altitude position about 4,000 feet above the skyline of Manhattan. Miraculously, she landed safely.

During her time on the island, Senator Bayne became her unofficial handler and caregiver, welcoming her to parties at Magnolia House. There, he introduced her to several prominent locals, two of whom had seen her play "Little Eva" in the stage version of *Uncle Tom's Cabin* at the age of six.

White is remembered today for a scene that she never appeared in—that of a virginal maiden being tied to railroad tracks, helpless before an onrushing train. That scene was depicted in another silent, *Barney Oldfield's Race for Life*.

The Perils of Pauline ran for 20 episodes, most of which were shot on Staten Island. Today, most of them have been lost, although collectively, they comprise an important chapter in the history of the cinema. [Decades later, in 1947, Betty Hutton starred in *The Perils of Pauline,* a hit movie based on that vintage, silent series originally filmed on Staten Island.]

Poor Pauline! Each of the short weekly installments focused on Pearl White, depicted with a swain in the photo on the right. Bayne might have fallen in love with her, endangering, it's said, his marriage.

Pearl White eventually faded from the public with the advent of the talkies, directors finding her voice "unsuitable" for sound. Also, it was said she could not scream convincingly.

"The last I heard of Miss Pearl," Bayne said, "was that she was very rich—some two million dollars—and living in Paris. There, she'd purchased the Hôtel de Paris, a château once occupied by the Empress Eugénie."

"She was said to have married two, maybe three times. Her first husband she vowed never to speak of again. Another husband just up and disappeared. Poor Pauline, unlucky in love. She traveled the globe in luxury, but ironically, never visited Hollywood."

***

Known for the expressiveness of her face, the silent screen actress, Mabel Normand, was hailed as the female Charlie Chaplin and blossomed into the first woman superstar. She was born in New Brighton, (i.e., this neighborhood of Staten Island), in November of 1892. Later, she bought a house at 125 St. Marks Place. A few doors away from Senator Bayne, her former home is interpreted by its neighbors today as a monument to silent films and the difficult life of the celebrity who owned it.

As she was growing up, she become very close to the senator, spending a lot of her time at his house. Her excuse was that he was a father figure to her. But Bayne's southern wife, Elizabeth, wasn't so sure, suspecting that the charming young girl was seducing her husband, who seemed devoted to her. Believing that she had a lot of talent, he was the one who urged her to break into films.

Normand became vastly intrigued with this handsome, courtly Southern gentleman, lawyer, and historian who introduced her to some of the people he knew who were making films. They didn't seem as deeply intrigued with Mabel as he was.

There was talk of a scandal, but no one knows for sure what it was. Neighbors speculated that Elizabeth had caught Mabel in bed with the senator. Just before news of whatever had happened got amplified, Mabel headed west to join the burgeoning film colony getting established in Hollywood.

Mabel, who has the dubious distinction of being the first female to endure having a pie thrown in her face on film, became a popular star, beginning a collaboration with Mack Sennett and his Keystone Cops in 1912. She was also instrumental in getting her by now lover, Sennett, to hire the English comedian, Charlie Chaplin. In time, she would co-star with him in a dozen pictures, and have an affair with him, too.

Bayne avidly followed Mabel's career, and wrote letters to her. In one of them, he claimed, "I remain your most devoted fan and servant. You will burn as a flame in my heart forever."

Normand quickly rose in box office power and prestige, forming her own production company. She also took as her lover William Desmond Taylor, one of the most famous directors in Hollywood, and was the last person to see him alive before his murder on February 1, 1922. Forever associated with the flamboyant 1920s, and still unsolved, it became one of Hollywood's most notorious murders. After extensive grilling by Los Angeles police, Mabel was ruled out as a suspect.

Mabel also made 17 silent films with Fatty Arbuckle, another "big" attraction at the box office. His career was destroyed when he was tried three times for the rape and murder of actress Virginia Rappe in San Francisco. Even though acquitted for the third time, his career was destroyed.

Mabel was indirectly involved in another murder when her chauffeur stole her pistol and fatally shot Courtland S. Dines, an oil baron. That murder and all the other scandals led to the destruction of her career. She was also revealed to be a dope addict.

Death came to Mabel in 1930, and Bayne would die three years later.

Top photo: Mabel Normand, comedienne in *Won in a Closet* (1914).

Lower photo: An ad for the saucy role she played that critics define as the early days of madcap cheesecake at which such later stars as Betty Grable became adept.

Rumors of a love affair with her St. Marks Place mentor, Howard Bayne, perhaps inside Magnolia House, were the talk of the neighborhood.

But as he told his assistant, "I mourn Mabel's death. She was the brightest bulb who ever lit up my life. A man gets only one great love this time around."

A psychic, Jeffrey R. Forrest, of Pasadena, California, visited 75 Saint Marks Place in 1966, and walked through all the rooms at night. He then proclaimed, "The ghost of Mabel Normand still roams through this old house after midnight."

***

Around 1911, Senator Bayne and his family decided to leave Staten Island for an extended trip to Europe. During his absence, he turned his home at 75 Saint Marks Place over to a friend he'd been cultivating with hopes that he'd settle and prosper in Staten Island. He was film producer and distributor William Fox. One of the most important players in the history of the film industry, his name lives on today in such companies as 20th Century Fox and Fox News. During his association with Bayne and his residency at Magnolia House, Fox commuted to his studio at Fort Lee, New Jersey.

Fox shot one of his earliest short silent films in the back yard of Magnolia House when the gardens were more extensive than they are today. Entitled *Far, Far from Home*, it was the frothy saga of a young girl from Indiana who arrives in New York to become a Broadway star. When she's menaced by three villains in black capes, she's rescued by a Prince Charming, in this case a screen version of a farm boy, also from Indiana, who tells her, according to the text flashed across the screen, "There's no place like home," a line made even more famous by Judy Garland in *The Wizard of Oz* in 1939.

In the original version of *Far, Far From Home*, Fox had depicted a rape scene, where the helpless maiden is overpowered by one of the villains. Faced with protests from exhibitors, this episode was cut before the film went into general release, so as not to offend the puritan audiences of the early 20th Century.

William K. Everson, one of the best film

Hungarian-American film producer William Fox in 1921. His depictions of violence and sex caused problems with the censors.

In the Beginning..... 23

historians of the silent era, wrote: "Fox films on the whole, perhaps overly influenced by those Theda Bara vamp movies, tended to be coarser and more brutal than those of any other company, and each had to be examined carefully by exhibitors so that any offending sequence could be cut."

Regrettably, almost none of Fox's early silent movies survived. Like literally thousands of other silent flickers, they're lost to history, since in the early days of moviemaking, no one really worried a lot about film preservation like archivists do today.

[The history of the movies could not be written without mentioning Fox, a Hungarian Jew who arrived in New York in 1879 when he was nine months old, one of dozen siblings, only six of whom survived. Recognizing the potential for the inclusion of sound in his movies before his competitors, he formed Fox Film Corporation in 1915, leasing space for his first film studio in Fort Lee, about 35 miles from the house Bayne offered him in Staten Island.

In his heyday, Fox's chain of movie theaters stretched across America and abroad. By 1915, he had developed a virtual monopoly on film production and distribution based on a policy of releasing his movies only to theaters he owned.

His multi-millionaire empire controlled a large portion of film exhibition and distribution in America during the silent film era.

He was the man who introduced organ accompaniment to movie screenings in theaters. He was also the producer who made the silent star, Theda Bara, the first screen vamp.

He created a fake and mysterious legend about her, asserting that she was born in the shadow of the Sphinx, despite the fact that medical records defined her birthplace as Cincin-

The photo immediately above shows superstar John Barrymore making love to an unidentified actress in the film shot on Staten Island that set hearts atwitter.

As part of a business deal that was brokered with input from Howard Bayne at Magnolia House, it was considered a public relations triumph for civic boosters eager to develop the borough into a centerpiece of the fast-emerging film industry nati.

Fox also became known for creating, in 1927, the first illustrated news series, MovieTone News, the first commercially developed movies with sound.

Faced with the coming of sound, he had to retrofit 1,100 theaters with the new-fangled technologies, which drove him into bankruptcy in 1936. His domination of the movie industry attracted powerful enemies who began anti-trust litigation against him. Trying to retain control of his empire, he impulsively tried to bribe a judge in 1942. For that transgression, he was convicted and sentenced to six months in jail.

After his release, he faded from the scene. In 1952, at the age of 73, he died and was buried in Salem Fields in Brooklyn.

Had Fox lived until today, and if he still controlled the company he'd founded, he might find the company he founded valued at $55 billion.]

***

Senator Bayne, still from his base at 75 St. Marks Place, lured both the producer and director of another silent film, *Raffles, the Amateur Cracksman*, to Staten Island in 1917, when most of the film industry's other players were settling into California.

[Adapted from a collection of short stories by E.W. Hornung that were first published in 1899, it focused on a gentleman thief, A.J. Raffles, a socially connected cricket champion, who steals expensive jewelry for sport and profit. Captions displayed at the bottom of the screen include "I've never stolen a farthing for personal gain. I've robbed the rich to give to the poor", and "Get the sparklers and be quick about it"]

Bayne's campaign to have that movie shot in Staten Island was supported by the film's star, the very temperamental John Barrymore, who insisted that

At the end of filming, Howard Bayne hosted an enormous party at Magnolia House for John Barrymore, the hottest, and perhaps the most eccentric, celebrity in town.

This movie still from *The Amateur Cracksman* (1917) depicts the film's profane and occasionally drunken star in a setting that's similar to what he encountered at the fashionable party hosted in his honor by Senator Bayne at Magnolia House.

Raffles be filmed near Manhattan because of his commitment to some theatrical productions being staged on Broadway at the time.

Like a prince arriving in triumph, The Great Profile, brother of Ethel and Lionel Barrymore, eventually commuted to Staten Island for its filming. During an interlude not associated with movie-making, Senator Bayne, still and always touting Staten Island's civic and commercial charms, escorted him to the Staten Island Cricket and Tennis Club, of which he was a charter member.

[Although primarily a stage actor, Barrymore had made his film debut in 1913 in *An American Citizen*. Senator Bayne had long admired his widely reviewed stage roles.

The members of the club welcomed Barrymore as an exotic and as a celebrity but found him eccentric and perhaps even a bit scary. Part of this derived from his drunken habit of urinating in public, either in or out of doors, wherever and whenever he felt like it.

Barrymore, as a visiting VIP, asked Bayne for only one thing: an introduction to "a steady supply of wenches" during his visit.

When the filming of Raffles, the Amateur Cracksman, was wrapped, Bayne threw a lawn party for Barrymore, its cast, and its crew. As the party was ending, The Great Profile, in drunken disarray, chased after two of Staten Island's fairest lassies—and may have done more than that. After all, he was John Barrymore.

Affairs with Tallulah Bankhead and countless others, including a marriage to the beautiful actress, Dolores Costello, lay in Barrymore's future.

During his drunken departure, he delivered some vulgar advice to Senator Bayne, which was overheard and later gossiped about by the late-departing guests: "Don't trust any wench as far as you can throw Fort Knox. They're all twittering vaginas."]

***

This old house has withstood wars, storms, various owners, and an association with the movies and the entertainment trades that this section has tried to unravel. We've discussed Magnolia House's association with the seminal days of silent films. This overview now moves on to other dramas—some of them tragic, some of them frothy, and all of them entertaining—that have unfolded here as well as abroad.

Darwin Porter and Danforth Prince have chased celebrities here, through the British Isles, and throughout the capitals of Europe. The pages that follow describe associated dramas and perhaps, some of their residual glamour.

Chapter Two

SEEKING SANCTUARY AT MAGNOLIA HOUSE
JULIA GARDINER TYLER

"THE MARIE ANTOINETTE OF THE WHITE HOUSE"

Two views of Julia Gardiner Tyler (left) before her marriage to U.S. President, John Tyler, and (right) as a controversial celebrity hated for her ostentation, her sense of privilege, her support of slavery, her lavish spending, her *coquetteries*, and for what her contemporaries defined as sexually equivalent to the loosest morals of the Napoleonic courts of Europe.

Of the many glamorous cultural and political figures who moved along St. Marks Place during its early heyday in the 19th Century, either visiting or staying here, none is as celebrated as the former First Lady, Julia Gardiner Tyler, wife of John Tyler, the 10th President of the United States.

She was born in 1820 on Gardiner's Island, off the coastline of Long Island, the largest privately owned island in the United States. She grew up there and blossomed into a rather dazzling teenager, hailed as "The Rose of Long Island."

As a captivating beauty, her looks and charm earned her a steady stream of male admirers. As a young coquette, she was rumored to be "wildly flirtatious." Decades later, when Margaret Mitchell's *Gone With the Wind* was published, a historian referred to Julia as "The Yankee Scarlett O'Hara."

Today, she lives in the history books as America's First Lady, a niche she occupied for nine months between June of 1844 and March of 1845.

She was schooled in refinement at the Chegary Institute in Manhattan, which daughters of wealthy families attended before making their debuts into the high society of that era.

After her graduation in 1840, it was almost mandatory to make the grand tour of Europe, reserved only for sons and daughters of the fabulously wealthy.

Sailing to Europe, she toured the Continent and lost her virginity, either to a Belgian nobleman, a count in Paris, or to a Duke who was related to the royal family in London. Returning to Long Island in the fall of 1841, the now-experienced beauty became a fun-loving *debutante*, known for her scandalous escapades. At least they were considered wild by the standards of the 1840s.

Once again, she attracted a string of slavering male admirers. During her time on the Continent, John Tyler, Vice President, had become President of the United States.

William Henry Harrison had been elected President of the United States, having run on a catchy platform derived from a popular song at the time, "Tippecanoe & Tyler, Too." Born in 1773 to a father who was one of the signers of the Declaration of Independence, Harrison was an Army officer who had fought against the Indians before becoming a hero of the War of 1812.

At his inauguration as a Whig President, he gave the longest inaugural speech in presidential history, running for 105 minutes. During its long-winded delivery on the steps of the Capitol, he preferred to stand without his overcoat on a blustery day in March when people not heavily

William Henry Harrison (1773-1841) not only had the shortest term of any U.S. President, but also had an undistinguished sex life.

"The only women he saw were officers' wives who he escorted to remote posts out West, and the Indian women who gleefully scalped dead soldiers and tortured the wounded to death," wrote Nigel Cawthorne.

bundled were freezing.

Later, back at the White House, he fell gravely ill, falling sick and becoming bedridden. White House doctors plied him with castor oil, lots of brandy, camphor, ipecac, and opium. All this medication brought on colitis and hepatitis. Harrison passed into history on April 4, 1841, having had the shortest term of office of any U.S. President.

As his replacement, Harrison's Vice President, John Tyler, was elevated to the office of U.S. President, fulfilling the term of office slated for Harrison.

As a Confederate, a son of the old South, and an advocate of slavery, Tyler received many death threats during his term of office (1841 to 1845).

Into the White House he moved First Lady Letitia Christian, with whom he had produced eight children. She had been born to a slave-owning plantation master in Richmond, Virginia. Having suffered a stroke, she spent most of her time at the White House in her bedroom reading from the King James Bible.

She once said, "I can't imagine a life without slaves waiting on me hand and foot. I expect the White House staff to assume the duty of my slaves in Virginia, tending to my every wish day or night."

She suffered another stroke and died on September 10, 1842, her term

Two views of John Tyler (left, from his tenure as Governor of Virginia in 1821; right from his later years) In the center is a portrait of his first wife, Letitia, whose popularity and chaste rigor, as well as her fecundity in childbirth, continued to haunt her replacement (Julia) long after Letitia's death.

Letitia was First Lady for only eighteen months, and in name only, paralyzed as she was from a stroke two years before her husband's election. She lived upstairs in the White House and never came down, except once, for the wedding of one of her daughters. She died in the White House in September of 1842, being the first First Lady to die "in office."

One of the Tyler daughters-in-law performed the social duties of First Lady until Julia became the new Mrs. Tyler.

as First Lady having been very brief. After her death, the newly inaugurated "replacement president," John Tyler, conspicuously lacked a First Lady.

A description of Julia in 1841 read: "She is raven-haired, with dark, dancing eyes, a radiant porcelain complexion, an hourglass waist, and luscious red lips you want to kiss." Eligible young suitors, plus some not so eligible, sent her love poems, one of which proclaimed his hopes of "this rose to pluck"—racy stuff in the early 19th Century.

Her prosperous landowning father, David Gardiner, a New York State Senator with enormous wealth and influence, decided to move his lovely and very eligible daughters, Julia and Margaret, to an elegant home he'd rented with a ballroom in Washington, D.C. There, he planned to throw lavish parties with hired musicians. As he explained to his wife, Juliana, "I'm going fishing for husbands for my daughters, but only those men in the highest echelons of power."

Julia's first affair in Washington was with one of the justices of the Supreme Court, a man who proposed marriage to her. She rejected his offer, perhaps because of her ambitions for a man in a loftier position.

Her most persistent suitor was John Tyler, Jr., son of the newly designated President. He was rather dashing, and politically well-connected. As a couple, Julia and John, Jr., were soon seen around Washington together.

Her sister Margaret claimed that Julia had taken him as her lover after dumping the Supreme Court Justice.

In Washington in 1842, John Tyler, Jr., made what he later defined as "the biggest mistake of my life." He escorted Julia to a White House recep-

AN IRONY OF FAME

The ad that provoked the loudest scandal of young Julia's then-sheltered but very prosperous life managed to associate her likeness with a depiction of the fashionable good life.

In 1839, Julia secretly posed for an engraving which was adapted into an advertisement for the dry-goods emporium Bogert & Mecamly, on lower Ninth Avenue in Manhattan.

In it, Julia's handbag was overlaid with the words "I'll purchase at Bogert and Mecamly's, No. 86 Ninth Avenue. Their Goods are Beautiful and Astonishingly Cheap."

At the bottom of the advertisement the lady was identified as "Miss Julia Gardiner, the Rose of Long Island."

It was an early example of celebrity endorsements, when a woman might be mentioned only at the time of her birth, her marriage, and her death. It was the first of Julia's many subsequent scandals.

tion and introduced her to "dear ol' Dad." She was 21, and he was in his 50s. Because of shorter life expectancies, a swain of that age was considered positively antique in those days.

The President recalled, "Julia stole my heart that night, and at the end of the evening, I took her to my private quarters, where I kissed her passionately. I wanted to assure her that despite my age, I was in the prime of life, a raging bull."

The next morning, when her father quizzed her about her impression of the President, she said, "A randy old man, but quite jolly." This high-spirited and independent-minded beauty was not at all attracted to this grave yet courtly Southerner.

Tragedy struck on February 28, 1844 when the President invited Julia, her father, David, and several Washington dignitaries for a cruise along the Potomac aboard the U.S. Navy's *Princeton*. On this ill-fated voyage, one of the gunboat's cannons exploded, killing David Gardiner and a few other politicos.

That night and during the nights that followed, the President comforted the grief-stricken Julia, who had been very close to her father. He was always seen with his arm around her, comforting her. They were drawn together in their mutual mourning, he for his late wife, and she for her father.

Within weeks, both of them seemed to bounce back, and she helped

A explosion aboard the presidential yacht, *Princeton*, ultimately led to love.

The tragedy struck on February 28, 1844. The widowed John Tyler had become the first U.S. Vice President to become President by the death of a sitting President.

He had invited VIP David Gardiner and his 23-year-old daughter, Julia, for a cruise aboard his yacht. A distinguished list of dignitaries was also invited.

The accidental explosion of a cannon killed Julia's father, as well as the Secretary of State, the Secretary of the Navy, an ambassador from Brussels, and the President's personal valet, an African-American.

Julia had become nauseated by the movement of the boat and had gone below, thereby saving her own life. It was President Tyler himself who delivered the news that her father had been killed in the explosion. She fell into his arms.

A wake followed in the East Room of the White House to honor the fallen.

Only four months later, Tyler married Julia, thereby creaing a unique episode in history wherein a U.S. President had two First Ladies during his term in office.

him plan a gala party, with music and dancing, to celebrate George Washington's birthday on February 22. He spotted Julia dancing with young Ralph Brooks, a handsome and rather studly young man from Westport, Connecticut. As commander-in-chief, Tyler banished the naval officer from the White House.

Jealous with rage, the President proposed to Julia later that night. She was wearing a Greek cap with long tassels. He proposed three times, and she answered "No, no, no." Each time she said that, she'd fling a tassel in his face. On his fourth try, she said, "Yes! Yes! Yes!" From then on, he wrote her a love poem every day.

The following day, a Washington reporter claimed, "Miss Julia Gardiner, escorted by John Tyler, Jr., was the star of the most recent reception at the White House. She seduced every man there with those flirty, flirty eyes."

At this point, by now quasi-committed to Tyler, Julia's list of suitors entered a bizarre phase. Her affair with John Jr. came to an end, but only temporarily. The President was in hot pursuit.

To compound matters, the President's younger son, Robert, fell madly in love with Julia, too, and pursued her almost daily at the White House behind the backs of the President and his older brother. In whispered corridors of the White House, the three Tylers became known as "The Love Triangle."

Julia became a regular daily visitor to the White House, not to mention at nights when the Secret Service, such as it was back then, kept the lovers concealed from the prying eyes of the press. The White House staff saw him chasing Julia—as she screamed with what was interpreted as a flirtatious actress's unconvincing screams—up and down the halls. Catching up with her, he usually wrestled her down onto the carpet. Once, when they were playing "catch me if you can" inside the Oval Office, his male secretary entered, suggesting that they should either retire to the President's bedchamber upstairs, or follow the day's schedule and receive the foreign dignitaries waiting outside.

Some White House historians attribute Julia with the most lovers of any other First Lady—that is, until Nancy Reagan. *[As an MGM starlet in the late 1940s, Nancy Davis numbers such suitors as Clark Gable, whom she wanted to marry, and Spencer Tracy, plus numerous others. But once Ronald impregnated her with the future Patti Davis, she settled into a happy marriage—that is, unless Frank Sinatra visited the White House when Reagan was away. Since the 1940s, she'd had a crush on Ol' Blue Eyes.]*

On June 20, 1844, "John & Julia," as they were known to their family and friends, became man and wife. He was 54 years old, she only 24. Taylor was known by the press as "Honest John." After marrying Julia, he was billed as "Lucky Honest John."

On July 6, he escorted her to his 1,100-acre plantation, Sherwood Forest, on the James River in Tidewater Virginia, introducing 70 of his slaves to their new mistress. In the romantic swirl of it all, she told him, "I'm Maid Marian and you're Robin Hood. I'll have a pair of green tights made for you."

[Tyler was one of the most unpopular Presidents in U.S. history, having alienated both political parties. Fearing a takeover of Texas by Mexico or Great Britain, he lobbied for annexation, which he later cited as his greatest achievement.

Some historians claim that the annexation of Texas is widely interpreted as a result of Julia's influence over both the President and certain key senators, with whom she flirted.

She pictured herself with another tile, "The Yellow Rose of Texas," having chosen yellow since "The Rose of Long Island," as she once was called, was thought to be red.

Tyler had another distinction as President, having had more children than any other President, eight with his first wife and seven with his second wife, Julia. At the time of Tyler's birth, George Washington was President. At the age of seventy, he sired a daughter named Mary. At her death, Harry S Truman ruled over post-war America.

The years that separated George Washington (winner of the Revolutionary War) from Truman (the man who dropped the Atomic Bomb) is a long stretch of time.]

Back at the White House, Julia threw a reception for some senators and the justices of the Supreme Court, including her former lover. She made her entrance in a red velvet gown with plunging *décolletage* and ostrich plumes in her hair.

She had assembled an entourage, a coterie of "ladies in waiting," each attired only in white, causing the Washington press to dub them the "Vestal Virgins." However, some of the more cynical senators didn't know them as virgins. "Julia came upon us like a goddess descended from Mount Olympus," claimed one senator.

Wherever Julia went in Washington, the Vestal Virgins accompanied her in a

View of Sherwood Forest in Charles City County, Virginia, a photo snapped in 1961.

Although vandalized and battered by the Yankees who occupied it, and later by the plantation's former slaves, it was not burned, like many others, and returned, uninhabitable, to the Tyler family.

It still remains, much-restored, in private hands today.

gold carriage pulled by four white horses. For this, she was loudly denounced as "Napoleonic" by her enemies.

It was for that reception that she commissioned the Marine Band to play "Hail to the Chief," a song that became a tradition from then on to announce the arrival of the president at social functions.

Shortly after her elevation to the rank of First Lady, Julia wrote to her mother, Juliana. "I am now in residence. I am the most powerful woman in America, a virtual queen. I will live like one, too."

The press didn't buy the queenly image, sometimes savaging it viciously. Regardless of their political affiliation, they seemed united, however, in referring to her as "The Marie Antoinette of the White House."

Julia immediately set about refurbishing the White House, evocative

Despite her perceived frivolity, the times through which Julia Tyler lived were truly desperate.

Upper left: Ruins of a house near Bull Run, Virginia. destroyed in the Civil War
Upper Right: the somber dedication of a memorial to those fallen during the same batle (Bull Run) and...
Lower center: Burying the dead at a battlefield in Pennsylvania.

of a future First Lady, Jacqueline Kennedy. For the master bedroom, she ordered an antique four-poster and draped it with white lace, adding a blue ribbon for every foot of it. Above the bed, she wanted a depiction of Cupid's heart with an arrow. On one wall, she commissioned a nude picture of Adam and Eve in the Garden of Eden. Adam would have Tyler's face, and she would be a very seductive Eve with a serpent dangling from a tree as a backdrop.

Throughout the remainder of her life, she would call Tyler her "beau," and he would refer to her as "Sweet Lady." She demanded he treat every night like their honeymoon night. Sometimes, her demands for passionate kisses at all hours interrupted important meetings. Once, while presiding over a cabinet session, he had to interrupt it for a kissing session. She also had to suffer the hostility of his original brood of children from his first wife. The sons and daughters of Letitia strongly resented her.

For her farewell to Washington and as an *adieu* to her status as the America's First Lady, she threw what is still considered the most spectacular gala in the history of the White House. Champagne flowed lavishly on the night of February 18, 1845, when she functioned as hostess to 3,000 illustrious guests.

A few days later, she abandoned the White House, taking along certain mementoes of her stay, and leaving the accountant "with a staggering number of bills equal to the national budget" (his words).

After her departure from Washington with Tyler, she returned to Sherwood Forest and their dozens of slaves. Although born a Yankee, she had been converted to the Southern cause, and, like her husband, was a strong advocate of slavery.

As regards the resumption of her role as a "civilian" in control of a massive plantation, a black servant there claimed that "when the Massa is away, the Massa John Junior takes over the duties of his Daddy. He spends the nights in Miss Julia's bedroom seein' no harm comes to her."

When Yankee soldiers overran the Tyler plantation in Virginia, Julia and her children fled to the Gardiner-Tyler residence on Staten Island. Her brother David, a strong supporter of the Union, was so horrified by her sympathies for the Southern Cause, he moved out.

She did not endear herself to the locals in the neighborhood when she displayed the Confederate flag from the top of the home. She so enraged veteran Yankee soldiers that they broke in, threatening to kill Julia and her children.

She fled to a hideaway on St. Marks Place, eventually returning to the South after a bitter legal battle, which she lost, with her brother David over her mother's estate.

In 1853, Julia wrote an article for the *New York Herald*, defending slavery, claiming that "Southern slaves live sumptuously compared to workers in modern industrial cities of Britain such as Birmingham."

From her new base in Virginia, she became best friends with Jefferson Davis, later President of the Confederate States of America, and his wife, Varina.

With the oncoming Civil War, and with the ascension of Abraham Lincoln as U.S. President, the lives of "John & Julia" were completely uprooted in the wake of the South withdrawing from the Union to form its own nation.

Tyler spent many of the subsequent months away, serving in the Confederate Congress. During his absence, the Confederate flag flew defiantly from flagpoles above Sherwood Forest. In Richmond, he suffered a stroke and died in January of 1862, before the true horrors of the Civil War unfolded.

Julia Gardiner Tyler, aged and chastened, in her later years.

By now a devout Roman Catholic, she referred to herself as "Mrs. Ex-President Tyler."

With the ascension of Abraham Lincoln as President of the Union, Julia's life, and that of her children were violently uprooted.

Virginia was the first Confederate state to be overrun with vengeful and sometimes uncontrolled and marauding Yankee soldiers. Julia and five of her children fled from the South, abandoning their plantation and its slaves, and returning to her native New York, carrying her Southern sympathies with her. Two of her older sons, John and David, were left behind to continue fighting with the Confederate Rebel Army.

Julia and her brood went to live with her mother, Juliana, at the historic Gardiner-Tyler home on Staten Island. It had been constructed in the Greek Revival style with Corinthian columns dominating its façade. Today, the mansion stands at 27 Tyler Street, about two miles away from St. Marks Place.

She was not a diplomat. In residence there, Julia infuriated her Yankee neighbors by flying a Confederate flag on its front lawn. Throughout the remainder of the war, she received numerous threats.

As the Civil War raged on and casualties increased, Julia threw herself into a new role as caregiver to wounded soldiers, viewing herself as the Florence Nightingale of Staten Island. *[She and the legendary "Lady of the*

Lamp" were each born in 1820.]

Julia tended to wounded Rebel soldiers hauled by train into New York City, and she lobbied to get Washington to free certain Southern prisoners whom she found living in "horrid conditions."

Her life took a drastic turn for the worse only hours after Lincoln was assassinated in Washington in April of 1865. Three enraged Union veterans broke into the Gardiner-Tyler house and threatened to kill Julia and her children. Along with her children, she was rescued by the local police, whose recommended that ex-First Lady move to a more secure location—and to do it in secret.

Her attorney was William M. Evarts, who, along with his close friend, Augustus Prentice, were the two most prominent and visible lawyers on the island.

Two years before, Prentice had acquired 75 St. Marks Place, and at Evarts' urging, he made that address her hideaway.

Under the blanket of night, she moved into Magnolia House with an entourage who included her five children, an Irish-born coachman, a tutor for her offspring, and two servants, each of them recent *emigrés* from the East End of London. Her travails were documented in *John Tyler, the Only President Who Had Two Wives in the White House*, a thesis by Dr. Margaret Boyles of Boston.

Things got really ugly when it became clear that Julia's brother, David, a passionate Yankee and defender of the Union, detested her because of her links to the Confederacy. When their mother died, she bequeathed most to her estate to Julia. David immediately sued, claiming that their mother had suffered from dementia and that Julia had used undue influence to influence her will.

John Tyler's Grave in Richmond

Before being buried with pomp and cirmstance, his body was wrapped in a Confederate flag and lay "in State" in Richmond at the Confederate Congress.

Julia, a New Yorker once famous as "The Rose of Long Island," is buried beside him.

The trial was held in Staten Island's courthouse.

Fearing for her safety, her lawyer advised her to go court, and to conduct her everyday errands, in disguise.

Ultimately, based on the strong resentment that raged against his Confederate sister, David won his case. Evarts appealed it twice but lost each time. Even *The New*

York Times described the trial as a venue for a jury that was unfairly biased against (Confederate, Southern and socially pretentious) Julia.

In the aftermath of the trial, Julia's late mother's homestead on Tyler Street reverted to Julia's brother, David.

Abandoning 75 St. Marks Place, and hard up for money, she returned to Virginia, living with her more prosperous children and converting to Roman Catholicism.

Julia's finances were depleted even further by the Depression of 1873, and she petitioned Congress to grant her its first pension to widows of former presidents. After some reluctance, she was granted $5,000 annually, beginning a policy that exists to this day.

She died in obscurity on July 10, 1889, at the age of 69. The setting was the Exchange Hotel in Richmond, a few doors down from the death site of her husband, the former U.S. president. Her remains rest today with those of President Tyler in the Hollywood Cemetery, in Richmond, Virginia.

Her final words to her children as they clustered around her deathbed were, "Life, my dears, sure does have its ups and downs."

Julia Tyler was the first First Lady to have publicly danced during her tenure in the White House.

She was also the first to be photographed. Here she is, without any of the expensive accessories for which she was frequently berated.

Chapter Three

MAGNOLIA HOUSE MEETS THE FROMMER TRAVEL GUIDES

How Decades as Their Most Prolific Writer Turned Darwin's Conventional Travel Writing into

A CELEBRITY-CHASING ADVENTURE

The publication of *England on $5 a Day* launched a stampede of low-budget post-war travel to the British Isles back in the days when there were bargains galore.

Europe on $5 a Day by Arthur Frommer spawned massive travel to the Continent and created a travel-publishing empire.

On the right, as authored by Porter and Prince, is one of the best guides to France ever published, showing that the Frommer guides were still moving aggressively forward into the 21st Century

The very strong point we want to make in this chapter is that before Blood Moon Productions ever existed, Magnolia House devoted itself to the research and production of travel guides, specifically, THE FROMMER GUIDES.

The venue was unique: We saw the world, experienced the wonders of Europe, and had a fabulous time.

But in 2013, the party ended. In the wake of a recession and radically new, Internet-related changes in how America opted to educate itself about travel, the Frommer guides were radically reorganized, curtailed, and diminished in their scope, research, and titles. A way of life had ended, and Magnolia House was reformatted as the headquarters of a bold new publishing venue, one associated with celebrity biographies, Blood Moon Productions.

In this section, we'll describe Magnolia House's early associations with the then revolutionary "Travel Revolution," and how Magnolia House managed to combine its links to Frommer with celebrity-watching and the gathering of the raw materials that were later adapted into Blood Moon's backlist of celebrity biographies.

How We Used Our Niche at the Frommer Guides as a Vehicle (a Disguise?) for the Meeting & Greeting of Celebrities

Here's How It Started

A Detail from Titian's *The Rape of Europa*.

In 1982, Simon & Schuster hired Danforth Prince, formerly of the Paris Bureau of *The New York Times*, to work on the Frommer Travel Series alongside veteran travel writer, Darwin Porter.

Darwin was already the featured Frommer writer, with roots that extended back to the early days of the series. He developed and turned out dozens of guides to Europe and later, the Caribbean, issuing both their original first editions, and then, later, radically updated followup editions.

[Darwin, incidentally, has been called a "journalistic phenomenon," because of his talent and speed at churning out journalistic copy. His ambition had been to become a top-flight investigative reporter. At the age of nineteen, he was already writing a column for The Miami Herald, *and he later evolved into the youngest-ever Bureau Chief of that newspaper's Key West office, just when the post was heating up over the political turmoil in neighboring Cuba because of the rise to power of Fidel Castro.]*

Unknown to him, Darwin's career goal was about to be derailed, and he soon ventured into a new type of publishing: travel guides.

In New York, Stanley Haggart, a well-known art director in both Hol-

The travel ambitions and visions of Maria Jane Haggart, and her son, Stanley, coincided with cheap prices before World War II and the rise of the travel empire of Arthur Frommer, for whom Darwin (through Stanley) later worked.

Traveling through Europe with her then-young son, and later a resident of Hollywood (where she knew everyone in the early film colony), Mrs. Haggart wrote the pioneering budget travel guide, *Europe on a Shoestring*.

lywood and New York, had returned form England. His advertising accounts had included, among others, working with Joan Crawford to promote Pepsi-Cola.

Born on the plains of Kansas in 1910, he and his widowed mother arrived in Hollywood to begin a new life in 1917. "It was a small town then," he said, "and you got to meet everybody, including Mary Pickford, Greta Garbo, Gloria Swanson, Lillian Gish, and Charlie Chaplin."

In the 1930s, he went to work for RKO, hanging out with such stars as Katharine Hepburn, along with Ginger Rogers, Randolph Scott, Lucille Ball, and Cary Grant. He was a movie extra, appearing in such hits as *Top Hat* with Rogers and Fred Astaire.

In the 1940s, he held several jobs—as radio announcer in Trinidad during the war, a decorating editor of *Family Circle*, and a designer of sets for films. But in 1960, he decided, as a change of pace, to go to England to write a budget travel guide.

Haggart, although a good researcher, was not a writer. As such, he spent several months researching budget accommodations, pubs, and dining spots. He'd been inspired by the publication of *Europe on $5 a Day*, written by a New York lawyer, Arthur Frommer, who had graduated from Yale, where he'd edited the *Yale Law Journal*.

Drafted into the Army during the Korean War, he had been posted in Europe. While a soldier, he also wrote *The G.I.'s Guide to Traveling in Europe*, which became widely popular with servicemen.

After he left the Army, he published the first edition of a budget travel guide, *Europe on $5 a Day*. It became an immediate best seller and launched, in time, a virtual empire devoted to travel.

Back in America, Haggart, with three suitcases of research notes he'd compiled in England, decided to assemble and edit his book in Key West. Before going to England, he had toured as a scenic designer with a play, *Crazy October*, written by his friend, James Leo Herlihy, who was also a novelist.

Travel guru Arthur Frommer, whose tumultuous work habits and busy schedule prevented him from actually writing his series.

TO THE RESCUE came Darwin, who actually wrote and quietly maintained the first and subsequent editions of many variations and many editions of the series that bore Arthur's name.

In addition to almost constant travel to the glam spots of Euorpe, Darwin got to meet scads of celebrities, often on their home turf, between gigs as movie stars

It was Herlihy who had lured him to Florida, but since Haggart was not a real writer, he asked another friend, Darwin Porter, if he'd write the book for Haggart. Accepting the challenge, Porter agreed, and in a few weeks, the book was ready. Both men, young and old, never knew how such a book would later affect their lives forever.

Returning to New York, Haggart submitted the book to Crown Publishers. It just so happened that Frommer, visiting the publisher's offices one afternoon, spotted Haggart's manuscript. He picked it up, took it home, read it that night, and called Haggart the following morning with an offer to publish it.

Of course, it had to be updated and greatly altered. Haggart had focused on B&B houses, pubs, and low-cost restaurants. Frommer, however, wanted a full-service guide to tourist facilities, helpful hints for travelers, and descriptions of shopping and nightlife.

Haggart phoned Porter in Key West and asked him to join him in creating what turned out to be a new series of guidebooks that changed the face of budget travel.

Two views of a young Darwin Porter, (left), as the youngest bureau chief (Key West) in the history of the *Miami Herald*, and (right) as snapped during a pensive moment on the road as the writer who eventually commandeered, as a prolific writer, the annual production of most of the Frommer Guides.

The gig afforded ample opportunity for the care, nurturing, and maintenance of celebrities, many of whose stories eventually made their way into biographies he crafted, through Blood Moon Productions at Magnolia House, in the years following their deaths.

Suddenly, breaking from the dollar-a-day format, Frommer wanted a new series that included the best values in first class, moderate, and budget. Porter wrote the first of the new Frommer Guides, beginning with Italy and England, and going on to cover most of the countries of Western Europe., even Morocco, over the next decades and until 2013. He was the chief Frommer writer, covering spots as far north as Greenland and as far South as the Sahara Desert, as well as the islands of the Caribbean, including The Bahamas and Bermuda. And throughout the many encounters and dramas and problems he encountered, he always brought them back to Magnolia House for solutions and respite.

***

Every now and then, Darwin takes a nostalgic look back at the prices he encountered during his first venture into budget travel in England in 1960.

One of his first stopovers in London was in a comfortable room with a wash basin near Earl's Court. It rented for 84¢ a night in U.S. currency. He paid another 35¢ for breakfast, and only 31¢ for a filling lunch. At night, he dined at Simpson's on the Strand, ordering the specialty, oyster, mushroom, and steak pie, for $1.19.

Moving out of London, he discovered truly astounding bargains. In a stopover at Lord Hurcomb's 18th-Century manor house in Dorking, he was charged only $23.80 for an entire week. In the resort city of Brighton, he found a little seaside hotel near West Pier, where—believe it or not—full board began at $13.23 for an entire week.

As the novelist Margaret Mitchell might say, prices like that are long *Gone With the Wind*. Surely, the world will never see figures like those again.

Here at 75 St. Marks Place, dozens upon dozens of Frommer Travel Guides, following research trips, were written. Haggart eventually went into retirement, living at his home in Key West, living with relatives in Pasadena, or renting a vacation home in Honolulu. He turned the business over to Darwin, before dying in 1980.

Porter worked on the guides from 1960 until he wrote the last one in 2013. During that time, Danforth Prince entered the fray, eventually earning and being promoted to the rank of a full partner.

***

Yet during a half century of traveling the globe, Darwin never abandoned his deeply entrenched goal of crafting celebrity biographies. Over the decades, he collected boxfuls of data, enough to eventually fill two large rooms, about his encounters with celebrities in Europe.

He often conjoined research of a travel destination for Frommer to when celebrities were there. Such was the case when he went to Rome for a travel project while Richard Burton and Elizabeth Taylor were filming *Cleopatra* (1963) and falling in love at the same time.

Many of those revelations appeared later in his biography of Elizabeth Taylor, *There Is Nothing Like a Dame* published in 2012.

The pages that follow are devoted to some other episodes in which travel journalism contributed to insights into celebrity oddities and foibles.

Here, Magnolia House appears as photographed in midsummer from a drone flying high overhead. The drone was operated by overnight guests from Tasmania, staying as overnight guests through AirBnb and availing themselves of the buidling's rich associations with the travel industry and with celebrity scandals.

"Oops!" one of them said after the drone crashed. "There certainly is a lot going on around here!"

Here, buxom Anita Ekberg at the Trevi Fountain in Rome lures her co-star, Marcello Mastroianni, in Fellini's *La Dolce Vita* (1960).

But when Darwin met her while researching *Frommer's Rome,* she was selling used cars in the Eternal City, her beauty having faded with the summer winds.

Italy, Italy!...it's magical, it's historic, and the time Darwin spent there provided huge op-portunities during LA DOLCE VITA period to better understand Hollywood on the Tiber.

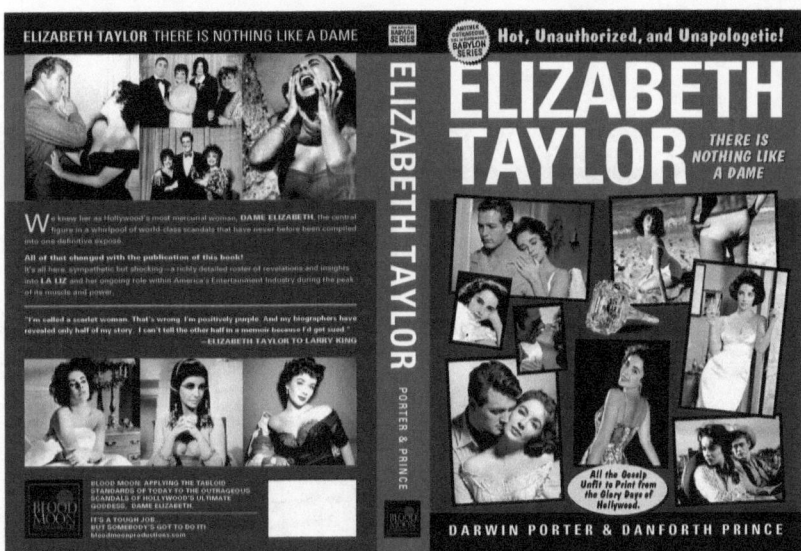

ELIZABETH TAYLOR, There is Nothing Like a Dame, published by Blood Moon in 2012, owed a lot to the on-site information Darwin picked up in Rome during the research of *Frommer's Italy*. It was the most comprehensive overview of Dame Elizabeth's life & career ever published. .

Darwin was in Rome at the time Elizabeth Taylor was impersonating the Queen of the Nile. Off and on the screen, she was having an affair with the Welsh actor, Richard Burton. Trouble was, both of the lovers were married at the time to other partners. The scandal went around the world.

One reporter in Rome labeled the *brouhaha* surrounding their affair and their film as "the most exciting development since the birth of Christ."

Darwin's research for the Frommer Guides in Europe unearthed information about more than just the travel scene. It uncovered salacious memories from dozens of witnesses to the hysteria and excesses of Hollywood on the Tiber, or in London or Paris, or Berlin, or wherever.

Some of those stories were included in two volumes of Blood Moon's Babylon series, both of which are now collector's items. They were marketed to thousands of enquiring minds with sales tags like these:

ALL THE SCANDAL PREVIOUSLY UNFIT TO PRINT

Lurid but little-known scandals from Hollywood's Golden Age, as well as SHOCKING RUNDOWNS OF TODAY'S HOLLYWOOD SCANDALS-IN-THE-MAKING. From the Golden Age of Beautiful Bombshells and Handsome Hunks to today's sleaziest, most corrupt, and most deliciously indecorous but still glamorous hotties.

As they were unfolding, these stories were known only within Hollywood's most decadent cliques. All of that has changed thanks to the release of this book!

BLOOD MOON: Applying the tabloid standards of Today to the Scandals of Hollywood's Golden Age. It's a tough job, but somebody's got to do it!

Chapter Four

THE PORTUGUESE RIVIERA
Where Kings Fled
After They'd Lost Their Thrones

Too often ignored by travelers to the Iberian Peninsula, who visit only Spain, Portugal is a land of fado, fishing villages, beach resorts, art, architecture...and the good life.

At least the European aristocracy, often former kings who had lost their crowns, thought so when they discovered the coastal resorts of Cascais and Estoril, near Lisbon.

The Portuguese Riviera, west of Lisbon, is known locally as the Costa do Sol. Its main resort is Estoril, the home of some of the wealthiest people in Europe. As a resort, it has been frequented by celebrities and movie stars of stage and screen.

Edward VIII came here with his new bride, the Duchess of Windsor, after he'd abandoned his throne for "the woman I love."

During World War II, in which Portugal remained neutral, ex-kings fled here after Nazi troops stormed and took over their kingdoms. Estoril became a retreat of European aristocracy: "a flock" of dukes, princes, counts, barons, and their titled ladies.

Bordering Estoril, Cascais was put on the map in the 1870s by King Luis I of Portugal. He established a summer residence for his family here, opening onto the sea. Portuguese aristocrats followed, and the resort blossomed.

World War II was an epic event, but particularly ironic in Estoril. Nazi officers drank in the same bars as Allied soldiers from England and America.

In 1941, the author, Ian Fleming, arrived, and found it a center of espionage. "Everybody was spying on everybody else," he said. "An idea came to me one night. Thus, my James Bond 007 master spy was born."

"I didn't order dry martinis anywhere except in Estoril," he said. "Usually, I like my gin wet. But sitting in a low antique chair at the wood-paneled Spy's Bar at the Hotel Palacio, nothing but a dry gin martini will do."

Spy's Bar is still here today, offering a menu of 23 gins, not just Gordon's.

In Estoril, the Palacio became the retreat of exiled royalty fleeing lost kingdoms as German tanks rolled through their capitals, confiscating power. Sometimes, they escaped with just the clothes on their backs...

Top top photo: King Luis I of Portugal
Top photo: the Pena Palace in Sintra
Center photo: Hotel Palacio in Estoril
Lower photo: The waterfront in Cascais

and their jewelry. Lacking local currency, they often paid their hotel bills in gold, rubies, and diamonds.

The Count of Paris, "pretender" to the throne of France, held what was arguably the most prestigious title. Had he still ruled, he'd have been identified as Henri VI. He was recognized in royal circles as the descendant in the male line of France's "Citizen King," Louis Philippe d'Orléans, who ruled until 1848. French Royalists also regarded the Count of Paris as the rightful heir to Henri de Bourbon, the last descendant of King Louis XVI.

Ian Fleming: "An idea has come to me. Why not create a master British spy character and call him James Bond?"

The now deceased Count of Paris was born in 1908 in France, but grew up in Morocco on his family plantation, raising livestock and crops.

The French government would not permit his family to live in France, so their European homestead was an estate near Brussels.

In 1926, the Count became the Dauphin of France in *prétence* when his father was designated as the Orléanist claimant to the throne.

By 1939, with the outbreak of World War II in Europe, the Count joined the French Foreign Legion fighting in North Africa.

In the winter of 1942, French Royalists clustered around the count, planning a future coup, hoping to overthrow any government

Le Comte de Paris, born 1908: "If my ancestors had held onto their territory, I would today control large land grants in North America, with New Orleans as my capital!"

Charles de Gaulle might form after the Allies defeated the Nazis.

They wanted to restore a king to rule over France, and the Count, as the pretender to the throne, heartily endorsed their plan. However, General Dwight Eisenhower, the Allied commander, nixed the idea, asserting "those days of Louis XIV, the Sun King, or Marie Antoinette, his wife, are gone forever—and will not return."

In 1950, the travel ban against the Count of Paris was rescinded, and he returned to France from exile, purchasing a château in Amboise in the Loire Valley.

He became a spendthrift, supporting residences in Morocco, Brazil, and Estoril. Faced with mounting bills, he had to spend a lot of his family's wealth, including jewelry, paintings by Old Masters, and centuries-old antiques, some of which had been rescued from Versailles.

Over dinner at the Estoril Palacio, the Count of Paris was rather blunt in assessing his current position in life: "I was a lowly farm boy growing up in Morocco. Now I preside in name only over a once great kingdom. My ancestors once owned a huge hunk of the United States. They should never have sold it."

At the end of the dinner, he rose to his feet, an act that was immediately replicated by everyone else at the dinner party, including Darwin Porter. First-timers at such an event had been carefully instructed in royal protocol.

"I have to get up at four in the morning to milk my cows," the pretender to the throne of France said, before leaving.

In 1984, the Count officially declared that his son, Henri VII, had forfeited his right to inherit his title because he had divorced his first wife and married a second one outside the Catholic Church. But two years later, he rescinded his mandate.

The Count of Paris died of prostate cancer at the age of 90 in Dreux, France. His son became the pretender to the Throne of France. This heir apparent, Prince Jean, Duc de Vendôme, was born in 1933.

He also assumed the title Duc de France, which was in use one thousand years ago.

Darwin was once asked by his editor at Simon & Schuster to write a book about the ex-royals in exile, including the Count of Paris. He always used the Palacio as his headquarters. Danforth Prince followed suit when assigned to write travel guides to Lisbon and also for the country of Portugal.

Darwin's friend was the American-born public relations director of the Palacio, and he made certain that Darwin was included in any visit or din-

The *Infante* Juan, aka the Count of Barcelona, born 1913.

"First, Franco takes my throne and then, in time, he turns it over to my son. I'm left to languish in exile."

His son, Juan Carlos, King of Spain, in a photo from the 1970s.

"I detested Franco. But he did restore the monarchy and made me king, but only after he died."

ner party with a former king.

At one dinner event, Darwin bowed low when he was introduced to the Count of Barcelona. Born in June of 1913 at the Royal Palace of La Granja, he was the third son and designated heir of King Alfonso XIII of Spain and Victoria Eugenie of Battenberg.

The Count's father was forced into exile when the Second Spanish Republic was proclaimed in 1931. His brothers renounced the throne, making Don Carlos next in line to the defunct royal seat. He bore the title of Prince of Asturias.

He served in the British Navy in 1935, stationed in Bombay. With the coming of the Spanish Civil War, Don Carlos remained in exile, and the Fascist dictator, Francisco Franco, became the ruler of Spain.

In 1935, through the efforts of Victor Emmanuel of Italy, Juan Carlos met his future wife, Doña Maria de las Mercedes de Borbón Dos-Sicilias y Orléans.

Franco declared Spain a monarchy in 1947, although he would remain as dictator until his death. But he passed over the ascension to the throne of Don Carlos and named his son, Juan Carlos, as the future king. After Franco's death, he became king. Perhaps as a consolation prize, Juan Carlos designated his father as Count of Barcelona. Born in 1938, Juan Carlos had married Princess Sophia of Greece and Denmark in 1962.

At the previously mentioned dinner party in Estoril, the Count of Barcelona did not conceal his loathing of Franco. "My son will rule instead of me," he said.

"There was a sadness in his voice," Darwin recalled. "I think he loved his son but resented him at the same time. He seemed to think his son, through no fault of his own, had taken from him his right to rule over a country he still loved,."

The Count of Barcelona died in April 1993. Given a state funeral, he was buried with honors in the Royal Crypt at the Monastery of San Lorenzo del Escorial, near Madrid. His wife survived him by seven years.

Umberto II of Italy, the "34-day King," in 1944.

In Cascais, he developed a fondness for handsome Portuguese soldiers.

***

The deposed king that Darwin most wanted to meet was Umberto II, the exiled

King of Italy, the last monarch to ever sit on that throne. He had been Italy's ruler for only 34 days, from May 9 to June 12 of 1946.

For years, Darwin had heard scandalous stories spread about him, and felt he'd make an intriguing chapter in his book on the ex-monarchs.

Umberto was the only son of five children of King Victor Emmanuel III and Queen Elena. But trouble lay ahead during Umberto's brief reign. A successful referendum voted to abolish the monarch, and Italy was declared a Republic. Umberto fled to Cascais in Portugal, never to set foot in Italy ever again.

Umberto had been born in the Castle of Racconigi in Racconigi, Italy (in the Piedmont, near Turin) in 1904. By 1930, he had married Princess Marie José of Belgium, but it was what was called a "lavender marriage." It was a continuation of many unsuccessful attempts to conceal his homosexuality. The attempt failed.

In exile, the king and his former queen separated, although they sometimes met for special occasions.

Mussolini had once had detectives file a dossier on Umberto's homosexual affairs, most often with soldiers in the Italian Army. Perhaps he planned to use it for blackmail. During the war, many Italian newspapers had run exposés of their king's homosexuality. His sexual preference had become an issue during the post war referendum to decide if Italy wanted to abolish the monarchy.

The PR director at the Palacio had arranged a 10AM meeting for Darwin with the former king within his residence in Cascais.

"It was more like a villa than a palace, and a handsome young man, rumored to be the king's lover, showed us into the living room," Darwin said. "Apparently, Umberto had forgotten about the appointment and emerged sleepily from his bedroom in his jockey shorts, not even bothering to put on his silk robe, which the young man soon brought to him. Coffee was served."

During the three hours Darwin spent there, Umberto surprised him with details of his private life. "Why not?" he said. "It's hardly a secret. A ton of newsprint has made that clear to the world."

But before that, he spoke of Hitler, of Mussolini, of Eisenhower, of his parents, and his life in exile. He said that a former lieutenant in the Portuguese army kept him supplied with a series of young soldiers. "He knows my type and is never wrong in the choices he picks for me. Each soldier leaves with a hundred-dollar bill, which is good for men used to living on a soldier's pay."

His surprised both Darwin and PR director by telling them he had had some notable high-profile affairs with both Luchino Visconti and Jean

Marias.

"Sometimes, celebrities seek me out just for the distinction of saying they have gone to bed with the former King of Italy." He cited Porfirio Rubirosa as his favorite "conquest."

He also claimed affairs with three male Italian movie stars, but "discretion prevents me from naming them."

He also cited as his "most exciting week ever spent with celebrities" was when Freddy McEvoy and his best friend, Errol Flynn, showed up on his doorstep. "Pure, unadulterated debauchery."

In that day, the celebrities' names were widely known. But for those born to an earlier generation, a quick thumbnail sketch might be in order.

[Most of the world knew (or once knew) who Errol Flynn was, the great lover and swashbuckler of such hits as Captain Blood, The Adventures of Robin Hood, and Don Juan.

Two notorious playboys, movie star Errol Flynn and heiress-marrying Freddy McEvoy show up in Monaco for the wedding of Grace Kelly to Prince Rainier.

The other men on Umberto's list of lovers are lesser known today. Luchino Visconti was an Italian theater, opera, and cinema director known for such first-rate pictures as the 1960 Rocco and His Brothers, the 1963 The Leopard, and the 1971 Death in Venice. Although he looked like a burly, macho truck driver, he made no secret of his homosexuality. Other lovers of Visconti included director Franco Zeffirelli and the Austrian actor Helmut Berger. Visconti, who smoked 120 cigarettes a day, died in Rome of a stroke at the age of 69.

Handsome and studly Jean Marais, a star of more than 100 French films, was hailed in the Parisian press as "a French God, our answer to the Viking warriors." He was also a writer, director, and sculptor. The famous

Film director Luchino Visconti always fell in love with his leading men.

French writer Jean Cocteau discovered him in 1937, and he and Marais were lovers until the author's death in 1963.

Marais lived on until 1998, dying at the age of 84 in Cannes. Two years earlier, the government had awarded him membership in the French Legion of Honor for his enormous contribution to French cinema.

Flynn's best friend and sometimes lover was Frederick McEvoy, an Australia-born sportsman and socialite. When not in bed with Flynn, he married several rich heiresses. He was given the nickname "Suicide Freddie" because of his love of danger, both in sports and in life.

Along with Porfirio Rubirosa, McEvoy was called "The Playboy of the Western World." The two men often indulged in a contest to see which one of them had the larger penis, as each of them was celebrated for their endowments.

Jean Marais posed with his own reflection in a mirror in *Orpheus* (1950). The handsome French actor was the lover and "discovery" of the then-scandalous and terribly famous French poet, writer, designer, playwright, artist and filmmaker, Jean Cocteau.

Women who became intimate with each of them claimed that they were exactly equal in size and dimensions.

Rubirosa, born in the Dominican Republic, was called "The World's Greatest Lover," marrying two of the planet's richest women, tobacco heiress Doris Duke and Woolworth heiress Barbara Hutton.

Waiters in Paris called giant peppermills "Rubirosas." He was fond of seducing Hollywood stars, notably Zsa Zsa Gabor, Ava Gardner, Susan Hayward, Eartha Kitt, Joan Crawford, Jayne Mansfield, Marilyn Monroe, and Kim Novak, as well as the Argentine dictator, Evita Perón.

He told Umberto, "I consider a day in which I make love only once a wasted day. If a woman is not available, although they usually are, I will grab some young man and send him to heaven…or else to the hospital."

***

Darwin was in Estoril when the latest James Bond thriller, *On Her Majesty's Secret Service* (1969), was being filmed at the Palacio. This was the first James Bond movie shot without 007 himself, Sean Connery. Taking over for the Scot was a newcomer from Australia, George Lazenby. [Originally, Sean Connery was to have reprised his now-familiar role alongside the French sex kitten, Brigitte Bardot. What a movie that would have been!]

On Darwin's last visit, he met and talked with some of the staff members who had been late teenaged bellhops when he'd met them. Now they were old and gray, planning their retirements.

Many memories were evoked, including the varieties of high heels that had clanked against the marble floors. Grace Kelly, Princess of Monaco, came to mind, and the silent screen vamp, Gloria Swanson, later to star in the classic *Sunset Blvd.* in 1950. Everyone on the staff remembered the arrival of Zsa Zsa Gabor dressed in shocking pink.

In the bar, Darwin sat in the same seat once warmed by the Count of Barcelona who had come by every afternoon for his dry martini.

But outside, the modern world had intruded. Darwin noted that the Estoril's old-fashioned Hotel Atlántico had been torn down. During the war, it had been the favorite of Nazi officers.

In its place was a gray hulk, the Intercontinental.

That moonlit night, Darwin walked along the beach where the romantic poet, Lord Byron, had once trod.

Wandering from country to country in exile, with widely publicized stopovers in Portugal, the Duke and Duchess of Windsor weren't welcomed in England, but were lavishly celebrated everywhere else and occasionally sighted by Porter and Prince.

The world didn't know until the publication of later *exposés* that he liked young men and that she "just adored" beautiful girls. And there were also those embarrassing outreaches to the Nazis before World War II that were so difficult to explain...

WHO ELSE WAS A TRAVELER LIKELY TO ENCOUNTER ON THE PORTUGUESE RIVIERA?

The twilight of a tabloid goddess is bitterly evident in this shocking photograph of an aging "professional socialite" (Woolworth heiress Barbara Hutton) on her last legs.

Here she is seen in 1972 with the handsome Spanish matador, twenty-four year old Angel Teruel. Draped in a mink stole, Hutton was sixty years old when the photo was taken but her so-called friends cattily remarked that she looked eighty-five.

Hailed in Madrid as the greatest bullfighter since Dominguin, Teruel was known in Spain for killing bulls in the arena, and for being a bull at night with the ladies. Hutton fell for him and, although she hated the brutality of bullfighting, had a bodyguard carry her to a front row so she could watch her beloved. As she aged, she wore more and more diamonds to the *corrida*. Teruel would present her with the blood-soaked ear of the bull at the end of the fight. In return, she showered him with gifts such as a gold-and-diamond ring and a new Rolls-Royce.

Hutton was bitterly attacked in the Spanish press for "tempting our national hero of the ring by waving her ill-gotten Woolworth millions in his bedazzled eyes." She got the point and bid her lover *adios* before fleeing back to the horrors of Tangier. In Tangier, party guests and her own staff were systematically looting her treasures, and her bank accounts dropped precariously.

One of the world's richest women died bankrupt on May 11, 1979, at the age of sixty-six. There were only ten mourners at her funeral, which took place at the Woodlawn Memorial Cemetery in the Bronx. One obit claimed, "America's Gilded Age officially ended today with the death of its last standard-bearer, Miss Barbara Hutton. Peace at last for the troubled heiress."

Chapter Five

TEA FOR TWO WITH MISS MARPLE

MARGARET RUTHERFORD

Spectacularly frumpy, Margaret Rutherford evolved into a universal stereotype for the well-bred, very polite older English eccentrics who made Britain Great.

Here's how Darwin Porter met and bonded with her during one of his early trips to the UK for research of *The Frommer Guides*.

"Chances are that there will never be another Margaret Rutherford," asserted Darwin Porter to Danforth Prince, his co-author of zillions of editions of *Frommer's England, Frommer's London, Frommer's Scotand & Wales*, and several commercially successful spin-offs.

He was referring to the indomitable Dame Margaret, a London-born character actress of stage, screen, and television.

She is best known for her interpretation of Agatha Christie's murder-sniffing amateur detective, Miss Marple.

Born in London in May of 1892 during the reign of Queen Victoria, Margaret experienced tragedy early in life.

Her father, William Rutherford, a journalist and poet, suffered a nervous breakdown the year of her birth and was committed to the Bathnal House Lunatic Asylum.

After his release, years later, he murdered his father, the Rev. Julius Benn, by bludgeoning him to death with a chamberpot before slashing his own throat with a pocket knife. Tragedy was also in store for her pregnant mother, who hung herself from a tree.

This led to Margaret suffering long months of depression, fearing for her own sanity.

In 1925, at the age of 33, she made her stage debut at the Old Vic. She soon became known for her "spaniel jowls" and bulky frame.

She waited a long time to gain much attention, which came only in 1939 as England went to war. She starred in John Gielgud's *The Importance of Being Earnest* at the Globe Theatre. In 1941, she had another hit with Noël Coward's *Blythe Spirit* at the Piccadilly Theatre.

Critic Kenneth Tynan wrote, "The unique thing about Margaret Rutherford is that she can act with her chin."

She repeated her stage role in *Blythe Spirit* on the screen in 1945, and, as she put it, "that part put me on the map. The public remembered me cycling through Kent, head held high, back straight, and a cape fluttering in the wind."

Role after role followed until she left the stage in 1966.

Back in the 1950s, when she was married to actor Stringer Davis, the couple adopted a son, the writer Gordon Hall, who was already in his 20s. He underwent gender reassignment and emerged as Dawn Langley Simmons, later writing a memoir of his mother a year after her death.

Margaret's greatest screen triumph came in the Terrence Rattigan's 1963 film, *The V.I.P.'s*, with an all-star cast headed by Elizabeth

Taylor and Richard Burton, with Dame Maggie Smith, Louis Jourdan, and Orson Welles in supporting roles. Margaret won both an Oscar and a Golden Globe.

One of her last parts was in a supporting role in *A Countess from Hong Kong* (1967), directed by Charlie Chaplin, and co-starring Marlon Brando and Sophia Loren. Margaret later told the press, "That trio...my oh my! All three of them were grand ladies. I was the only commoner."

Darwin first encountered Margaret when he was scouting for bed and breakfast houses on Earl's Court to recommend for inclusion in *England on $5 and $10 a Day*. The hostess there told him that Margaret came for tea in their old-fashioned salon every afternoon at 4:30PM. He asked if he could be introduced.

The next day, Margaret welcomed him to join her, claiming, "I could use some company, especially from a man so young...and an American at that. Is it really true that in America you heat a kettle of water, pour it over a tea bag in a cup, and actually drink the vile potion?"

He admitted that was true.

Day after day, for two weeks in a row, he showed up to have a "cuppa" with her. She amused him, telling stories of her life. Her assessments were often blunt.

"I knew or worked with such actors as John Gielgud, Noël Coward, and Sir Larry (Olivier). Each had a fondness for young men. I think all of them seduced a young Richard Burton. Of course, I see nothing wrong with that. A person can't help who they are attracted to. I'd rather men make love to each other than kill each other on the battlefield."

"Diana Dors, our version of Marilyn Monroe, liked anything in trousers walking on Piccadilly Circus. I admire a woman who reaches out and takes what she wants."

"Peter Sellers...Oh Peter. He was so full of himself."

"Perhaps my greatest disappoint-

In addition to many portrayals of Miss Marple, Margaret Rutherford received enormous acclaim after co-starring with Richard Burton and Elizabeth Taylor in *The V.I.P.s.*

She was honored again when the Queen of England, Elizabeth II, elevated her to the rank of a Dame of the British Empire.

Miss Marple fans worldwide applauded wildly.

ment was my loss of the Mrs. Danvers role in the film *Rebecca* (1940) with Sir Larry and Joan Fontaine. It went to Judith Anderson. But since the role called for a dangerous lesbian, Judith would know more about that life than I would."

"I think what ruins a marriage is having a woman forced to have sex with her husband: Couples can have a happy marriage without her being summoned to bed like a sex slave. Stringer and I have the happiest marriage in England, without all those demands on a woman. What do you think?"

"Miss Rutherford, if you say that is so, then I believe it is true," Darwin said, gallantly.

Suffering from Alzheimer's, Margaret died in her home in Buckinghamshire on May 22, 1972. Stringer was at her bedside. He died the following year.

"That was sad, and it did not surprise me," Darwin said. "They were always known as 'the odd couple,' but I knew one could not go on living without the other."

Miss Marple, sleuthing and doing the Twist with her real-life husband and movie cohort, Stringer.

Relentlessly deadpan, and relentlessly funny, she successfully satirized both herself and the times in which she lived. Her fans and most of the U.K. adored her.

Chapter Six

AN OASIS IN MARRAKECH
THE VILLA TAYLOR

MEMORIES OF SIR WINSTON, FDR, & THE FRENCH COLONIAL EMPIRE

Winston Churchill with Franklin Roosevelt, discuss war strategies together in the tower at the Villa Taylor. Newsworthy clients who arrived later in the century included JFK, Averill Harriman, Brigitte Bardot, the Aly Khan, Rita Hayworth, Charlie Chaplin, Peter O'Toole, Mick Jagger, and at least a dozen others.

"Of all the private homes, grand hotels, not-so-grand hotels, country houses, converted mansions, modest B&Bs, or castles at which Darwin Porter and I stayed, none equaled the Villa Taylor," said Danforth Prince. It lies in the European quarter of exotic Marrakech, hailed as 'The Paris of the Sahara.' We were there researching *Frommer's Morocco*.

The Villa Taylor and its gardens, surrounded by walls of pink stucco, lies about a mile from the 12th-Century ramparts that enclose the ancient city.

Darwin's invitation—and ultimately Danforth's, too—came from his long-time friend, Mrs. Virginia Peirce, the socialite and fashion designer who spent part of her adult life in Key West, Florida.

In her heyday, she'd once turned down a marriage proposal from J. Paul Getty, then the richest man in the world. She used the ridiculous excuse that she wasn't in love with him.

Villa Taylor takes its name from its original owner, a railroad heiress and granddaughter of Ulysses S. Grant, the super-rich Mrs. Moses Taylor, who had it constructed between 1923 and 1926 as a vacation retreat for herself. During World War II, the villa became the Moroccan headquarters of the U.S. Army.

Two years after the war, Villa Taylor was offered as a wedding gift to her son from the Boston-born mother of Comte Charles de Breteuil. In 1947, the count moved in with his bride, the newly rechristened Contesse Madeleine de Breteuil. To her international coterie of famous guests to the years to come, she was known as "Boule."

The count was one of the most famous publishers in the world. A "monument" to the French colonial regime in north and Central Africa, he owned newspapers in Paris, Marrakech, Casablanca, Tangier, Dakar, and Senegal.

As you approach the villa, the street scene outside looks like a portrait from the 15th Century. Old sheep herders lead donkey carts carrying wool for sale in the Souk. Their faces concealed, Arab women scurry past on their way to open-air stalls selling fruits and vegetables. Nearly all the men passing by are clad in hooded kaftans.

Villa Taylor is a serene oasis set

LONG AGO AND FAR AWAY, WHEN PARTS OF AFRICA WERE COLONIES OF FRANCE

The left figure in the photo here is the Comte Charles de Breteuil, scion of one of the most illustrious families of the *ancien regime*.

Snapped in 1931 in the Gare St.-Lazare in Paris, at the time of the International Colonial Exposition of 1931, he evolved into one of the major publishers of French-language newspapers in French Colonial Africa.

His mother, the Boston-born American heiress, Mrs. Moses Taylor, presented the Villa Taylor to him and his bride, the former Solange de Ganay ("Boule") as a wedding gift.

Years later, during time when they were headquartered at Magnolia House, Darwin Porter and Danforth Prince soaked up the atmosphere at the most impressive and evocative private monument in Africa.

apart from the bustle and noise of the Medina. But even from within its walls one could hear the *muezzins* in the distance, calling the faithful to prayer. The chant of *"Allah u Akbar"* resounds through the desert air. These chants compete with the birdsongs from the villa's gardens.

You come up to the gatehouse that is cut out of the walls enveloping the exclusive property. The wall is closeted in rich foliage and vines. An armed guard in a kaftan checks the approved list of guests and allows them entrance.

Before meeting the countess, visitors enter a veritable Garden of Eden minus Adam and Eve. Spider ferns and flowering shrubs flank your pathway as you roam in a world of flowers and trees that include palms, lemon, cypress, and olive. Among the many flowers are larkspur, jasmine, gardenias, amaryllis, multi-hued snapdragons, and bougainvillea in a rainbow of colors, in bloom throughout the year.

A male might feel like a Sultan straight out of *Arabian Nights* exploring his gardens before heading inside palace to deflower the beauties waiting for him.

At last you come face to face with the Comtesse herself, a formidable but gracious woman who has hosted kings, ex-kings who had lost their thrones in Europe or the Middle East, international beauties such as Brigitte Bardot in the late 1950s, movie stars such as Peter O'Toole, and politicians. She also hosted, among others, two famous women, Jacqueline Kennedy Onassis, who showed up with a gentleman Boule didn't want to name, and Princess Margaret with another gentleman she didn't want to name. It was the kind of place where indiscretions were strictly off the record.

Boule is your guide through elegant rooms crafted by skilled artisans from the imperial city of Fez. You see painted plaster walls, traditional mosaic tile work, and elaborately carved ceilings.

You are assigned your suite, Darwin the chamber occupied in 1943 by Sir Winston Churchill. "The marble bathtub could hold ten corpulent Churchills," he said.

"I was shown to the other suite, also with a large marble bathtub, once occupied by Franklin D. Roosevelt when he met with Churchill in 1943," Danforth said.

Towering over the villa and its gardens is a majestic five-story tower with tiny sitting rooms on each level. From its balconies, panoramic views can be seen, not only over all of Marrakech, but over to the landmark Koutoubia Minaret built in the 12th Century of pink sandstone. In the far distance loom the Atlas Mountains.

The dinner setting is one of the grand experiences of life at the villa. The dining table is set in the gardens, with an ornamental pool of sapphire waters. Green tiles here have the subdued tone of the mimosa trees and cypresses. Next to the pool is a garden planted with lilies.

You come upon a towering nude statue of a male, that of the Comtesse's late son, Jean de Breteuil. The statue stands in the midst of clumps of ivy. You learn later that he was a celebrated male beauty of his day, and that he was murdered by his gay lover.

You're shown into the poolside bar for pre-dinner champagne. The posters decorating the bar were a gift from Boule's neighbor, the Parisian designer Yves St. Laurent, her neighbor up the street where he, too, lives in a lavish villa with his lover.

The following night, St. Laurent and friend showed up for dinner: "As it turned out, he learned that I, too, had worked in *haute couture* fashion in Paris, so we chatted for a while," Danforth said. "He had marvelous stories about the Parisian fashion world, sharing his opinions about Coco Chanel—'a former Nazi' (his words)—and Christian Dior. He also spoke of Pierre Cardin and Pierre Balmain, who also owned villas in Marrakech, which they visited during escapes from the rigors of Paris and its fashion scene."

Among the visitors who followed was the deposed Shah of Iran who, in 1979, fled his country as a fundamentalist Islamic revolution swept his world and its premises away.

"The next evening, as we dined alone with Boul, she shared a dark secret," Danforth said. "She informed us that the King of Morocco and his entourage arrived one night to inform her that he was taking over the Villa with the intention of converting it into another of his royal palaces, but with the understanding that she'd be granted a lifetime residency. He pointedly noted that with the murder of her son, she had no other living heir."

In the interim, during the remainder of his lifetime, he assigned five gardeners to keep her grounds in mint condition. Also, at the gate, he would post a rotating series of armed guards, three a day, each employed in eight-hour shifts. Not only that, but he would bring in craftsmen from Fez to keep the villa in top condition, ready for his immediate occupancy after her death.

***

Unknown to most of the world, Villa Taylor played an important role in the history of World War II.

Between January 14 and 24, the fabled Casablanca Conference between Sir Winston Churchill and the U.S. President Franklin D. Roosevelt, was held in Casablanca, French Morocco. Also present was General Charles de Gaulle, representing the Free French Forces. Joseph Stalin was invited, but could not attend, as he was engaged in the deadly Battle of Stalingrad against Hitler's Nazi soldiers.

In his memoirs, Churchill wrote about his invitation at the time FDR was departing Casablanca. "You cannot come all the way to Morocco without seeing Marrakech," he told FDR. "Let us spend two more days here. Wait until you see the sunset over the snows of the Atlas Mountains."

The only suitable abode in Marrakech at the time was the luxurious Villa Taylor, then in American hands.

Roosevelt accepted, and elaborate precautions were set into play. Along the 150-mile route to Marrakech, thousands of American troops stood guard. A double assassination of these two Allied leaders would have forced the rewriting of the history of the 20th Century.

At the Villa, great security measures were taken, and anti-aircraft guns were installed outside. Bright red boxes called "scramblers" were installed at strategic points to safeguard wartime communications.

Photo displays Jean-Francois de Breteuil, stepson of **Solange de Ganay,** (Marie Madeleine Jacqueline Solange de Ganay; aka La Comtesse de Breteuil; aka "Boul"), born December 17, 1902 in Salbris, France, deceased August 25, 2003 in the 8th arondissement of Paris.

A distinguished ethnologist noted for her documentation of the Dogon tribes of Mali, she is remembered by hundreds of guests who met and admired her during her ownership and administration of the Villa Taylor in Marrakech.

In the background is the Chateau de Breteuil, the symbol of a family prominently featured in the cultural and history of France. Three of the chief ministers to the Kings of France derived from here,

Located 32 miles southwest of Paris and still nominally under the control of the family who built it, it now receives 120,000 visitors a year as a showcase for the patrimony of France.

Roosevelt was said to have fallen in love with the villa after being escorted inside. A highlight for him was when his security guards carried him up five flights right before sunset, so that he could admire the panorama over the Atlas Mountains. "It was everything that Winston said it was...and more," the President claimed.

Before a lavish dinner, FDR sat in the elegant salon on cushions. Henry Hopkins, his chief aide, entered as the President held out his hand. "I am the Pasha. You can kiss my hand."

"That's a hell of a lot better than having to kiss your ass," Hopkins countered.

Later that night, Averell Harriman joined them for dinner. It was reported that Roosevelt and Churchill stayed up until 3:30AM drafting the historic document, the "Casablanca Declaration of Unconditional Surrender." Both leaders agreed they would accept "nothing less" from the Axis powers, including Hitler and Mussolini, and the military leaders of Japan. Back in the United States, on February 12, 1943, FDR, in a radio address to the nation, outlined a commitment: "We mean no harm to the common people of the Axis nations. But we do mean to impose punishment and retribution upon their guilty, barbaric leaders."

That December of 1943, Churchill, feeling ill and tired from the strain of World War II, had returned to the Villa Taylor to recuperate and to paint. His painting from the top of the tower had been the only known artwork he had crafted throughout the entire course of the war.

He wrote to FDR about his visit. "I wish you could be here with me. Last night, Eisenhower was with us. Montgomery is here tonight."

He expressed his desire to stay here in "this delectable asylum," but he had to fly to the British stronghold of Gibraltar and on the dangerous flight back to London at war. Big plans were on the way, none bigger than the Allied invasion of the Continent, scheduled to begin in occupied France in June of 1944.

IF THE VILLA TAYLOR COULD TALK

It would reveal the secrets of some of the most famous people in the world, many of whom did their best to conceal their off-the-record flings.

Jacqueline Kennedy Onassis showed up with a secret lover. Princess Margaret slipped behind its walls with her "discovery" from the Caribbean island of Mustique.

Even General Eisenhower came here with his wartime mistress, far from the prying eyes of his wife, Mamie.

The Countess Charles de Breteuil was, according to Pierre Bergé (long time companion and business director for Yves St.-Laurent) and other French expatriates, "a pillar around which the entire community revolved." She lived in the Villa Taylor, the most sumptuous residence in Marrakech, a mix of Berber architecture, Arab artisanship, and American-inspired Art Deco.

She was a natural, blue-eyed blonde with an extraordinary personality and a hostess unlike anyone else. Thin and elongated like a thread, a model of kindness, she organized dinners that were perfectly presented by uniformed majordomos in a very French style with perfect etiquette.

Because she didn't have a lot of money, she invented the system of "paying guests." According to Danforth, "As the years passed, she evolved into one of my role models because of the style of hospitality she extended. Some of it, to the degree that I could, I tried to replicate at Magnolia House."

Chapter Seven

PURSUING THOR HEYERDAHL

The "Neo-Viking" Who Sailed in a Handmade Balsa Raft Across 5,000 Miles of Pacific Ocean

This replication of how Thor Heyerdahl looked during his "insane" but successful expedition on a raft from the coast of Peru to the islands of Polynesia is a press and PR photo from the documentary made in 1950 in the wake of his transformation into one of Norway's most widely publicized heroes.

Before setting out to write the first edition of *Frommer's Norway*, the editor at Simon & Schuster requested a special feature on famous Norwegians. That would most definitely include Leif Eriksson (circa 1,000 AD), son of Erik the Red.

Leif had sailed west, perhaps to what is now Labrador, Newfoundland, and Greenland. Heyerdahl always believed he was the reincarnation of Leif, a time traveler who had nothing to do with God, since he was an atheist.

Born in Larvik, Norway, in 1914, Thor Heyerdahl was named after the

Norse god of thunder, weather, and crops.

In Oslo, Darwin met with the director of tourism, who asked how he might assist in Darwin's coverage of Norway. He wanted an interview with Heyerdahl for his feature. The director doubted if the explorer would meet with him, but in a surprise move, he agreed to see Darwin the following night at his home. He would meet him from 7 to 8PM, but the two men bonded and talked until around 3AM, with a few drinks along the way.

Of course, the whole world knew at that point that Heyerdahl, in 1947, had taken his balsa wood raft and sailed from the coast of Peru to the Tuamotu Islands, a French-controlled archipelago in the South Pacific, east of the Society Islands.

In person, Heyerdahl was a big, strapping Viking who to Darwin evoked Stewart Granger in the best of his swashbuckling adventures.

The explorer was both an adventurer and an ethnographer with a background in zoology, botany, and geography. He attributed his interest in zoology to his brilliant mother, Alison Lyng. Born in 1873, she maintained a life-long fascination with Charles Darwin's theory of evolution.

As a boy, Heyerdahl established a zoological museum in his back yard, its chief attraction being an adder, the venomous viper.

As a student at the University of Oslo, he developed a passion with Polynesian culture and history.

He settled for a while in Berlin, where he became involved with experts in ethnography. After a few months, they banded together and contributed enough marks to finance Heyderdahl's exploratory flights to isolated Pacific islands with the intention of studying how local animals had found their way to such far and distant corners of the globe. In 1936, he set out for the Marquesas Island, thus launching his career as one of the world's greatest explorers.

Eventually, he returned to Oslo to resume his work but was horrified when Nazi soldiers overran Norway and the king was forced to flee. He endured the deprivations of occupation until 1944, when he joined the Free Norwegian Forces. As resistance fighters based in the northern province of Finnmark, they were determined to drive the Germans from their homeland.

In 1947, two years after the war's end, Heyerdahl embarked on an adventure that would be documented in books about the world's greatest sea voyages. In Peru, he and five brave sailors constructed a raft made of balsa wood and bamboo, lashed together with other local materials. He dubbed his little raft in honor of the supreme creator god of the pre-Incans, Viracocha (aka *Kon-Tiki*).

Thor Heyerdahl holds a shark fished from the ocean in 1947 aboard the *Kon Tiki*

In the bleak aftermath of WWII, Heyerdahl captured the imagination of the world.

They set out on this wild adventure, which would last for 101 days. On April 7, they crashed onto a reef offshore from the then-uninhabited atoll of Raroia in the Tuamotu Islands, about 450 miles from Tahiti. Everyone aboard survived.

Thor had proved his theory that ancient Incas could have migrated from South America to the islands of Polynesia, using rafts like the one he'd used. Old drawing of Inca rafts by Spanish *conquistadores* and native legends backed up his theory.

A book on the Kon-Tiki voyage was translated into 70 languages, and a documentary film based on its saga won an Oscar in 1951.

Today, visitors to Oslo can see the *Kon-Tiki* on Bygdøy Island in a museum custom-designed to display it.

A while later, Darwin went on to write yet another article about Thor, since visitors to Norway often asked where he was. He claimed that Thor was living in Colla Micheri *[a well-preserved medieval village in northwestern Italy, near Genoa]* as a "tax exile" to avoid the crippling income taxes of his native land.

Weeks later, Darwin received a blistering letter from Heyerdahl: "Mind your own god damn business. My personal affairs are of no concern to you. If I ever meet up with you again, I'll bash your face in."

Darwin was not offended—in fact, he framed the letter and kept it on display in his office for years.

"Perhaps he was right," Darwin said. "Regardless of what he thought of me, I will always be honored to have spent an amazing evening in the presence of this incredible man who set out to unravel one of the mysteries of history."

In 1991, Heyerdahl married for the third time, to Jacqueline Beer, a former Miss France, the couple settling in Tenerife in the Canary Islands. At the age of 87, in 2002, his doctor told him he had incurable brain cancer. He made a ghastly decision, refusing to take medication or eat any food.

As his wife said, "Thor just wasted away, meeting death on his own terms, the way he'd lived his life."

Chapter Eight

WHO'S HIDING IN MAJORCA?

Faye Emerson, George Sanders, Charles Boyer, & Broderick Crawford

How Darwin found himself in a Strange Interlude with "The First Lady of Television;" Zsa Zsa Gabor's Ex-Husband; a French Matinée Idol; and the Oscar-nominated Actor who portrayed the Corrupt Governor of Louisiana, Huey Long.

During the research of *Frommer's Spain*, Darwin was getting his shoes shined in the departure lounge at the Barcelona airport. He was waiting for the departure of the next flight to Majorca, the largest of Spain's Balearic Islands.

A rather burly, brutish-looking man took the seat next to him to get his shoes shined, too. When the man said hello, Darwin turned to look at him. He knew at once that he was staring into the face of the famous screen actor Broderick Crawford.

When he'd portrayed the fascist egomaniac, Willie Stark (aka Huey Long), in *All the King's Men* in 1949, he'd won the Best Actor Oscar. Later, as gangster Harry Brock, he gave his second-greatest performance in *Born Yesterday* (1950) opposite Judy Holliday (cast as his mistress), and William Holden.

In one of the biggest upsets in Hollywood history, Holliday won the Best Actress Oscar that year. She beat out Gloria Swanson, delivering the performance of her life as the fading silent screen star, Norma Desmond, in *Sunset Blvd*. Also competing against each other—an unfortunate coincidence—were Bette Davis as Margo Channing and Anne Baxter as Eve Harrington for roles they'd delivered in the same film, *All About Eve* (1950). By dividing the judges' votes, they'd more or less canceled each other's chances of a direct win.

As was discovered later, Crawford was flying to Majorca during its peak season without a reservation. Since a lavish suite had been booked for Darwin at the upscale Son Vida Hotel, he asked Broderick to stay with him during his holiday. The invitation was gladly accepted.

The next day, Darwin gave Broderick a scenic tour of the island before accepting his dining invitation at the home of two of his friends. Broderick was deliberately

Casting the 6'1", craggy-faced Broderick Crawford seemed like the ideal choice for Huey Long, the governor/dictator of Louisiana. The role was for the film adaptation of Robert Penn Warren's hard-hitting novel, *All the King's Men*, an exposé of political corruption that earned for him the Pulitzer Prize.

At the Academy Awards for Best Actor in 1949, Crawford beat out Kirk Douglas in *Champion;* Gregory Peck in *Twelve O'Clock High;* Richard Todd in *The Hasty Heart;* and John Wayne in *Sands of Iwo Jima.*

mysterious about their names, concealing them until Darwin arrived at the designated address. The door was opened by Charles Boyer, who ushered both of them inside to greet another famous actor, George Sanders.

"As a celebrity writer, I had hit the jackpot," Darwin recalled. "I noticed that Charles and George seemed very, very close, real dear friends."

Boyer, a former matinée idol, had been born in France in 1899, the same year as Humphrey Bogart. On the short list of Darwin's favorite Boyer films was *Algiers* (1938) with Hedy Lamarr; and *Gaslight* (1944) with Ingrid Bergman. Over the course of his career, he'd co-starred with such leading ladies as Bette Davis, Greta Garbo, Jean Harlow, Irene Dunne, Loretta Young, and Claudette Colbert.

Boyer had also been nominated for a Best Actor Oscar four times.

"Both Sanders and Boyer seemed equally matched in style, sophistication, wit, and charm, although Broderick, my new buddy, was the bear in the china shop," Darwin said.

Born in St. Petersburg, then part of the Russian Empire, in 1906, Sanders had been married to Zsa Zsa Gabor from 1949 to 1954. At the time of that dinner party in Majorca, he had not yet married Zsa Zsa's older sister, Magda, which was quickly annulled.

Darwin knew a lot about Sanders, having followed a trail of gossip of his seductions, everyone from matinee Tyrone Power to tobacco heiress Doris Duke. Other conquests included Hedy Lamarr, Gene Tierney, and Noël Coward. He'd also seduced starlet Marilyn Monroe during the filming of *All About Eve* (1950).

Despite all that, he said, "I don't like women. They bore me."

He went on to tell fascinating stories of his life, as when, as a young man in Chile, he'd wounded his opponent in a duel and was asked to leave the country. He'd been challenged to a duel using pistols after his landlord had caught him in bed with his wife.

"Of all my many seductions, I still find that for me, the greatest aphrodisiac is money," he said.

Some of the revelations Sanders made that night ended up in

Charles Boyer with Jennifer Jones in *Cluny Brown*, a 1946 comedy which charts the evolving relationship between orphan Jones and a penniless Czech refugee in pre-World War II England.

a biography that Darwin wrote, *Those Glamorous Gabors, Bombshells from Budapest* published in 2013 by Blood Moon Productions.

The next evening, Broderick asked Darwin to join him and a surprise female guest, who was vacationing on the island. Until the surprise guest entered the dining room, Darwin didn't know who she'd be.

When she made her entrance, he immediately recognized her as the actress Faye Emerson, long ago known as "The First Lady of Television." Because she wore evening gowns on camera, always with plunging *décolletage*, it was said she put the "V" in TV. She'd been famously married in 1944 to Elliott Roosevelt, the son of Franklin and Eleanor Roosevelt. Self-styled as "First Daughter-in-Law," Faye—during the closing months of World War II—lived for long periods in the White House.

Their matchmaker had been none other than her former lover, Howard Hughes, who had brought them together in Hollywood. Hughes had spread the word that later earned Fay the title of "Fellatio Queen of Hollywood," a few years before Nancy Davis (later Reagan) was anointed with the same title when she was a starlet at MGM.

After the war, Faye and Elliott had lived with Eleanor at Hyde Park, New York.

Left photo: Faye Emerson as half of the most famous newlywed couple in America: with her then-husband, Elliott Roosevelt, son of FDR.

On the right, Emerson got a rare top billing over Zachory Scott in *Danger Signal*, a thriller he made in 1945 right after playing his most memorable role as the cad who was shot during the opening scene of *Mildred Pierce*, starring Joan Crawford, that year's Oscar winner for Best Actress.

Darwin's conversations with George Sanders aided tremendously in his characterization s of Zsa Zsa Gabor, his ex-wife. So did the arrival of Jolie Gabor, their mother, at Magnolia House.
Alongside Zsa Zsa's sisters, Eva and Magda, these captivationg ladies were the stars of Darwin's trilogy biography, *Those Glamorous Gabors, Bombshells from Budapest*, published by Blood Moon Productions in 2013.

Travel Writing as a Celebrity Adventure/ Who's Hiding in Malloca?

In 1948, despondent over her failed marriage, Faye had cut her wrists but had survived. She'd later married band leader Skitch Henderson in 1950. He was known to millions as the leader of the band on Johnny Carson's *Tonight* Show.

They divorced seven years later, before a scandal broke loose. Henderson was accused of molesting teenaged girls and was dropped by the network.

Broderick and Darwin spent most of the weekend with Faye, who told them she was shopping for a villa with the idea of retiring one day in Majorca.

Many of the stories she told Darwin about Howard Hughes ended up in his 2005 biography published by Blood Moon under the title *Howard Hughes, Hells's Angel*.

Three stars that Darwin met and dined with on Majorca ended in either tragedy or a long, bittersweet exile from their home countries.

In April of 1972, Sanders committed suicide in a villa on Spain's Costa Brava. The note he left said, "Dear world. I am leaving because I am bored. I have lived long enough. I am leaving you with your worries in this sweet cesspool."

Boyer, too, in August of 1978, committed suicide in Phoenix, Arizona, after the death of his beloved wife, Pat Paterson, whom he'd married in 1934.

In lonely self-exile, Emerson died in March of 1983, suffering from stomach cancer. She'd been living on Majorca since 1975.

"I found her a great lady," Darwin said. "Witty, intelligent, and charming, but also a tragic figure."

Despite a long list of film credits, Crawford, in the late 1960s, found that his roles in Hollywood had dried up. He crossed the Atlantic to work in Europe—"anything for a paycheck," he said. He starred in trash like the campy *The Private Life of J. Edgar Hoover* in 1978. Facing bankruptcy, his career more or less over, and in failing health, he told a few friends, "I welcome death." It came on April 26, 1986.

Chapter Nine

PETER O'TOOLE

His Strange and Stylish Affair with the Duchess of Alba During His Filming of *Lawrence of Arabia*

"That Galumping Camel Drama"

As was his wont, Darwin Porter became adept at multi-tasking during his endless research trips for the Frommer Guides. Depicted above are the front and back covers of his award-winning biography of the Anglo-Irish megastar, Peter O'Toole, parts of which were investigated during Darwin's research of southern Spain, where O'Toole was filming what he defined as "That Galumping Camel Drama"

Darwin was in Spain, researching *Frommer's Spain* and a spin-off smaller guide to Andalusia, when the cast and crew shooting *Lawrence of Arabia* arrived after months in the Jordanian desert to shoot segments of the film in Seville.

Picking up gossip and scandal, Darwin also added another chapter on his research on O'Toole. As a full-length biography, it was published in 2015 as the most comprehensive biography of this star ever written. Entitled *Peter O'Toole—Hellraiser, Sexual Outlaw, Irish Rebel*. Danforth Prince was its co-author.

Released in December of 1962, the film version of *Lawrence of Arabia* was produced by Sam Spiegel and directed by David Lean. The movie transformed O'Toole, known for his carousing, drinking, and what he called "wenching," from a relatively minor actor into an international star. Today, according to the *Los Angeles Times*, *Lawrence of Arabia* is "one of the Seven Wonders of the cinematic world."

The movie was based on the life of T.E. Lawrence, the British guerilla leader of Arab tribesmen during World War I in their battles against the Turks of the Ottoman Empire. *[The Turks were allied at the time with the Kaiser's German soldiers against the British.]* More than anything else, the O'Toole film transformed the real-life Lawrence into a mythical hero.

Appearing on the screen in flowing white robes, O'Toole was a dazzler in this epic set against the backdrop of a foreboding desert, racing camels, larger-than-life sheiks, bloody battles, and massive explosions.

Before signing a contract to star in what he called "This Galumping Camel Drama" O'Toole held a meeting with its director, Lean, in London. You might call it a face-to-face. Subject matter? Giving O'Toole a new face.

Lean told him that before he'd sign O'Toole into the role, he'd have to submit to a plastic surgeon to have his nose reshaped. "I want to turn you into one of the pretty boys of England," he said. "You know, the type of flashy male chased by horny women and faggots."

Without protest, O'Toole agreed and showed up three weeks later in the aftermath of his surgery. His face was bandaged, and he wore extra black sunglasses. "Since you're paying for it, I also had an operation on my eyelids to correct my squint. I want movie audiences to swoon over my baby blues. As you can see, and according to your instructions, I had my hair dyed

After *Lawrence of Arabia* was released, the till-then relatively unknown Anglo-Irish actor, Peter O'Toole exploded onto the public consciousness, evolving into an instant mega-celebrity and sex symbol.

In this publicity still, he appears as an idealized version of the ultimate British romantic hero, T.E. Lawrence, a historical figure who soldiered together an alliance between the Saudi Arabs and the British colonial forces figthting the Ottoman Turks in the years before World War I.

blonde."

For 117 days, O'Toole and Lean shot scenes in the Middle East, notably Jordan. Cast and crew were then flown to Seville for more shooting before being sent off to Morocco. "I'd become a desert rat," O'Toole claimed.

Flying into Seville, O'Toole was captivated by the legendary capital of Andalusia, the abode of Don Juan, Carmen, and the *Reconquista*. He wandered the streets at night, passing old homes opening onto flower-filled patios, taking in castanet-rattling gypsies, beautiful olive-skinned beauties in *mantillas*, and lovesick *torreos*.

For what was going on behind the scenes in Seville, we turn to Darwin, who became fascinated by the off-screen dramas being acted out during those torrid nights in that city.

Shortly after O'Toole's arrival, a hand-delivered invitation was sent to him by Cayetana Fitz-James Stuart, the 18th Duchess of Alba. She also held 40 other titles. According to *Guinness World Records*, that made her the most titled aristocrat in the world.

The flamboyant *duenna* was known for her lavish lifestyle, her vast wealth, and her fondness for young men. O'Toole was only six years her junior. She invited him for dinner at her palace two nights hence.

Other than having seen Ava Gardner emote as an 18th-century earlier version of Duchess in *The Naked Maja* (1959), O'Toole knew very little about his hostess. [*It was rumored that her 18th-century ancestor, the 13th Duchess of Alba, had posed for Francisco Goya's famous nude portrait of a desirable woman, now hanging in the Prado.*]

Dressed in a rented tuxedo, O'Toole arrived at her palace and was ushered in by a liveried doorman in 18th century dress. The Duchess received him in an emerald-green gown with a diamond-and-ruby necklace once owned by Marie Antoinette at Versailles.

According to Darwin, "All of Seville, or so it seemed, was buzzing with rumors of the Duchess having seduced O'Toole. He was seen leaving her palace at 7AM. Not only that, but for the next five nights in a row, he was seen coming and going from her palace. In Seville, the night has a thousand eyes."

The fabulously sought-after Duchess of Alba in 1956, a few years before she met O'Toole.

"Two days after O'Toole departed from Seville, another rumor spread," Darwin asserted. "One of Spain's leading matadors was rumored to be seen coming and going from the palace at night, too. It seemed that whenever a young man, either on the screen or in the bullring, whomever, was summoned to the Duchess's palace, it was with the understanding that it was an invitation to sample her charms. Too bad Goya wasn't around anymore to capture the latest Duchess's allure on canvas."

"As for O'Toole, he headed to Morocco for more filming...and for further adventures."

***

In 1963, at the 35th Academy Awards presentation in Santa Monica, an event hosted by Frank Sinatra, *Lawrence of Arabia* was nominated for ten Oscars, seven of which it won, including Best Picture and Best Director. O'Toole received the first of his eight Oscar nominations, none of which ever evolved into an actual win.

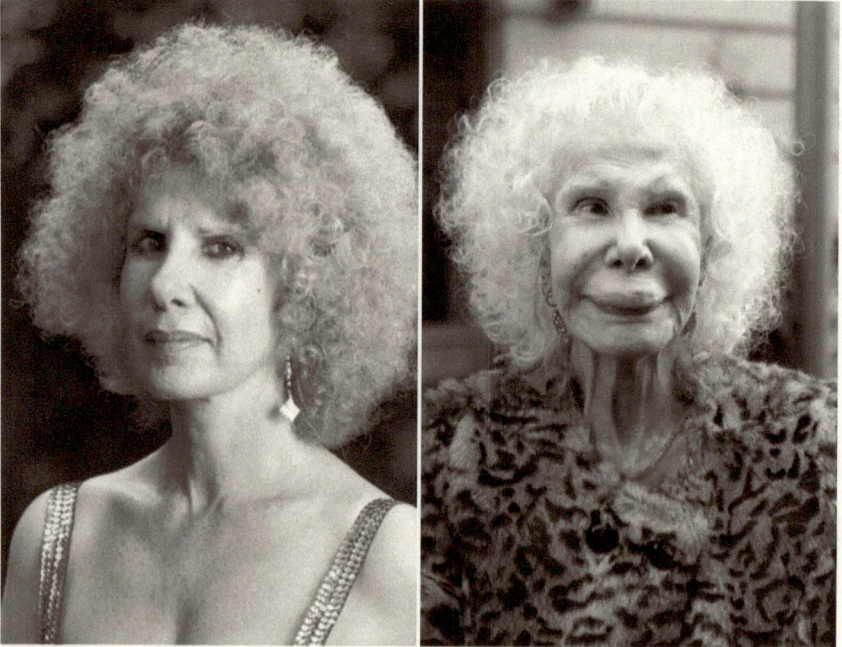

Sadly, in the years that preceeded her death in 2014, the 18th Duchess of Alba—one of the richest and most titled woman in Europe—became a poster child for how NOT to have a facelift. Tabloids throughout the Spanish-speaking world, from Spain to Argentina to Peru, plastered "before and after shots" of her facial wreckage as a symbol of the negative aspects of too much privilege and too much wealth.

Chapter Ten

"ICH BIN EIN BERLINER"

A MILLION BESIEGED BERLINERS WELCOME JFK AS HE DELIVERS THE MOST FAMOUS SPEECH OF THE COLD WAR

East Germany: The Cold War was immediate and real. The Soviet Union encircled Berlin on all sides, clanking their weapons and threatening to invade. President Kennedy arrived during the peak of the tensions to deliver his address. Here's what Darwin saw.

Darwin was in Berlin on June 26, 1963, and was a witness to a moment in world history. He was updating his annual guidebook, *Frommer's Germany*.

As he woke up and had breakfast in a sidewalk café, he noticed the buzz in the air. Everyone seemed to be talking about the arrival of President John F. Kennedy, who was flying into Berlin, this time without Jacqueline.

Berliners were excited by his visit, but some expressed disappointment that his charismatic First Lady would not be accompanying him.

"It was a tense time to be in Berlin," Darwin said.

The city was still recovering from its almost complete devastation in World War II. Berlin was like an island surrounded by hostile forces. Soviet tanks were ready to move in at a moment's notice. Tensions had reached a new boiling point when East Germany, acting on orders from Moscow, had tried to isolate Berlin from the rest of the world. That had led to the famous Berlin Airlift, as U.S. planes flew desperately needed supplies into a beleaguered city.

In 1961, the East German, Moscow-controlled government of Walter Ulbricht erected a barbed wire barrier around the city of West Berlin, under the pretense of keeping spies out of East Berlin. In time, that led to the erection of the dreaded Berlin Wall.

In East Berlin, buildings near the wall were demolished to create a "death zone." East Germans trying to escape would be shot. The Wall closed the biggest loophole in the Iron Curtain, which had been given its name by Sir Winston Churchill.

The Wall had become necessary because thousands of East Germans had fled to West Berlin, seriously threatening the economy of East Berlin. The government feared an economic collapse if something wasn't done... and quick.

There was a certain optimism Darwin noted in the air as word spread that JFK was landing in Air Force One at the Berlin airport. It is estimated that a million Berliners turned out to greet him.

Earlier that day, JFK had made a moving speech in Frankfurt, asserting

The response to his speech from listeners, including Darwin Porter, was virtually ecstatic.

that, "The United States will risk its cities to defend yours because we need your freedom to protect ours."

As the first item on his agenda, JFK was driven to the Berlin Wall to look out over "No Man's Land" in which hundreds of East Germans had been shot during attempts to escape to the West. After surveying the scene of such massacre, he left in disgust.

He was then taken to Rudolph Wilde Platz where at least 500,000 Berliners, including Darwin, were crowded together to hear the President's address.

"JFK did not disappoint us that day," Darwin said. "His speech was not only a high point for The New Frontier, but a historical moment in the Cold War."

He spoke from a hastily erected platform on the steps of the Rathaus Schöneberg, his words mesmerizing the crowd.

In a Bostonian accent, he said, "Two thousand years ago, the proudest boast was *civis romanus sum,* or 'I am a Roman citizen.' Today, in the world of freedom, the proudest boast in *Ich bin ein Berliner*. All free men, wherever they may live, are citizens of Berlin, and therefore, as a free man, I take pride in the words *'Ich bin ein Berliner!"*

Stepping down from the platform, JFK, with the cheers of the crowd ringing in his ears, told McGeorge Bundy, his National Security Advisor, "We'll never have another day like this one."

Hordes of Berliners went wild after the President's departure. Darwin joined in the whirlwind of partying and beer drinking which lasted into the pre-dawn hours.

"I've visited many cities celebrating—Mardi Gras in New Orleans, Carnival in Rio de Janeiro, but I have never seen anything like Berlin that June night."

Richard D. Mahoney, Kennedy scholar emeritus, wrote: "On the world stage, the President's demeanor and mastery of symbol had never seemed more sure. He was tacking smoothly among the currents of time, shaping them with his own view of history, his romantic sense of self, and his passion for freedom."

Sadly, in November, five months later, the President was dead, the victim of an assassination in Dallas. Much of Berlin mourned.

The mayor announced, "President Kennedy is no more with us, but the inspiration, the hope, he gave us as spring blanketed our city will never die."

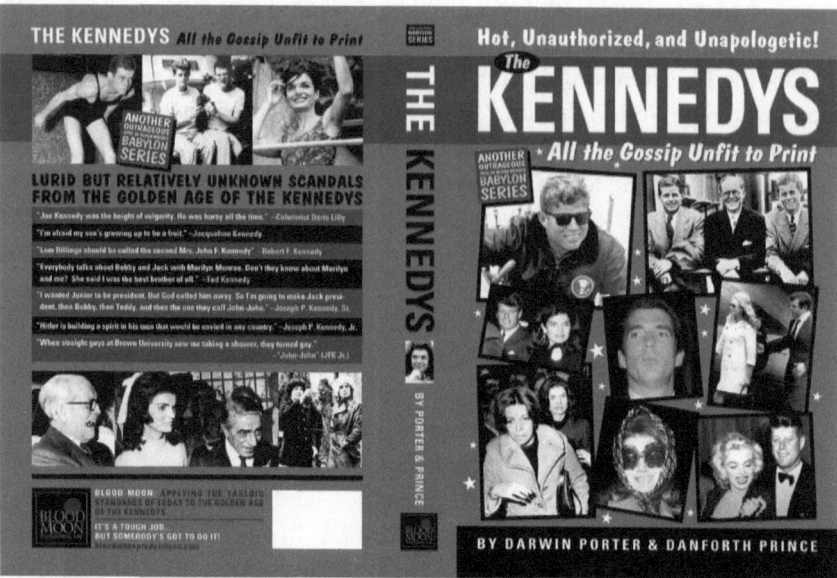

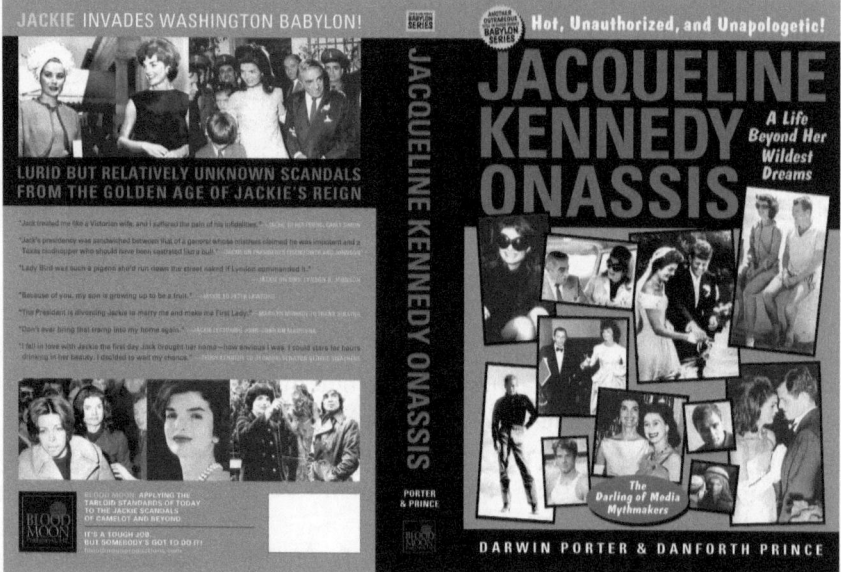

Everyone agrees that JFK was a national hero and much-adored. Along with his wife, Jacqueline, he was also the most fascinating and charismatic celebrity of his age.

Those were some of the factors which prompted and inspired Darwin, in the aftermath of decades of Kennedy-watching, either on location or from within Magnolia House, to commit to print some of the episodes for which the Kennedys were (and are) universally and on-goingly fascinating.

Chapter Eleven

CLEOPATRA

After Filming It in Rome, Its Stars —Elizabeth Taylor, Richard Burton, & Rex Harrison— Descend on Portofino to Dish the Dirt

As Queen of the Nile, Cleopatra (Elizabeth Taylor) is torn between two lovers. Shall it be Julius Caesar (left, Rex Harrison) or Marc Antony (right) as played by Richard Burton?

Obviously, she chose Burton, almost simultaneously dumping husband, singer Eddie Fisher.

As she told he press, "It is his powerful voice hat is the physical allured. And, if you believe that, I have a bridge over the Tiber to sell you!"

Even though today it's overrun by day-trippers eating ice cream, Portofino, Italy, has gone down in the annals of world chicdom as a haven for the élite who occupy villas in the hills and arrive on yachts. They only appear at the portside bars when the day trippers have mercifully departed. The resident locals call the visitors "barbarians," although most working people in Portofino live exclusively off them.

No one seems to know for sure who launched this tiny fishing village as a fashionable destination, making it famous worldwide as "the Pearl of the Italian Riviera." Perhaps it was Guy de Maupassant arriving in 1889 aboard his sailboat *Bel-Ami*, titled after the French author's frivolous but successful novel.

Critics—snobbish ones, that is—claim that Portofino was never chic but more like a circus. Consider Darwin's impressions of his visit there during his research of *Frommer's Italy* in the 1960s and make your own judgment:

"There I was a *La Gritta American Bar*, entertaining a party of three villa owners (two from England and one from Germany) when Rex Harrison (alone for a change) arrived and sat at the bar's only reserved table," Darwin said. "He already knew both of the Brits and acknowledged our table briefly with weak handshakes before assuming a center position at his own reserved table. Then he asked the bartender to do something about the lighting. It was a bit harsh, and he appeared to have had a bad night."

Harrison wasn't going to be drinking alone. He was at the bar to greet Elizabeth Taylor and Richard Burton, who were about to make an entrance in Portofino from aboard a yacht. All three actors had finally recovered from the debacle of *Cleopatra* (1963) in which Elizabeth had starred as the Queen of the Nile, Burton as Marc Antony, and Harrison as Julius Caesar.

Elizabeth made a stunning entrance into the bar in a shimmering silver gown with a plunging décolletage. She wore a diamond bracelet around her neck, a gift from Burton.

She kissed Harrison on the lips, promising to return in half an hour. "I'm going shopping," she told the men.

Burton began to drink heavily with Harrison, and Darwin listened in on their dialogue. When his guests got up to leave, he walked out with them to tell them good night.

The Burton/Taylor yacht was clearly visible in the harbor. Elizabeth was staging a minor riot among the tourists and locals as she went boutique-hopping at the upscale stores with their overpriced merchandise that lined the edge of the harbor.

Word of her presence spread quickly, and at least a dozen women, most of them wives of fishermen, rushed to descend on the port. They held up their babies for Elizabeth to admire, often aggressively thrusting them into her face. It soon became obvious that these women were offering their babies for sale. It was widely known that the beautiful movie star had a history of adopting children.

As she strolled along the waterfront, liquor glass in hand, her butler from the yacht trailed her. Every time he saw her glass only half full, he returned to the yacht and came back to hand her a fresh glass of scotch. After spending $5,000 in one boutique, which tripled its prices for her, she returned to the bar, which had emptied out.

Trailing her, Darwin returned too, taking a table in the bar's far corner. Since the bar consisted of just one rather small room, he could hear every word spoken at her table. So as not to give the impression that he was eavesdropping, he slipped the bartender one hundred dollars in lire and asked him to make it appear that he worked for the bar. Positioning himself near a wine rack, he checked the labels on some of the bottles it contained, scribbling notes. Although giving the impression that he was an associate of the bar, he was actually making notes of what Harrison and Burton were saying. Their conversation heated up as Elizabeth, after her shopping, returned to dish the dirt on what had happened in Rome during the filming of their movie, *Cleopatra*.

As tabloid readers knew, Elizabeth had arrived in Rome for filming with her then-husband, singer Eddie Fisher. But when the movie was wrapped and she eventually fled from Rome, she was with Burton, who at the time was still married to his faithful wife, Sybil.

Elizabeth had flown into The Eternal City with an entourage, whom she'd installed in the rented "Villa Papa."

On her first day at work at Cinecittà, she was told that wardrobe was preparing seventy costume changes for her, including her startling ceremonial dress for the scene depicting her triumphant arrival in Rome.

In Portofino that long-ago afternoon, each member of her trio revealed some casting news about what might have been: "We weren't the first choices," Elizabeth said. "The British Open—yes, I'm speaking of Joan Collins—was at first considered by Fox for the role I eventually played."

As was revealed, Fox, at least for one daring moment, also considered casting Dorothy Dandridge, an African-American actress, as Cleopatra.

"Perhaps that was type casting," Elizabeth said. "I heard that historically, Cleopatra was actually a black woman."

Fox also considered Cary Grant for the role of Caesar and Burt Lancaster as Marc Antony. Producer Walter Wanger said he'd have preferred either Susan Hayward or Jennifer Jones as Cleo.

As was also revealed to Darwin that evening in Portofino, Director Joseph Mankiewicz originally offered the role of Marc Antony to Marlon Brando. Stephen Boyd had also been considered for the role, and Peter Finch was an alternative choice for Caesar.

From the beginning, however, Roddy McDowall, one of Elizabeth's closest friends, was relatively secure in his selection as the actor who'd play Augustus.

As the evening in Portofino progressed, no one else entered the bar during long interludes, and the drinks kept arriving for the Burton/Taylor party. Darwin, meanwhile, supposedly taking inventories of the wine bottles, was completely ignored.

He heard Burton refer to Elizabeth as "Miss Tits" or "Fat Little." The husband she'd deserted, Eddie Fisher, was referred to as "The Busboy."

Burton gloated a bit over the fact he was paid far more money for the role he'd played than Harrison, but Elizabeth had each of them beat, taking home a staggering one million dollars, which was the highest fee for a movie role ever offered to a film actress.

Burton spoke of his early career where he had been called England's answer to Marlon Brando, as well as "the working man's Laurence Olivier. I am myself unique and godly," he claimed. "I can act circles around those two homos."

Between revelations and drinks, the drunken actor, seemingly for no reason at all, would suddenly recite lines from the poems of Dylan Thomas, a fellow Welshman.

Elizabeth wanted to discuss more recent matters and seemed especially worried that she might be labeled "box office poison" because of the negative publicity associated with her affair with Burton. *[Each of them was married at the time.]*

"I think that under normal circumstance, I would be nominated—and probably would win—my second Oscar. I also feel that under normal circumstances, Richard would also be

Roddy McDowall as Octavian in *Cleopatra* (1963). A Brit, he was one of Elizabeth's closest friends, dating from the time they were child actors. They often got together to dish their male lovers.

nominated for his role as Marc Antony."

"What about me?" Harrison asked. "Just a mushy mess of blood pudding sitting across from you?"

"You were terrific as Julius Caesar, and you, too, might be nominated," Burton said. "But I've got to ask a favor. I hope you'll have your agents approach the Academy and put you in the Best Supporting Actor slot. As history as shown, when two actors are nominated for roles in the same film, they cancel each other out."

"I'll think about that," Harrison said, guardedly.

Both Elizabeth and Burton lamented the way the press had treated them. "Rome's *Il Tiempo* called me a vamp who destroys families and shucks husbands like a praying mantis."

"I heard over Vatican Radio that your affair with Richard endangered the 'moral health of society,'" Harrison said. "And, get this—Pope John XXIII called our beloved angel here an 'erotic vagrant.'"

"I don't give a rat's piss what the Pope or the Vatican says about my morals," Elizabeth said. "I'm not Catholic, I'm a Jewess—converted, that is."

"I was really surprised when you two started to dance the tango together," Harrison said. "Richard told me of his first impression of you."

"That stuff about her being the most beautiful woman in the world is pure nonsense," Burton had said. "She's a pretty girl, of course, and she has those wonderful eyes. But she has a double chin and an overdeveloped chest—and she's rather short in the leg—no Betty Grable."

She told Harrison of her first meeting with Burton. It had been on the set of *Cleopatra*. "He'd obviously arrived with a hangover from a night of carousing. He was kind of quivering from head to foot, and his face was covered with grog blossoms (skin blemishes). Instead of that turning me off, it made me more sympathetic to him."

He ordered coffee to steady his trembling hands. "I had to hold the cup to his mouth so he could drink it. This brought out my motherly in-

Pope John XXIII in 1962, around the time he was denouncing Elizabeth Taylor as an "erotic vagrant"

stincts. He was so vulnerable, so shaky. In my heart, I *cvtched* him—that's Welsh for 'hug.'"

From this unlikely beginning one of the world's most scandalous romances was launched. Soon, Fisher was lurking around the set, hawkeying their every move.

Fortunately, Fisher was not around on January 22, 1962, when Mankiewicz directed Elizabeth and Burton in their first love scene.

As the director reported to Harrison, "Their succulent lips came together. He locked her into a deep, wet kiss. I ordered the scene reshot four times. I could feel their passion for each other. It was almost frightening—like an oncoming tornado. Finally, I called 'Cut!'"

The following afternoon, according to Harrison, "The gossip was floating around the set. From what I was told," he said, turning to Burton, "you lured Elizabeth behind one of the fake ancient Roman sets, where you proceeded to masturbate her. Later, you were seen emerging from behind that set, licking your fingers."

"That's the bloody truth," Burton confessed.

"Not only that," he said, "but after working with Miss Tits here for only five days, I came onto the set the following morning and announced to some of the cast in my marvelous stentorian voice: 'Gents, I nailed Miss Taylor last night in the back seat of my rented Cadillac.'"

"That very day," Burton revealed, "I was taking a shower in my dressing room. There was a tap on the glass panel. I pulled it back to see this woman in a blonde Marlene Dietrich wig, and I didn't recognize Elizabeth

Liz and Dick: The Hottest Show in Portofino and everywhere else, too.

at first. She dropped the towel and asked, 'how much do you charge, luv?'"

Harrison seemed to want to interject himself into the romance department. "I had my own affair going on, too. In fact, you know, I married Rachel Roberts in March."

Burton wasn't interested, as he wanted to talk about himself. "When I was a young actor, I got my start in the theater by lying on the casting couch of some of England's most stately homos—Larry Oliver, John Gielgud, Emlyn Williams, and Noël Coward—but not you, Sexy Rexy. By the way, Elizabeth here adores bisexuals—take her marriage to Michael Wilding, who was often shacked up with Stewart Granger. She also adores homosexuals—take Monty Clift, for example."

"Speaking of gay men," Harrison responded. "Our mutual friend, Roddy McDowall, told me The Busboy was acting more like Elizabeth's business manager than her husband."

"I had a private confab with Walter (Wanger, the producer), and he chastised me, telling me to go back to Sybil," Burton said. "He claimed I could fuck Elizabeth on the side, but, to save my career, I'd better go back to home, hearth, and those bedroom slippers. He was right. So I told Elizabeth I was leaving her. She became hysterical."

She backed up his account: "That night, I overdosed on sleeping pills. Someone leaked the story. The next morning, I was greeted with headlines in Italian."

[Dick Hanley, her assistant, translated them into English: TAYLOR ATTEMPTS SUICIDE OVER BURTON AFFAIR.]

"When I felt Richard slipping away, I went crazy. I had to be with him. I knew it was wrong. I knew, I knew. But I also knew I had to do it. God help me. I had to be with Richard."

"Two days later, Mankiewicz faced the press. He told those boys they had it all wrong. 'I am the one,' the director announced, 'who is having the affair with Burton—not Elizabeth.'"

After signaling to the barman for yet another drink, Elizabeth went into a rage. "John F. Kennedy was the most famous man on the planet, and he was fucking the most famous woman on the planet, Marilyn Monroe, who is part dyke, you know. She once came on to me. But during the white heat of their illicit affair, it didn't make one headline. But when Richard plowed into my quim [*an Elizabethan word for vagina*], it was treated like the Second Coming."

"One afternoon, my darling friend Roddy (McDowall) arrived at the Villa Papa," she said. Did I ever give him an earful. I had heard that before I came into Richard's life, Roddy was servicing him. Not that I objected to that. Better Roddy than Brigitte Bardot. I told him that Richard was a devious snakepit of contradictions. If a prefrontal lobotomy was performed on him, *[like Katharine Hepburn wanted to do to me in Suddenly, Last Summer]*, out of Richard's skull would emerge poisonous snakes, tadpoles, frogs, worms, and bats from hell. What a man! I can experience an orgasm just listening to his voice!"

"You're not telling us anything about Richard here that we don't already know," Harrison said. "But how did Eddie handle the scandal?"

"He came onto the set one afternoon after the news broke," Burton said. "He sat down possessively close to Elizabeth. I walked over to where they were sitting and reached down and began to fondle her breasts. As I have said before, those breasts, before they wither, will topple empires. I turned to Eddie and said, 'You know, ol' thing, I'm in love with your girl.'"

"She's not my girl," Fisher snapped. "She's my wife and she's gonna remain my wife."

"Okay, *Dummkopf*," Burton replied. "I'm in love with your bloody wife, then. Lizzie sat silently through this exchange, and all the while, I kept fondling that delectable breast."

"Even a guy as dumb as Eddie got the message," Elizabeth chimed in.

***

Finally, the trio got up and left the bar, leaving the equivalent of five hundred dollars in lire. Darwin departed soon after, watching Harrison bid farewell to Elizabeth and Burton, who then sailed away on their yacht, heading for the Côte d'Azur, where a berth awaited their yacht in Cannes.

At last, Darwin felt free to retire to one of his favorite hotels, the Splendido in Portofino. Years later, the revelations he overheard that night appeared in the biography he crafted, *Elizabeth Taylor—There's Nothing Like a Dame* (©2012, Blood Moon Productions).

Darwin always stayed at the Splendido during his annual research trips to Portofino. "If only the walls could talk," he said. "It was filled with memories of visits by Greta Garbo, the Duke and Duchess of Windsor, Ernest Hemingway, Ingrid Bergman, Aristotle Onassis, Clark Gable, and John Wayne."

Chapter Twelve

LUNCH WITH MISS BERGMAN
INGRID'S INDISCRETIONS

"Yes, Bogie and I Had an Affair During Our Filming of Casablanca."

"As Time Goes By," Ingrid Bergman and Humphrey Bogart were lovers (or former lovers) on the screen in *Casablanca*, while carrying on an affair after the cameras shut down for the night.

Both of them denied their liaison, of course, since each of them was married at the time. Bogie was ready to divorce his crazed wife, Mayo Methot, as a means of perpetuating their love affair, but Ingrid rejected his offer.

In 1966, when Darwin was assigned to write the first-ever edition of *Frommer's Scandinavia* and later, *Frommer's Sweden*, he met with the nation's director of tourism in Stockholm.

After plotting a plan for the best coverage of the country, the director asked if he had any special request.

As a matter of fact, Darwin did. He had read that Ingrid Bergman had returned to her native country for a vacation. He explained that not only was she among his most admired actresses, but that he was compiling material for a biography of Humphrey Bogart, to be entitled *The Making of a Legend.* "I plan to devote an entire chapter to *Casablanca,* and I've contacted anyone still alive who worked on the film. Naturally, it would be a great honor to get Miss Bergman's insights."

"I don't think Miss Bergman will grant you an interview," the director said. "but I'll give it a try."

The following morning, he phoned Darwin at the Grand Hotel. "I was wrong. Miss Bergman will receive you. I told her you were promoting tourism to our country. She agreed to do it, providing you don't reveal where she is staying. We'll call you later today with the details, and we'll also provide you with one of our drivers."

The meeting was set up for the following afternoon. That night, Darwin reviewed in his mind the many factoids he had collected about Bergman.

"Some of the opinions were quite graphic," Darwin said. "I knew she wasn't as pure as Joan of Arc, whom she'd played on the screen, but her screen image was pristine."

Her director, Alfred Hitchcock, had delivered the most unkind dig. "She'd do it with a doorknob."

Anthony Perkins, a closeted homosexual, claimed that he had a hard time avoiding her clutches when they had co-starred in *Goodbye*

Michael Curtiz directed Bogie and Ingrid Bergman in *Casablanca.*

"Every day we were shooting off the cuff," she said. "Every day they were handing out new dialogue, and Bogie and I were trying to make sense of it. No one knew where the picture was going, and no one knew how it was going to end. Every day, I had to ask Cutiz, 'who am I still in love with? Bogie or Paul Henreid?'"

Again in 1961.

The musician, Larry Adler, with whom she'd had an affair, said, "Ingrid wasn't interested in sex all that much. She did it like a girl."

Her former husband, the Italian director, Roberto Rossellini, had gotten her pregnant and destroyed her first marriage to Petter Lindstrom. Lindstrom told a reporter in Rome, "She doesn't do what a whore does," and went on to complain that she would not fellate him.

She had shocked Lindstrom when she told him she couldn't work well on any film unless she was in love with her leading man, or else the director."

In Hollywood, she'd seduced from the A-List: Yul Brynner, Gary Cooper, Gregory Peck, Joseph Cotten, Bing Crosby, Leslie Howard, Burgess Meredith, Anthony Quinn, Omar Shariff, and Spencer Tracy, with whom she'd co-starred in the 1941 *Dr. Jekyll & Mr. Hyde*.

She was also known to have had affairs with Cary Grant, Charles Boyer, Michael Wilding, Curt Jurgens, Jean Marais, and, inevitably, Howard Hughes, who had offered to make her the Queen of RKO.

To that list should also be added Robert Capa, the *Life* magazine photographer. Their romance began in Paris during that heady time after VE Day in Europe.

There was also Victor Fleming, director of *Gone With the Wind*. He was many years married and twice her age. She said, "No fool like an old fool. He did not merely fall, he toppled over the edge. For him, it was more agony than ecstasy."

Darwin later said, "After all those stories, I arrived on Miss Bergman's doorstep, fully expecting to be seduced. I wore an Italian suit I'd had tailored in Florence and designer underwear. But I was wrong—It didn't happen."

"What took place instead was my introduction to one of the most gracious film stars I'd ever met. She wore no makeup, but her natural beauty shone through. She even invited me for lunch. I will never forget it. She served just one course: A huge boiled beet with fresh bread and country butter. I later learned that many Swedes have lunches like that in summer."

"When Miss Bergman told me goodbye, she gave me such a light kiss on the lips, it was like a feather. In parting, she said, "I might win seven Oscars, highly doubtful, but whatever happens when I die, *The New York Times* headline will read—STAR OF CASABLANCA DIES."

A few years later, shortly before her death, she said, "I wish I could live long enough to see the autumn leaves turn." She died of cancer at the age of 67 on August 29, 1982.

What follows are some tantalizing excerpts from Darwin's biography of Humphrey Bogart, *The Making of a Legend*. In recent polls, *Casablanca* has beat out Orson Welles' *Citizen Kane* as the best movie ever made.

***

In January of 1942 Bogie read an item in the *Hollywood Reporter*, claiming that Ronald Reagan and Ann Sheridan, the lovers in *Kings Row*, had been selected to head the cast of *Casablanca*, with Dennis Morgan as the third lead in this romantic triangle.

This may have been a trial balloon. Years later, Reagan claimed that he was made no serious offer to play Rick. Speculative casting was a common practice to attract publicity for a forthcoming film.

The producer Hal Wallis wanted to cast Bogie in the lead, Jack Warner preferring George Raft. Warner prevailed.

Raft at the time was trying to escape the taint of gangster roles. In the films of the 40s, the Nazis had become the gangsters of the 1930s. Raft felt that Rick Blaine, an ex-smuggler, was really a gangster. "The script doesn't make clear why Rick can't return to America," Raft said. "Obviously he was involved in some illegal activity. I won't do it."

But after turning it down, he had second thoughts. He then notified Wallis that he would accept the role. It was too late. Warner had agreed to let Wallis cast Bogie.

The screenplay for *Casablanca* was based on an unproduced play, *Everybody Comes to Rick's*, written by Murray Burnett and Joan Alison..

The script of the play arrived on the Warner lot on December 8, 1941, one day after the Japanese attack on Pearl Harbor.

Jack Warner, the studio chief, agreed to pay $20,000 for it, the highest amount ever paid for an unproduced script.

Thinking of the success of the film, *Algiers* (1938), Warner had already ordered that the play be retitled *Casablanca*.

After several attempts to get a workable screenplay, Wallis had long talks with Julius J. Epstein and Philip G. Epstein, two brothers. These writers were known on the lot as "The Boys" or else "Phil and Julie."

Identical twins, they were both bald and rather lanky, but each of them was known for their snappy dialogue. The Epsteins set their romance/drama in unoccupied Morocco during the early days of World War II. An embittered American expatriate, Rick Blaine (Bogie), meets a former lover Ilsa Lund (Ingrid Bergman), with unforeseen complications. She's being torn between two lovers. Paul Henreid, as Victor Laszlo, would later be cast as the third member of the triangle.

To bail out the brothers, whose script was judged as inadequate, screenwriter Howard Koch was summoned to develop a screenplay from scratch.

Wallis considered casting Hedy Lamarr as Ilsa, because of her success in the film *Algiers*, but in the final negotiation, MGM refused to release her.

David Selznick agreed to lend Bergman to Warners for $25,000.

During her luncheon with Darwin, many years later, Bergman confessed that the role she really wanted was that of Maria in *For Whom the Bell Tolls* (1943), which she eventually won, appearing with Gary Cooper, who became her temporary lover.

Just before the beginning of filming, feeling negative about the project, with a visiting actress, Geraldine Fitzgerald, listening, Bergman pointedly asked Bogie, "How can I play Ilsa in *Casablanca*? I'm supposed to be the world's most beautiful woman. I look like a Swedish milkmaid."

According to Bergman, Bogie retorted, "If that's what you think you look like, I'm taking up a new profession—that of milking cows."

"Don't be vulgar," Bergman cautioned him. "I hardly know you."

"When you get to know me, we can get down and dirty together."

According to Fitzgerald, "The whole subject at lunch that day involved

DOUBLE THE PLEASURE, DOUBLE THE FUN.

The insights gleaned during Darwin's lunch with Ingrid Bergman near Stockholm eventually made their way into the second of the two biographies, published in 2003 (left) and 2010 (right), he wrote about Humphrey Bogart.

how both Bogie and Ingrid could get out of making that movie. They thought the dialogue was ridiculous and the situations were unbelievable. Yet Bogie had campaigned for months to play Rick Blaine. Why would he suddenly want to bolt from *Casablanca?*

According to Bergman, "Both Bogie and I hated working from an unfinished script. Things just weren't working out."

The film's scriptwriting team, which by now was composed of five writers, had still not crafted a suitable script. Many problems in the plot had not been worked out. *[Some loopholes in the plot were never answered even after the film was released—for example, why had Rick been banished from America?]*

***

After filming began, Bogie did everything he could to rush through the film because he had agreed to star in *Sahara* (1943) for Columbia in return for a Cary Grant commitment.

"Bogie told Curtiz, "The audience won't believe that a looker like Ingrid would fall for a guy with a mug like mine."

But later, after viewing the first rushes with her, he changed his mind. "When the camera moves in on that Bergman face, and she's saying she loves you, it would make anybody look romantic."

Spencer Tracy advised Bogie, "This is the first time you've played the romantic lead against a major star. You should stand still and always make her come to you. Curtiz probably won't notice it. If she complains, you can tell her it's in the script. You've got something she wants, so she has to come to you."

In spite of his initial com-

An unproduced play, *Everybody Comes to Rick's,* arrived on the Warner lot on December 8, 1941, one day after the Japanese attack on Pearl Harbor.

The script was evaluated as "sophisticated hokum, but it will play."

Alert to the success of *Algiers* (1938), with Charles Boyer and Hedy Lamarr, Warner changed the title to *Casablanca,* and put it into production in time for a morale-boosting midwar release in 1942.

plaints, Bogie was actually pleased with the role, yet didn't want to admit it to anybody.

He did demand that his character be made stronger. "The world is at war, and Rick is crying in his champagne about some whore he dumped in Paris."

The difference in height between his stars caused some problems for Curtiz. Bergman towered over Bogie, who stood on a box in some scenes or else sat on a pillow. In one scene which was shot while Bogie and Bergman were sitting together on a couch—the famous "franc for your thoughts" moment—Curtiz directed Bergman "to slouch down." Bogie also had to wear platform shoes in some scenes.

When Bergman appeared on the set, Curtiz attacked her. "You're playing a decent woman, not a whore from 10th Avenue. Take off pounds of makeup. No lipstick."

Bergman pestered Curtiz, asking him, "Which man am I in love with?" Since the director hadn't decided, he told her to "play it in between."

Until deep into the shoot, Curtiz and the writers could not make up their minds about how the film should end. Bergman later said, "I never knew from day to day which man I was in love with, Rick or Victor."

Curtiz was not without female companionship on the set. "But I didn't go for Bergman," Curtiz recalled. "I decided to give Bogie a chance. I had plenty of other broads."

At the end of the film, after Ilsa, accompanied by her husband, is airborne, the captain walks away with his man. Bogie famously drawls, "Louis, I think this is the beginning of a beautiful friendship." World War II audiences didn't get this homoerotic overtone.

The line, "Louis, I think this is the beginning of a beautiful friendship" was voted No. 54 among "The 100 Greatest Movie Lines" of all time.

Wallis came up with this line after the film was finished. Bogie was called back to the Warner lot to dub it in.

Bogie had his greatest moment on film when he stood on the gray tarmac with those fog machines blasting away. In his rumpled trench coat and fedora, he looked into Bergman's eyes welling with tears.

"You're saying this only to make me go," Bergman says.

"I'm saying it because it's true. You belong with Victor. If that plane leaves the ground and you're not on it, you'll regret it. Maybe not today, maybe not tomorrow, but soon, and for the rest of your life. I'm not good at being noble, but it doesn't take much to see that the problems of three little people don't amount to a hill of beans in this crazy world. Here's looking at you, kid."

***

As Laurence Leamer, Bergman's biographer, put it: "For Bogie, it was booze, blood, and brawls, a butcher knife in the back, a fistfight in the living room, pistol shots in the ceiling. It was a wife so jealous of Ingrid that he didn't dare get near his co-star. It was life as a forty-two-year-old balding actor with an alcoholic wife, a drinking problem of his own, and a co-star so beautiful, so irresistible, so shrewdly professional, that he was likely to lose the movie to her."

Night after night, Mayo Methot, Bogie's wife, fought bitterly with him over his alleged affair with Bergman. Finally, Bogie had had it. He told Curtiz, "If you have the name, why not play the game? I'm going after the Swedish broad."

As a Hollywood insider, Mrs. Humphrey Bogart, knew much of what was going on, especially off camera. From the very beginning of her marriage, she'd suspected that Bogie was a "whoremonger" [her words], and she never changed that opinion. She'd known many actresses personally with whom he'd had brief flings in the 1930s.

Methot also knew that Bergman's screen image had nothing to do with the private woman.

Bergman with "the real love of her life," Italian film director Roberto Rossellini.

On a spring evening in March of 1948, Ingrid and her husband, Petter Lindstrom, walked into an art house movie theater and saw Rosselini's *Open City*. At the time, Bergman was one of the most successful and popular actresses in the world.

Ironically, she would eventually fall for the Italian who had directed the film she enjoyed that night. The ensuing scandal destroyed her film career, at least for many years.

Bergman was wise not to allow any of the details of her affairs with her leading men of the 1940s to be revealed. Her virginal image as a model of propriety was shattered when her affair with the Italian director, Roberto Rossellini, was revealed in 1949. The affair and her subsequent pregnancy shocked her fans and sent her into exile from America for seven long years.

Although it seems silly today, her affair caused national outrage and she was denounced for her "immorality" on the floor of the U.S. Senate. In the wake of that, the press tore her reputation to shreds. She was temporarily "soiled" among puritanical moviegoers who refused to even tolerate her image on the screen.

One of Bergman's most famous off-screen remarks about Bogie was when she said, "I kissed Bogie. But I never got to know him."

Later, when she had nothing more to lose career-wise, she admitted, "I did say that. Can't a woman say something that is not true? That happens all the time. Why should the world at that time have known about my private relationship with Bogie? I didn't announce any of my other affairs with leading men. Why should I have with Bogie? It would not have helped either of us. Besides, what went on between Bogie and me is our own personal business."

In an interview with Darwin in her native Sweden, she recalled, "What could I say? That we were carrying on passionately and had a brief but torrid fling? We were both married at the time. An adulterous affair—look at what happened to me later—could have destroyed my career. It probably would not have affected Bogie's own career that much."

When Curtiz found Bogie becoming "love sick," he warned him, "Ingrid's trapped in a bad marriage. For her fun, she screws her leading men, then forgets them. Don't fall in love with her. She's poison. She'll break your heart."

"After marrying Mayo Methot," he said, "I no longer have a heart to break."

He confided to Ann Sheridan that he'd fallen in love with Bergman and had asked her to marry him, after both of them had gotten divorces from Methot and Bergman's Swedish doctor husband, Petter Lindstrom.

Claude Rains later told Bette Davis that when he dropped by Bogie's dressing room for a drink, Bergman was adjusting her dress and Bogie zipping up. "I assumed that they had been rehearsing their love scenes," he said sarcastically. "What else could it have been?"

Henreid also told Davis that Bogie and Bergman were having an affair.

Bob Williams, Bogie's publicist on *Casablanca*, later claimed. "I think Bogie fell in love with Ingrid. He was so jealous that if I brought anyone on the set, especially another man, to see her he was furious at me. He would sulk. I had a feeling he wanted Ingrid for himself."

Jack Warner seemed to know about the affair. When Bogie showed up late on the set two days in a row, Warner fired off a memo to Curtiz: "Tell Bogart to quit screwing the Swedish broad all night long and report on time. In one of the rushes, he looks sixty years old. Tell him to clean up his act."

Vincent Sherman, Bogie's sometimes director, claimed that Bogie told him that he had an affair with Bergman all throughout the shooting of *Casablanca*. "Forget all those stupid biographies that claimed Bergman and Bogie didn't have an affair. He screwed her during the entire making of *Casablanca* and fell madly in love with her."

That chemistry was undeniable both on and off the screen, although biographers for years have perpetuated a myth, spread by Bergman herself, that she had almost no contact with Bogie off camera. Methot knew better.

On the final night Bogie saw Bergman, he invited her to an out-of-the way restaurant to celebrate the end of filming.

It was on that fateful night that Bergman gave Bogie "the worst news of my life." She rejected his proposal to marry him after their respective divorces from Lindstrom and Methot.

She explained to him that she was going back to her husband in "dreary, boring" Rochester, New York. "There is no great romance there, but I have a daughter, Pia. I owe it to her to go back and be a mother. I can't leave either of them."

Bogie was said to have cried that night, and he was a man who didn't cry very often.

Although it may be apocryphal, Ann Sheridan later claimed that Bergman, as a final goodbye, told Bogie, "We'll always have Paris."

Chapter Thirteen

CHASING IGUANAS & SEX IN MEXICO

Elizabeth Taylor, Richard Burton, Ava Gardner, & Tennessee Williams During the Filming of *The Night of the Iguana*

On his third night back in New York, having flown in from Key West, Darwin's friend, Tennessee Williams, phoned for a catch-up talk. Darwin agreed to pick him up in his car and drive him to his home on Staten Island where he could spend the night.

He was eager for the latest gossip which the playwright always delivered with style.

Tennessee was about to fly to Puerto Vallarta on the West Coast of Mexico for the filming of his play, *The Night of the Iguana,* to be directed by John

Huston and starring Richard Burton and Ava Gardner. Elizabeth Taylor had not been cast in the film but would conspicuously be on location anyone to chaperone her errant husband.

Huston had offered the male lead to actor James Garner, but he had rejected it, claiming, "It's just too Tennessee Williams for me."

At Magnolia House, Tennessee told Darwin that as a journalist who liked "hot copy," he should join him in Puerto Vallarta for a scoop about what was going on behind the scenes. He eagerly jumped at the chance and promised he'd be in Puerto Vallarta two days after Tennessee arrived.

He had another reason to be in the region: He was negotiating to write the first edition of *Frommer's Acapulco*.

What follows is the report he published on the events surrounding the filming of that movie in Puerto Vallarta.

***

On September 22, 1963, in advance of the debut of filming, the arrival of the "scandalous" Elizabeth Taylor and Richard Burton in Mexico City caused mobs to descend on the city's airport and the generation of an international media event. Although she hadn't been cast in the movie, Elizabeth was nonetheless accompanying Burton (some said "guarding him from female predators") to Mexico.

Liz & Dick were the most famous and scandalous celebrity couple of the 20th Century, and even though Elizabeth was technically not associated with filming in any way, she made more headlines than the actual actresses who appeared with Burton in the film.

Here they appear with the young son of a Vallarta friend. Blaring headlines announced (incorrectly) that they had adopted him.

Losing her purse, part of her wardrobe, and even her shoes, Elizabeth made it through the crowd with the help of strong-armed security guards. "Fuck this!" she shouted at Burton. "They think we're the Beatles!"

Even before they left the airport, "The Liz & Dick" show entertained the masses by staging a big fight over a missing case of jewelry, each blaming the other for its disappearance. The box later turned up in a packed suitcase.

A press conference had

been scheduled, but Burton refused to attend. However, he did issue an ungallant statement. "This is my first visit to Mexico. I hope it will be my last."

In a short time he would change his mind and buy a vacation home there.

Elizabeth had a different opinion. She told the press, "I have always wanted to come back to fucking Mexico. I like fucking Mexico." The Mexican reporters printed her remarks but left out the two adjectives.

Initially, there was a lot of misunderstanding in the press, headlines claiming that Elizabeth, not Ava Gardner, would be the female star of the movie.

John Huston, the project's director, had wanted Marlon Brando to play the defrocked priest, but Ray Stark, the producer, favored either Richard Harris or William Holden. Finally, they settled on Burton. Ava Gardner had been their first choice as the notorious innkeeper, but Melina Mercouri was also held out as a replacement.

For the role of Deborah Kerr's grandfather, Nonno, Tennessee wanted Carl Sandburg, America's most famous playwright, but he was in failing health. The role instead went to Cyril Delevanti.

According to Elizabeth's secretary, Dick Hanley, who accompanied the famous pair, Elizabeth arrived "pissed off" at director John Huston. In fact, by the second day, she was already lambasting him as "an ugly, old, mean, withering fart," charging that he had mentally abused her friend Monty Clift during the filming of both *The Misfits* (1961) and *Freud* (1962).

Zoe Sallis showed up in Puerto Vallarta. It was common knowledge that she was Huston's mistress.

In 1963, Puerto Vallarta was a seedy little fishing village lying three hundred miles north of Acapulco. Tacky and not very well known, it became instantly famous when Elizabeth and Burton arrived and put it on the international tourist map. Tennessee would soon join in the chaos.

The actual shooting of *Iguana* took place on the isolated peninsula of Mismaloya, which had no road access to the mainland and could be reached only by

Long after her marriage (1951-1957) to Frank Sinatra, Ava was appropriately (some said brilliantly) cast as a blowsy, promiscuous, and alcoholic chaser of men who—in the film at least—included a bevy of Mexican laborers and, as depicted above, Richard Burton playing an emotionally tormented defrocked priest.

The sexual dramas offscreen more than matched the plot devised by Tennessee Williams.

boat. The only inhabitants on Mismaloya were ethnic Indians who lived in thatched huts and survived on fishing.

Elizabeth and Burton and all their massive amounts of luggage were taken to Puerto Vallarta and delivered to "Gringo Gulch," an upscale neighborhood where Americans had purchased a number of vacation homes. Locals had another name for it, referring to it as La Casa de Zoplotes (the House of the Buzzards) because it lay near a garbage dump.

Whereas Burton had an actual part in the filming, Elizabeth was on site to see that he didn't go astray in the arms of any of his female co-stars. They included man-eating Ava Gardner, Deborah Kerr, and Sue ("Lolita") Lyon.

Elizabeth also had to keep her eye out for at least fifty whores, some of them diseased, who had arrived from Mexico City to service the film crew. At least half of that number of male hustlers had also come to Puerto Vallarta to service homosexual members of the crew. "I'm sure Tennessee will be royally entertained," Burton said.

Arriving at the port, Elizabeth feared she'd be assigned to some shack, but was delighted by Casa Kimberley, the villa provided for her. In fact, she liked it so much that she eventually bought it for $40,000.

Burton liked the ramshackle port, too, and in time, he built a villa across the street from Casa Kimberley, connecting the two properties with a footbridge that linked the two buildings from points within their respective second floors. Its design was inspired by the Bridge of Sighs in Venice. "I can run across the bridge and escape from Liz when she becomes a raging harridan," Burton told his assistant, Michael Wilding, who—as her former husband— was all too familiar with her rages.

It would take almost a novel to untangle the past and present romantic entanglements that whirled around the cast and crew of *Iguana*. Before it was over, Kerr told the press, "I'm the only one here not shacked up with somebody."

She left out the fact that she was accompanied by her husband, Peter Viertel, the scriptwriter who had previously worked with Huston on *The African Queen* (1951) with Humphrey Bogart and Katharine

"The Bridge of Sighs," as defined by Burton, which interconnected the face-to-face villas owned by Burton & Taylor in downtown Puerto Vallarta. Gossipy fans used to watch the pedestrians, in varying states of drunkenness or undress, who crossed it

Hepburn. Viertel had also been the former lover of Ava Gardner.

Other sexual embarrassments unfolded during the course of the filming. Huston had a reunion with Gardner, with whom he'd once had a torrid affair. Huston had also pursued Kerr.

Elizabeth knew that Kerr had had a sexual tryst years before with Stewart Granger, but she was not certain if Burton had had an affair with her in Britain.

Relationships between Burton and Wilding were still friendly, and Elizabeth had no animosity toward him. It had not been a bitter divorce. They were involved in the rearing of their two sons, and both of them loved their boys very much, even though neither of them would ever win any awards for parenting.

Wilding was no longer lusting for Elizabeth. He showed up with a beautiful Swedish actress, Karen von Unge. She recalled, "Michael was a dear, sensitive man who should have been a great painter. Here he was, carrying suitcases of chili for Elizabeth from Chasen's in Los Angeles because she asked for them. She simply asked, and men did—it was that simple."

Huston looked upon Wilding as "a pathetic figure. He was once a big star in England, but he gave it up for Elizabeth. What did it get him? Now he serves her drinks and picks up dog poop for her. He's like the Erich von Stroheim character in *Sunset Blvd.*. Formerly married to Gloria Swanson in the movie, he becomes her butler."

Anticipating feuds or muggings, Huston passed out Derringers to key members of his cast. These were the kind of small pistols that late 19th-century card sharps were known for concealing within their sleeves. With the pistols, he gave each person a silver bullet with a name etched onto it. Even though she was not a member of the cast, the derringer he gave Elizabeth was gold-plated.

Dutiful and demure daughter Deborah Kerr noting the words of her father's spontaneously composed poem, functioning as what was described as the only sexually chaste player on the set of *The Night of the Iguana*.

Cyril Delevanti played her aging father.

Unlike the others, Elizabeth received five bullets, each with a name on it—Richard Burton, Sue Lyon, Ava Gardner, and Deborah Kerr. The director also included one with the name of John Huston.

On seeing Elizabeth again over drinks, Gardner said, "Dear heart, you and Richard are the Frank (Sinatra) and

Ava (Gardner) of the 1960s."

Evelyn Keyes, though not in Mexico, was present—at least in the group's collective memory. Following her divorce from John Huston, Keyes had had an extended affair with Mike Todd, who would later marry Elizabeth. Currently, Keyes was married to musician Artie Shaw, Ava Gardner's former husband.

The plot thickened when Budd Schulberg, author of the Hollywood novel, *What Makes Sammy Run?* and the screenplay for *On the Waterfront*, arrived to seduce Gardner. Viertel had once been married to Schulberg's former wife, Virginia Ray.

In a conversation one day at the beach with Elizabeth and Dick Hanley, Viertel confessed that he had abandoned his pregnant wife to run away with Bettina, arguably the most famous French fashion model of the 1950s. "She later dumped me for Aly Khan."

"I know Bettina," Elizabeth said. "I know Aly Khan, too. Oh do I know Aly Khan!"

"Huston tried to console me when I lost Bettina," Viertel said. "He told me 'Aly Khan is one swell guy.' Then, when Aly Khan fucked Huston's wife, Evelyn Keyes, I told him, 'It's okay, John, Aly is one swell guy.' He punched me in the mouth. I love John, though. He's fucked everybody from Marilyn Monroe on the set of *The Asphalt Jungle* to Truman Capote on the set of *Beat the Devil* when they shared a double bed. He even screwed a neo-Nazi woman in London who gave him syphilis—something he later referred to as 'the Hitler clap.'"

When Viertel left to return to the set, he, as a man of the world, kissed both Elizabeth and Hanley on the lips before departing.

Tennessee arrived in Puerto Vallarta with Frederick Nicklaus, a young recent graduate of Ohio State University. Tennessee told Huston, "Frederick is the world's greatest living poet, though not discovered as of yet."

"You've already introduced Freddie boy to me in Key West," Huston reminded the drugged playwright.

"I've dealt with Bogie, so I know how to handle difficult, temperamental personalities," Huston later said. "Williams is an odd bird, always in flight. He can also 'fly' off the handle at just a perceived insult. Not only that, but he is eccentric, a sex addict, a pill pusher, an alcoholic, and, perhaps, a genius. A genius is always difficult to handle. I already had Ava Gardner, Richard Burton, and Elizabeth fucking around. Now, Tennessee with his fat wallet would soon be buying every good-looking Mexican lad at the port."

Darwin flew in two nights later and was quickly caught up on what had happened before his arrival.

Tom Shaw, Huston's assistant director, detested Tennessee and his volatile personality. In his bulldog manner, he said, "I hated the mean son of a bitch. I was having a drink at the bar, and he was berating the shit out of this poor Mexican bartender. At the time, I didn't recognize who he was. I said to myself, 'Who is this asshole?' He was a vicious kind of faggot."

One night over drinks, the key players were asked by Herb Caen, the San Francisco columnist, what they most wanted in life. Huston said, "Interest." Gardner wished for "Health." Burton opted for "Adventure," Viertel for "Success," and Deborah Kerr "Happiness." Elizabeth chose "Wealth."

Tennessee requested, "Better sex."

One night in a tavern, Burton downed twenty-five straight shots of tequila, using Carta Blanca beer as a chaser.

Tennessee and Huston could almost keep up with him.

"I was in no condition myself, but I often had to put Burton to bed at his villa long after Elizabeth had retired," Tennessee said. "He begged me to help him get undressed, so I took advantage. He didn't specifically ask me to, but I also removed the Welshman's jockey shorts. I figured I wouldn't get a chance like this very often—to see what appealed to the stately homos of the British theater like Olivier and Gielgud in the 1940s, and to so many fine ladies."

The cast and crew were constantly besieged by reporters, Elizabeth claiming, "There are more press guys and paparazzi here than fucking iguanas."

Whereas reporters from California relished writing about the heavy drinking and the behind-the-scenes romances, the Mexican newspaper *Siempre* denounced the entire cast and crew of *The Night of the Iguana*. It attacked the "sex, drinking, drugs, vice, and carnal bestiality of this gringo garbage that has descended on our country." *Siempre* also cited "gangsters, nymphomaniacs, heroin-taking blondes, and the degenerate American playwright, Tennessee Williams."

One night, while drinking with Elizabeth, it became clear that her body was a sea of insect bites. "Welcome to Puerto Vallarta," she said,

Memories of decadence and the Old South: Tennessee Williams on the sands of Puerto Vallarta.

"with its tropical heat, cheating lovers, poisonous snakes, deadly scorpions, hot pussies, and giant land crabs. Of them all, the most devouring are the goddamn chiggers, which dig in real deep and can only be removed with scalpels."

The local Catholic priest attacked Elizabeth as a "wanton Jezebel" and called on the President of Mexico to deport her as an undesirable alien. When Tennessee's arrival was publicized in the press, the priest also called for his removal from Mexico as well. "We do not need another notorious homosexual coming to Mexico to corrupt the morals of our young men."

A drunken Elizabeth was asked one night how she'd describe the three women in the cast. She obliged: "Gardner is lushly ripe for a middle-aged woman; Kerr is refined and ladylike until you get her in bed, or so I'm told; and Lyon is…well, let's just say nubile. No wonder James Mason had the hots for her. When making *Lolita* (1962), he temporarily gave up his interest in boys."

When Tennessee, in a Puerto Vallarta tavern known as the Casablanca Bar, was asked for his opinion of the Taylor/Burton romance, he said, "They are artists on a special pedestal and therefore the rules of bourgeois morality do not apply to them."

Burton was sitting with Tennessee when he made that pronouncement. When Burton himself was asked for a comment, he said, "I am bewitched by the cunt of Elizabeth Taylor and her cunning ways. Cunt and cunning—that's what the attraction is."

***

Before his departure from Mexico in October of 1963 for New York, Tennessee hosted a party at his rented villa near Elizabeth and Burton in Gringo Gulch. He'd invited both of them to attend, but only Elizabeth had shown up.

TWO VIEWS OF SUE LYONS

Top photo: playing the title role in *Lolita* (1962) and (lower photo) dancing with Puerto Vallarta locals in this press photo snapped on the set of *The Night of the Iguana*.

There, she met Jose Bolaños, a Mexican screen writer who was enjoying a certain vogue. After the murder of Marilyn Monroe on August 4, 1962, he was getting a lot of press attention and being widely hailed as her last and final boyfriend.

Bolaños told Tennessee that he and Monroe had mutually committed themselves to get married, although some of her friends said that Monroe had promised to remarry Joe DiMaggio.

Bolaños was working on a TV commercial twenty-five miles to the south but had come to Puerto Vallarta with the hope of meeting and ingratiating himself with Elizabeth as he had with Monroe.

Tennessee had been charmed by the charismatic young Mexican and had set up the meeting for him with Elizabeth, presumably without Burton.

Tennessee defined him as a Latin lover archetype, evocative of both Fernando Lamas and Ricardo Montalban. Bolaños was dark and handsome, with a magnetic personality. The night of their meeting, Bolaños told Elizabeth and Tennessee that his dream involved coming to Hollywood and putting both Lamas and Montalban "out of business." Secretly, he hoped that by attaching himself to Elizabeth, she could use her influence to help him break into the American film industry.

She might have paid scant attention to Bolaños except for two reasons: He was the only man she'd met in Puerto Vallarta who qualified for that "revenge fuck" she'd planned as a means of getting even with Burton for seducing Gardner. Also, she was tempted by the idea of learning intimate secrets about Monroe's last lover, especially if the fallen star had considered Bolaños as marriage material.

At Tennessee's party, Bolaños exuded masculinity, and as Elizabeth would tell Dick Hanley, "He stood so close to me he was practically rubbing that big package up against me."

On his own turf within Mexico's film community, Bolaños was known as a "star fucker," having previously seduced such aging screen divas as Merle Oberon and Dolores Del Rio.

On the patio of Tennessee's rented villa, lit by colored lights, Bolaños

Jose Bolaños, depicted above with Marilyn on the cover of a Spanish-language biography of the Mexican actor/stud by Xavier Navaza.

danced both the rumba and the samba with Elizabeth. Tennessee had hired a six-member band, each of the members appearing in tight white pants and shirtless, as per the playwright's request.

According to his reputation, Bolaños specialized in making a woman feel like she was the only female on earth.

The screenwriter mesmerized Elizabeth with his tales of working in the film industry in Mexico. He had been an intimate friend of the late, great modernist painter, Diego Rivera, and was also close to the Spain-born director Luís Buñuel, a towering figure in experimental cinema.

Bolaños also invited Elizabeth to see the Mexican historical epic, *La Cucaracha* (aka *The Soldiers of Pancho Villa*; 1959), whose screenplay he had written.

She pumped Bolaños for any details he could supply about Monroe's final weeks alive. Hanley came over to join them. "Bolaños was very clever," he said. "He did not speak unkindly of Marilyn, but he placed Elizabeth on a higher pedestal. About three times, he told her that 'you are, of course, a far greater star than Marilyn, who possessed neither your talent nor your beauty.'"

"Your beauty is a natural beauty," Bolaños told Elizabeth in front of Hanley. "Marilyn had to become Marilyn Monroe by acting the part, dressing up, and painting her face. With no make-up on, I'm sure you'd look stunning. Surely no one on the planet has eyes as beautiful as yours."

Hanley drove Elizabeth and Bolaños to his apartment, where they disappeared upstairs. He waited downstairs in his car for two hours. When Elizabeth finally came down the steps, he drove her home. She told him that Bolaños had asked to remain in Hanley's apartment for the night, not wanting to drive after dark on the impossibly treacherous roads.

Back in his own apartment, he found a nude Bolaños asleep on his bed. Very gently, Hanley draped a sheet over him. "Lucky Marilyn, lucky Elizabeth," he later told Roddy McDowall.

"The next morning, I made breakfast for him," Hanley said. "He also let me make love to him, but only in exchange for a big favor."

"I know you're her secretary," Bolaños said, "and you can arrange for me to have a rendezvous with her in Hollywood. I want to be in her life. She'll tire of Burton. He's an old man of failing powers, I heard. I want to be nearby when she replaces Burton."

"You've got yourself a deal, but I'll expect my pound of flesh."

Bolaños sighed. "All of you *mariposas* want that. So if you deliver Elizabeth Taylor to me, you can have me on occasion. After all, I'm the most sought-after male in all of Mexico."

Bolaños was already aware of the important roles Tennessee had written for men, including the character of Stanley Kowalski in *A Streetcar Named Desire*, and the role of Brick in *Cat on a Hot Tin Roof*.

Consequently, Bolaños asked Hanley to call Tennessee immediately to ask if he could spend the day with him, and possibly the night.

Tennessee was only too eager to invite Bolaños over, telling Hanley, "If Marilyn and Elizabeth can go for him, why not me?"

In the aftermath of that call, Tennessee spent a day and a night with Bolaños before he headed out of Puerto Vallarta the following morning.

He was so taken with Bolaños that he promised to write a role for him based on the archetype of a dashing young Mexican. "The part will be ideal for you."

Of course that was an empty promise. He never came through for Bolaños.

***

On most mornings, Tennessee met Elizabeth at her villa. Together, they headed out, wading through chickens, naked children, and mange-encrusted mongrel dogs. He and Hanley carried the makings of a picnic with them, to be shared with Burton later when they reached the remote peninsula where filming was occurring.

Huston liked to launch his day with five Bloody Marys, and Elizabeth and Tennessee joined him.

One day, Elizabeth was feeling ill and Tennessee went alone, telling Huston that he stood ready to write additional dialogue.

Huston told him, "I don't think we're going to get much shooting done today. The heat is crushing, and Burton disappeared into Ava's dressing room at ten o'clock. They may be in there for the day."

As author Nancy Schoenberger wrote: "Ava seemed to come alive in Burton's presence. The press was not just covering a congregation of some of the world's greatest talents and personalities in a remote Mexican village, they were waiting—hoping?—that Burton and Taylor's vaunted love affair might founder on Ava Gardner's dangerous shoulders."

The coming together of the drunken, poetry-spouting, lust-filled Welsh actor and the Tarheel *femme fatale* and sex symbol had sparked "meaningful eye contact," as Huston described it to Tennessee.

One day before noon, both Gardner and Burton got drunk on a local moonshine known as *raicilla*. It was made from the agave plant. Gardner called it "cactus piss."

Huston defined it to Tennessee as "a cactus brandy stronger than tequila." Burton told him that the way to drink *raicilla* was straight down.

"That way you can feel it going into each individual intestine." When Elizabeth tried it, she said, "I hear it's made from cactus. Tell the fuckers who brewed it that they left the god damn needles in it."

One evening when Elizabeth was suffering from *"turista,"* Hanley drove Tennessee and Burton to the Casablanca Bar. To Hanley's surprise, a sultry Gardner was waiting there for him. Burton turned to Dick, "I can always count on you for being discreet around Her Ladyship."

Actually, Burton was wrong about the degree to which Hanley would remain discreet.

"After Ava and Richard consumed enough alcohol to resink the *Titanic*, they retired to one of the hot-bed shanties out back, where they disappeared," Hanley said. "I wondered if Richard would be able to get it up in his condition. I sat in the bar with this beach boy hustler waiting for their return."

"Tennessee hired this other hustler and seduced him in our car. Ava and Richard were gone for about three hours. When both of them finally emerged, they were barely able to stand up."

"I literally had to toss them into the back of our car, where they cuddled up with Tennessee for the ride back home," Hanley said.

***

Tennessee could not wait around for the shooting to end. He had to fly back to New York to face other commitments. He was in a Broadway theater when he heard the news about John F. Kennedy's assassination. He later heard that both Elizabeth and Ava Gardner took the news rather badly. Both of them had had flings with the assassinated President.

"So did I," Tennessee said enigmatically, with no explanation.

In the future, Tennessee would deal with Elizabeth and Burton again when they filmed *Boom!* in Sardinia, based on his play, *The Milk Train Doesn't Stop Here Anymore*.

Broadway had cast Tallulah Bankhead and Tab Hunter in Tennessee Williams' *The Milk Train Doesn't Stop Here Anymore*.

Retitled as *Boom!*, the 1968 movie adaptation starred a miscast Elizabeth Taylor as an aging, dying actress and Richard Burton as a young poet who tries to both hustle her and save her from despair.

An abject flop much scorned by critics, it marked the end of Burton and Taylor's reign as the hot box office team of the 1960s.

Chapter Fourteen

WHEN TITANS (OR DIVAS) CLASH

JACQUELINE KENNEDY ONASSIS VS. GRACE KELLY, PRINCESS OF MONACO

RIVALRY AT THE FAIR IN SEVILLE

"I dated Jack before she did. He should have married me. Then I could have been First Lady of the United Sates instead of a mere Princess."
—**Grace Kelly**

During an official State Visit to the White House, First lady Jacqueline Kennedy was forced to entertain Grace Kelly, now the Princess of Monaco, with her Prince. She didn't want to do it, because she knew of Grace's early affair with her husband, John F. Kennedy.

On May 4, 1961, when President John F. Kennedy and Jacqueline entertained Prince Rainier and Princess Grace at a White House luncheon, the two combatants were later forced to have a cup of tea together when JFK excused himself to talk to Prince Rainier. Jackie at this point had heard about Grace's affair with her husband.

When they were seated, according to a White House staff member, Jackie provocatively asked, "Of the Seven Graces, which one are you?"

"I try to have the qualities of all of them," Grace shot back.

Continuing her provocation, Jackie asked, "Jack and I heard that when Prince Rainier was shopping for a bride, he first considered Marilyn Monroe. At least that was the plan that Aristotle Onassis said he proposed to your prince."

"Yes, I know," Grace responded. "He found the idea disgusting. We're not promoting Monaco as a destination for Las Vegas style whorehouses."

Jackie wanted the last word, "Oh, I forgot to tell you how much I adore your hat. Did Oleg Cassini design it for you?"

She told her staff a different story. "Oleg must have had too much wine. That silly hat looked like something Esther Williams might wear if she were impersonating Neptune's Daughter."

While Grace was making *To Catch a Thief* (1955) with her co-star, Cary Grant, she confessed to him that "I fell in love with Jack Kennedy when I was working as a model in New York. I never got over him. He's the man I should have married. I only say that because you didn't ask me."

Their fathers, Joe Kennedy and Jack Kelly, were two rich Irishmen who decided that their children should meet. Soon, JFK was seen escorting Grace in and out of the Barbizon Hotel for Women in Manhattan. Their affair was in full bloom.

When the subject of a possible marriage came up, Joe nixed it for his son. His father had learned from Jack Kelly that Grace planned to be a Hollywood star.

"Have you ever heard of a President of the United States bringing an actress to the White House as his First Lady?" Joe asked.

[At that time, Ronald Reagan hadn't married the former B-actress, Nancy Davis.]

Although marriage was out of the question, JFK and Grace got together at certain intervals.

Until Grace married Prince Rainier of Monaco in April of 1956, Jackie had been only vaguely aware that the future princess and her husband had had an affair before her string of seductions that included Marlon

New evidence of Grace's enduring romantic fascination for JFK, as shown in this photo of Grace during her lunch at the White House shortly after his election.

Brando, Ray Milland, Gary Cooper, Bing Crosby, William Holden, Frank Sinatra, Cary Grant, James Stewart, Clark Gable, David Niven, Spencer Tracy, Jean-Pierre Aumont, Oleg Cassini, Prince Aly Khan, et al.

Jackie's loathing of Princess Grace spilled over into the White House after Jack was elected president in 1960. JFK asked Jackie to organize an official White House visit for Prince and Princess Rainier during the royal couple's visit to Washington.

Biographer Wendy Leigh quoted Letitia ("Tish") Baldrige, Jackie's social secretary, about what happened next. "Grace had a relationship with the President before his marriage to Jackie, and Jackie knew about it. That, in my opinion, is why Jackie changed the White House meal in their honor from a four-hour black-tie dinner dance to a small luncheon. A bit of jealousy perhaps. Jackie never said anything, but you could tell. She didn't really want to talk about the arrangements and was very offhand about how they were made. A luncheon meant that Princess Grace wouldn't look as gorgeous as she usually did at night."

Grace and Jackie were often compared in the press, and both women were considered valuable assets to their husbands. President Kennedy claimed he was the man who accompanied Jackie to Paris, and Prince Rainier called Grace "the best ambassador I have."

In 1966, three years after JFK's assassination in Dallas, Jackie took one of her publicized trips abroad. She accepted an invitation to visit the famous *Feria de Abril* held every year in Seville, the capital of Andalusia.

Hearing of the event, Darwin decided to fly there, both to update his annual guidebook to Spain and to see if the tension between the two old rivals, Jackie and Princess Grace, would erupt into a catfight.

In Seville, Darwin joined the Madrid journalist, Diego Fernandez, who promised to keep him abreast of all the latest gossip. Since Darwin wanted to gather material for a future book about Jackie, and since Diego was a self-styled scoop artist specializing in newspaper exposés, he didn't view Darwin as competition. So he hung out with him in the *tascas* and fed him secret data he'd gathered.

The Duke and Duchess of Alba had installed Jackie in the Palacio de Las Dueñas.

Grace opened the festivities clad in a ruffled, pink lace, Andalusian dress presented to her by local flamenco dancers.

Jackie "completely stole Princess Grace's thunder," wrote a journalist "when America's former First Lady agreed to ride a horse in the Feria."

Looking spectacular, Jackie had dressed for the occasion in the traditional riding costume, a *traje corio*, the black trimmed red jacket, a black flat-brimmed hat, and flowing chaps.

Jackie, the *equestrienne supreme*, mounted a white stallion and made a leisurely *paseo* around the gaily decorated fairgrounds, to the delight of the paparazzi and her local fans.

Perhaps Grace never got to read a review that appeared in a Seville paper of Jackie's appearance. "America's former First Lady revealed to all the world that she should not only have been made a princess like Prince Rainier's wife, but Jacqueline should be anointed Queen of the World." Grace's name wasn't even mentioned, except for the reference to her as "wife."

As part of the festivities, Princess Grace and Jackie encountered each other at Seville's splendid bullring. At that time, the celebrated, handsome, and well-built El Cordobés (actually Manuel Benítez Pérez) was the leading matador of Spain.

Bypassing Grace—actually, ignoring her completely—El Cordobés passed his matador hat to Jackie, who placed a Kennedy half-dollar into it before returning it. He then dedicated "the first bull" to Jackie.

In front of Jackie, El Cordobés performed his most dangerous stunt, as

Jacqueline Kennedy *(right photo)* survived Princess Grace and the Fair in Seville, and went on to marry the Greek shipping tycoon, Aristotle Onassis. But then she had to deal with another challenge in the form of the great opera diva, Maria Callas *(left photo)*, depicted here as Violetta in *La Traviata*.

she watched in horror. He broke his *banderillas* down to the size of a pencil, then stood with his back to the bull as it rampaged toward him. A moment before impact, he deftly moved his right leg out of the way of the bull's path. As the bull swerved, he thrust in the *banderillas* at a crippling point just behind its left horn. The audience went wild.

***

Fernandez, the scoop artist, filled Darwin in on all the juicy details. He later sent his *exposé* to his newspaper in Madrid, which caused a sensation in the days after its publication.

He claimed that El Cordobés was seen entering the palace of the Duke and Duchess of Alba where Jackie awaited him. Ostensibly it was for drinks and dinner.

The reporter said he waited outside the palace until three o'clock that morning when El Cordobés was seen leaving the palace and getting into a limousine. In print, he claimed, "It is all but certain that El Cordobés and the widow of President John F. Kennedy had an affair that night. In seducing her matador, Mrs. Kennedy was blazing a trail originally taken by the movie star, Ava Gardner, who had a particular fascination for Spanish bullfighters, especially Luís Miguel Dominguin. What is it with this fascination celebrated American women have for Spanish bullfighters? I think it has something to do with the bull."

Jackie allegedly found *El Cordobés* (The Cordoban), fascinating, though he was barely literate.

She met him during his heyday in the 1960s when he was the most famous matador of Spain, renowned for his unorthodox, acrobatic, and theatrical style in the ring.

He's young, virile, dashing, and with a legendary stamina. He's EL CORDOBES!, Spain's leading matador. When his eyes met Jacqueline's, it was passion at first sight.

She felt his story would not only make a great book, but an intriguing movie.

In Spain, he became a symbol of hope for poor boys around the country. He had risen fast within the celebrity circuit of Spain, driving a Rolls-Royce and flying his own airplane. Orphaned during the wrenching agonies of Spain's Civil War, young Manuel stole chickens to bring home for his mother to put into the pot, and worked as a ditchdigger, a pickpocket, a bricklayer, and a field worker as a means of earning a few pesetas.

Reportedly, El Cordobés showed Jackie his wounds as "badges of courage." Only two years before meeting her, he had experienced a near-fatal goring at the Plaza de Toros in Madrid on the horns of an enraged, half-blind bull named "Impulsivo."

Because of his ability to draw so many fans, the press dubbed him "The Beatle of the Bullring." Receiving $50,000 per fight, he was one of the highest paid entertainers in the world.

When he met Jackie, he was known for having seduced some of the most celebrated women anywhere. As Gregory Hemingway, son of Ernesto, said, "If these women weren't attracted to his bullfighting skills, they were to that package he encased in his tight-fitting suit of lights."

Jackie commented on the young man's theatricality in the ring: "He was a great showman, exhibiting a kind of razzle-dazzle. He would crouch, then leap away from the onrushing horns in just the nick of time. Talk about Hemingway's *Death in the Afternoon*. Or else he'd rest his head against the bull's hindquarters one moment and mock-box the beast the next moment. Of course, he flashed a smile suited for toothpaste commercials. At one point, I screamed when he flicked his red *muleta*. The beast was charging at him, and he wasn't moving until the last second."

To Jackie, El Cordobés said, "I fight for the masses. Those smart guys who think they know so much write great stuff on how to fight bulls. But there's just one trouble: The bulls can't read."

Based on the time he spent in Seville with Jackie, El Cordobés later claimed that he was going to transform her into a motion picture star. As Jackie biographer Freda Kramer wrote: "El Cordobés told everyone that Jackie was going to appear in a picture he was making. He swore on it." The claim merited some space in newspapers. It was even said that Jackie was going to donate her salary to charity.

This was not the only time the press speculated that Jackie was going to star in a movie. For a time, her dear friend, director Mike Nichols, was said to have cast her in a romantic comedy opposite Rock Hudson.

When asked about that rumor, Jackie said, "I'm leaving the acting in the family to my sister Lee."

The highlight of the Feria was the International Red Cross Ball, a charity debutante party for 2,500 guests hosted by the Duke of Medinaceli.

As usual, Princess Grace expected to be the belle of the ball. She went all out and appeared wrapped in white mink. Her hair was upswept and she was wearing a prince's ransom in diamonds. But she was virtually ignored as the guests rushed to get a glimpse of Jackie when she entered the courtyard bare shouldered and wearing a blue gown designed by Oleg Cassini. Jackie had fashionably arrived an hour late.

Grace was also jealous that the designer, Cassini, her former lover who'd once passionately wanted to marry her, was now showering his attention on the creation of chic *couture* for Jackie.

After battling through the hordes of reporters and photographers, Jackie finally made it to the table of their host, the Duke de Medinaceli. Grace extended a limp handshake to Jackie, then turned her head to avoid her throughout the rest of the evening.

With the poor Duke sandwiched in between them, he tried to make conversation to no avail. The next morning the *New York Herald Tribune* captioned a picture of them, headlining, "Cool Conversation," and noting that Grace and Jackie had little to say to each other. In response, Grace wrote a letter to the newspaper, claiming "I have great respect and admiration for Mrs. Kennedy."

Prince Rainier seemed dazzled by Jackie, but Princess Grace remained frosty, and Jackie turned an Arctic shoulder to Her Serene Highness. Jackie had long ago learned the details of Grace's romantic involvement with Jack

Hot nights and chilly din-dins with two princesses as refereed by the Duke of Medinaceli.

as well as her seduction of Bobby, who was Jackie's lover at the time. "Jackie had reasons to detest Grace," Truman Capote later said, "especially when eagle-eyed Grace detected a gleam in the eyes of her prince."

In a huff, the Princess departed for an hour to the powder room. During her absence, Prince Rainier was seen in a secluded area of a patio smoking a cigarette with Jackie, away from the prying eyes of the paparazzi.

At the time of this flirtation between Jackie and Prince Rainier, international rumors were swirling that she was all but engaged to Antonio Garrigues, a widower with eight children. At the age of 62, he'd been appointed Spain's Ambassador to the Vatican. He and Jackie were later spotted together in Rome.

Unknown except to many of her friends, Jackie was a great mimic. After leaving Seville, she headed for some R&R at the swank Marbella Club on Spain's Costa del Sol. Once there, she delivered a devastating satire of Grace as she'd appeared in *Rear Window* (1954) opposite James Stewart, another of Grace's sexual conquests.

"It should have been taped," said Antonio Cordova, a member of the chic clique who had gathered at the Marbella Club. "Jackie appeared with long white gloves and imitated Grace's speech pattern to perfection. Slowly those gloves were removed, and Jackie did the world's most amusing rendition of Grace Kelly imitating Rita Hayworth in her 'Put the Blame on Mame' number in *Gilda* (1946). What an evening!"

CELEBRITIES WITH OTHER CELEBRITIES IN OPEN-AIR CARS

JFK with Jackie during one of the Senator's early political campaigns, and Prince Rainier I of Monaco with his bride, Grace Kelly, after their wedding nuptials in 1956.

Chapter Fifteen

REPLICATING ANCIENT ROME IN ALL ITS DECADENCE

CALIGULA

KEEPING TABS ON
"THE MOST DEPRAVED & DECADENT FILM EVER MADE"

Caligula, released in 1979. was an Italo-American erotic biography financed by the guru of *Penthouse* magazine, Bob Guccione. With such stars as Peter O'Toole, Helen Mirren, John Gielgud, and Malcolm McDowell, it became the first motion picture to feature prominent movie stars interspersed with pornographic scenes. Even today, it remains the most infamous cult film ever made, and it is still banned in some nations.

In 1977, Darwin flew to Rome to update *Frommer's Rome* and his annual guide to Italy. This time, he had another purpose in mind.

As a celebrity journalist, he wanted to pick up some of the secrets unfolding behind the scenes during the making of *Caligula*.

Produced by Bob Guccione of *Penthouse* magazine, and released after horrific setbacks and controversies in 1979, it featured an all-star cast. Behind the scenes, rumors spread that it was the most daring, the most controversial, the most depraved major film ever made. There were rivers of intrigue and scandal both on the screen and off, and Darwin wanted to learn firsthand what was going on.

One day, he planned to write a biography—eventually published in 2015—called *Peter O'Toole—Hellraiser, Sexual Outlaw, Irish Rebel*. He also wanted to gather data for a chapter in another biography—eventually published in 2014—entitled *Pink Triangle—The Feuds & Private Lives of Tennessee Williams, Gore Vidal, & Truman Capote*. Vidal played a vital role during the crafting of the film because Guccione had hired him to write the movie's script.

Darwin began his "voyage of discovery" a few hours after his arrival in Rome, later remembering, "The city was as vibrant as ever, and the stories circulating about the making of *Caligula* were, for the most part, XXX rated."

How did it all begin?

***

In London, Peter O'Toole was startled to hear that Bob Guccione was on the other end of the phone, calling from his suite at the Savoy Hotel.

The founder and publisher of *Penthouse* was one of the most controversial media persons in the United States and Britain. Picking up the receiver, O'Toole said to Guccione, "If you're calling me to pose for a nude

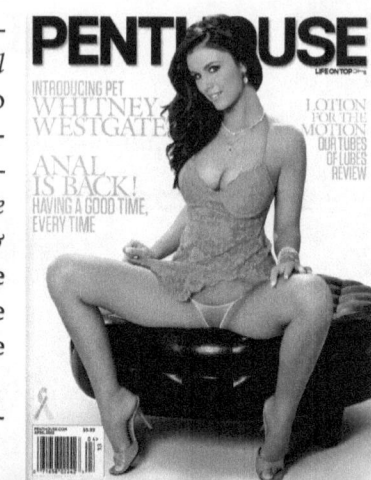

Although Bob Guccione (lower photo) viewed Hugh Hefner of *Playboy* as his major competitor, he also battled with another more provocative rival, Larry Flynt of *Hustler*.

After *Hustler* ran a cartoon insinuating that Guccione had transmitted a venereal disease to his girlfriend, Guccione got even by arranging for the woman to sue both Flynt and his magazine.

The (hugely expensive) lawsuit ended up in the Supreme Court. When the verdict went against Flynt, he denounced the Justices, calling them "nine assholes and one token cunt."

In response, Justice Warren Berger shouted, "Arrest that man!"

centerfold, the answer is an emphatic *no.*"

"I've got a better offer," Guccione said. "How would you like to play the Emperor Tiberius in an epic to be shot in Rome?"

"That sounds mighty intriguing," O'Toole said.

"If you'll meet me at eight tonight in the Savoy Grill, I'll discuss all the details with you."

Although a more ardent reader of Hugh Hefner's *Playboy* than Guccione's *Penthouse*, O'Toole had long admired Guccione as a champion of freedom of the press.

Guccione, "The Caesar of sex magazine gurus," believed in breaking taboos and outraging the so-called "guardians of taste." He made millions before drowning in a slough of bad investments, one of which involved financing the controversial pornographic epic, *Caligula*. *[To his embittered horror, most movie houses refused to show it.]*

Before having drinks and dinner with him, O'Toole read some recent articles about him that traced his amazing, trail-blazing career. A breaker of taboos, an outrage to bluenoses trying to maintain some semblance of Victorian taste in a rapidly changing, permissive society, Guccione had created a pornographic empire.

As a struggling artist, he had taken out a loan for $1,170 for the establishment, in 1965, of a magazine that featured female nudes in positions far more explicit than those within *Playboy*. "I wanted to be the first publisher to depict the clitoris," he announced to the press.

Forbes listed him as one of the world's richest men, with a fortune spiraling toward $400 million. Each edition of his magazine, at its peak, reached nearly five million readers. His art collection, filled with works by Dalí, Picasso, Matisse, and Renoir, was worth some $150 million.

Over drinks, O'Toole encountered a flamboyant publisher that to him evoked a "libidinous pornographer," as he later described his encounter to his ever-loyal confidant, Kenneth Griffith.

Dark, haunted eyes stared at O'Toole from under thick, grizzled brows. "He was tanned, really, really tanned," O'Toole told Griffith. "Either from the Palm Beach sun, or else from a sun lamp in a massage parlor attended by bare-breasted Amazons."

Guccione was dressed in an Italian silk suit with a black silk shirt open to the waist, exposing a hairy chest. Around his neck was a series of gold chains, many of them containing charms. He showed one charm which was a depiction of the first-ever cover of *Penthouse*; yet another was a miniature replica of a man's genitals.

"This is a reproduction of my cock and balls," Guccione said. "My dick is big enough, but, like all men, I wish it extended at least another two inches."

Two years older than O'Toole, Guccione revealed that he had been born in Brooklyn to parents of Sicilian roots. As an altar boy, he had considered the priesthood. "But as a teenager, my testosterone won out, and I began to deflower what virgins remained in Brooklyn. By eighteen, I was married."

He seemed very familiar with the geography of London, and O'Toole soon learned why. In 1960, he'd settled here, running a dry-cleaning business. "I sold pinup pictures of mostly naked women as a sideline." For a while, he became a cartoonist for *The London American*, where he feuded with his editor, Derek Jameson. "He constantly complained to me, 'Bob you can't put tits and arse on the front page, or we'll all end up in the nick.'"

He launched *Penthouse*, a magazine he described as devoted to "sex, politics, and protests."

"My kind of man," O'Toole said.

"I'm the enemy of all feminists and conservatives," he said. "And although I'm a publisher, my real interest in life is as a painter. I'm damn good. Better than Picasso."

"I've revolutionized men's magazines," he said, "Hefner wasn't showing pubic hair. From the beginning, I showed female genitalia, beginning with fuzzy pictures of the pudenda, without the inner labia parted. Now, I'm showing sharper views of the vulva."

"It took a while to get around to male genitalia, including erections."

"As you may know, in media, I'm known for breaking down barriers to censorship. I want to show actual oral, vaginal, and anal penetration. I also pioneered girl-on-girl shots. I know guys like to watch how much lesbians like each other's pussies. In the trade, we call it 'going pink.' I plan to break the final taboo."

"My god, man, what else is left for you to do?"

"I want to depict female models urinating," Guccione said. "That would cross the last frontier in men's magazines. What I'd really like to show is a man urinating into the face of a bitch, but that may be too much. Lezzie feminists wouldn't like it."

"I can't imagine why," O'Toole said, sarcastically.

"Working together, we'll get to know each other better," Guccione said. "I'd like to invite you to my parties. You'll learn that I believe in open marriages, and so do my guests."

"So do I, dear man," O'Toole said. "What man likes to walk around with a ball and chain?"

Guccione revealed that he was prepared to spend as much as $20 million on a film epic that graphically portrayed the decadence of Imperial Rome. "If it's successful, I'll do other biopics. I have two in mind, *Catherine the Great*, and a biopic based on Defoe's *Moll Flanders*. Perhaps there would be roles in both movies for you if you get through our first venture. I saw your film, *Great Catherine* (1968), so you already know your way around a Russian court."

"What are you calling your Roman epic?" O'Toole asked. "Perhaps just *Tiberius* would be enough, since even the name of that madman suggests all sorts of wicked things."

"You don't understand," Guccione said. "I'm hiring you to perform a cameo. The movie is to be called *Caligula* in honor of the main character."

"You mean, my successor, my great nephew?"

"Exactly. You know your ancient Roman history, I see."

"Who do you have in mind to play Caligula?" O'Toole asked. "Of course, it would have to be an actor younger than me."

"I'd prefer an English actor. He's got to agree to appear in a full frontal nude scene. You know most of the major actors. Who would you recommend?"

"Over here, we call it the Full Monty," O'Toole said. "The obvious choices would be either Alan Bates or Oliver Reed. After all, they showed their family jewels in *Women in Love* (1969). Alan is only two years younger than me, but Reed was born in 1938."

"Actually, I was thinking about pitching the role to Malcolm McDowell," Guccione said. "Do you know how he's hung?"

"I never gave him a blow-job, but he might go for it. After all, he made *A Clockwork Orange*, so he might be up for doing anything. He and I both grew up in Leeds."

"Right as we speak, Lina Wertmüller is at work on the script," Guccione said. "I'm thinking of asking her to direct the picture as well."

"I admire her work," O'Toole said.

[*At that time in the mid-1970s, Wertmüller was enjoying an international vogue. She was called "a modern Aristophanes and a Chaplinesque defender of humble individuals."*

An article by Ellen Willis had appeared about her in Rolling Stone, *making her a very dubious*

The English actor, Malcolm McDowell, played the title role—that of the depraved Emperor Caligula. His slightly startled look was defined by critics as "emotionally greedy."

He was not ashamed to appear fully nude in the movie. Thanks to his striptease in *Caligula*, the star of Stanley Kubrick's *A Clockwork Orange* (1971) developed a whole new fan base.

candidate for Caligula: "She is a woman hater who pretends to be a feminist. Her basic appeal is a clever double-dealing that allows high-minded people to indulge their lowest-minded prejudice."]

In the days that followed, Guccione stayed in frequent contact with O'Toole. One afternoon, he called from New York. "I detested Wertmüller's script. She and I had a big row. I'm asking John Huston to direct. I'll get back to you when I've found out his reaction. In the meantime, I've hired Gore Vidal to come up with a script. He and his lover live in Rome, and he's said to be an expert and scholar on ancient Greek and Roman history."

"A wise choice, I'm sure."

In the meantime, O'Toole was researching whatever he could on Tiberius, who ruled the Roman Empire from 14-37 A.D. Tiberius was the stepson of Augustus, the paternal uncle of Claudius, and great-grand uncle of Nero. He also was one of Rome's greatest generals.

In his later years, Tiberius became reclusive on the island of Capri, where he was said to have indulged in "the most wicked of all known perversions." Pliny the Elder labeled him "the gloomiest of men." Caligula, his adopted grandson, became his successor after his death in 37 AD.

O'Toole had agreed in advance that he would have to wear grotesque make-up for his depiction of the depraved, half-mad, syphilitic, and *débauché* Emperor during the final stages of his venereal disease. He amused himself swimming with his "minnows and little fishes," nubile youths ages 9 to 13, who swam below the waters to tantalize his rotting sex organs. For amusement, Tiberius liked to watch degrading sexual scenes, including both children and deformed people.

Before leaving for Rome, O'Toole speculated to his friends, "How in hell will Guccione and Vidal depict such debauchery of the court? They'll certainly have to sanitize the stories of Tiberius and Caligula to bring that pair to the screen. Otherwise, Caligula will degenerate into hard-corn porn."

As it turned out, he was correct.

CALIGULA, CATACOMBS, & CHICKEN GIZZARDS

Long before he co-starred with him in Caligula, Malcolm McDowell, who played the insane emperor, first met Peter O'Toole in 1965 at a "bring-a-bottle party" in Hampstead. He recalled McDowell as "an extraordinary-looking man with flaxen hair, jeans tucked into his boots, looking every inch a Greek god."

When O'Toole died, McDowell shared his memories of the actor with

The Guardian: When both of them met John Gielgud, also cast in *Caligula*, O'Toole said to him, "Hello, Johnny! What is a knight of the realm doing in a porno movie?"

McDowell recalled being summoned to the set with O'Toole at midnight, when the extras were "engaging in every sexual perversion in the book."

"Peter asked me if they were doing the Irish jig. I looked over to discover two dwarves and an amputee dancing around some girls splayed out on a giant dildo."

The most revolting scene occurred with McDowell and O'Toole when they encountered an inattentive Roman sentry. "Caligula," O'Toole (as Tiberius) asked. "Do you think this man is drunk?" When assured that he was, O'Toole, as Tiberius, orders two sentries to restrain him and to tie up his foreskin. Wine was then forced down his throat, enough so that his belly looked like that of a pregnant woman near term.

At that moment, O'Toole was supposed to take his sword and ram it into the sentry's bloated stomach, which was fronted with a goat's bladder filled with blood, wine, and chicken gizzards. When they spilled onto the floor, they evoked the sentry's decimated innards.

O'Toole inserted the sword under the sentry's breastplate, and then snapped it with such force that it hit the extra in the face, knocking him out.

He didn't pierce the goat's bladder but cut only the cord that positioned it into place around the sentry's waist. Instead of spilling out the sentry's simulated intestines, it plopped onto the floor and rolled along like a bouncing beach ball.

Observing what had happened, O'Toole, in one of the most arch and appropriate-to-the-situation comments he ever made in public, something that convulsed observers with laughter, said, "I think she's dropped her fucking handbag."

After seven takes, he finally got it right, puncturing the goat-skin bladder, causing the grisly blend of wine, blood, and gizzards to (supposedly) flow from the sentry's dying bowels.

Between takes, O'Toole told McDowell how he collected Etruscan jewelry and ancient artifacts: "I break into the tombs at night as a grave-robber. I then enter a tomb and sift very gingerly through the drains with my fingers. I know that when these ancient bodies decomposed, all the artifacts are eventually washed into these drainpipes."

"Gore Vidal Imagines Everyone as a Homosexual," Charges Caligula's Director, Tinto Brass

On a Monday morning, a chauffeur-driven limousine arrived at O'Toole's rented villa to transport him to the studio at Cinecittà, where *Caligula* was to be filmed. There, he was introduced to Tinto Brass, the film's newly appointed director. Guccione had designated him to helm the picture after John Huston rejected his offer.

As O'Toole recalled, "I didn't exactly hate the director on sight, but after working with him for a few days, I did. I mocked him behind his back, nicknaming him 'Tinto Zinc.' As a director, his usual instruction was to 'turn over,' and that was about it."

Guccione had hired Brass because of the reputation associated with his 1976 film, *Salon Kitty*, in which he fused explicit sex scenes with dramatic re-enactments of specific historic events.

[Salon Kitty *was an erotic drama, among the prototypes of the "Nazi-sploitation genre," set in an expensive brothel in Berlin. According to the plot, the bedrooms were wiretapped, and the whores were trained as spies, gathering various incriminating data on "rebellious" or disloyal members of the Nazi hierarchy during World War II.*]

Within the hour, Brass had delivered a blistering attack on Vidal's original script. "Everybody in the goddamn movie, according to Vidal, is supposed to be engaged in homosexual acts. Clearly, that is his fantasy of ancient Rome. I personally have nothing against gays, but *Penthouse* fans of Guccione want to see straight sex on the screen."

"Vidal did write a scene focusing on conventional hetero sex, but even that was tinged with depravity, since it depicted the co-dependent, incestuous passion between Caligula and his half-sister Drusilla," Brass said. Guccione paid Vidal $200,000 for the script, and it's a piece of shit. I'm rewriting it. Instead of *Gore Vidal's Caligula*, I want him to retitle it *Tinto Brass's Caligula*. If challenged, I'll denounce Vidal in the press as an aging arteriosclerotic."

In his attack on Vidal, Brass claimed that

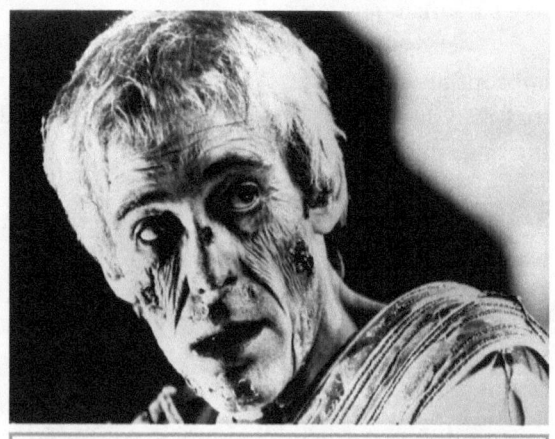

In one of the most artful of screen makeup jobs, Peter OToole played Caligula's great-uncle, the half-mad, syphilitic *débauché* Tiberius, who killed little boys for his own amusement.

Vidal had depicted Caligula as a good man driven to madness by absolute power. "In my rewrite, I'm depicting him as a born monster."

"That is pure delight to hear, darling, but I really want to know how Tiberius is being written," O'Toole said.

"We're still working on that. There's one sequence being debated. On the island of Capri, Tiberius was known for sodomizing nine-year-old boys. After he'd gotten their asses all bloody, he ordered his guards to toss the youths over a cliff to certain death."

Bringing Arrogance to New Levels

Probably the worst thing for Guccione's finances (and the movie, too) was its spendthrift director, Tinto Brass.

"How utterly enchanting," O'Toole said, mockingly. "Such a scene would surely guarantee me that long, elusive Oscar, which is certainly overdue me."

"In a perfect world," Vidal told the press, "Tinto Brass would be washing windows."

After hearing that, Brass countercharged, claiming, "If I really get mad at Vidal, I will publish the original script he submitted to us. It was laughable, it was so horrible."

***

O'Toole was amazed at the impressive lineup of stars who had contracted with Guccione to star in the movie. Malcolm McDowell had agreed to play the star role of Caligula.

John Gielgud, cast as Nerva, a trusted friend of Tiberius, commits suicide at the prospect of having Caligula proclaimed as the new emperor. Gielgud would maintain his artistic dignity throughout the curse of this bacchanialian, orgiastic film. His farewell to Tiberius (and to life itself) begins when he slits his wrists and submerges himself into a bath of hot water.

Unaware of the sex scenes that Guccione would later insert into the context of the film, Gielgud, after seeing the final cut, announced, "*Caligula* is my first porno movie."

Back in London, he told his friend Noël Coward, "I didn't regret making the movie. After all, Guccione had rounded up at least one hundred of the best-looking and the best hung young Romans, a feast for any old Queen. Nearly all of them were available."

Helen Mirren would play Caesonia, "the most promiscuous woman in Rome," who marries Caligula. Mirren was to appear in most scenes dressed like a flamboyant drag queen of the ancient world. Maria Schneider was cast—temporarily, as it turned out—as Drusilla, Caligula's half-sister.

John Gielgud: "Suicide was the only way out for me."

Appearing in a porno flick did not prevent Mirren in 2003 from receiving a Damehood in the Order of the British Empire for services to the performing arts.

She would later define the film as 'an irresistible mix of art and genitals."

McDowell, cast as the depraved emperor, had a slightly startled look in many scenes, which some critics would label as "emotionally greedy." He was not ashamed to appear fully nude.

Thanks to his striptease, he developed a whole new fan base, which included author Truman Capote. He told the press, "I can't abide anything written by Gore Vidal. But I went to see *Caligula* just to get a glimpse of Malcolm's cock."

Helen Mirren...a raging nymphomaniac...and wife of Caligula.

"For me, seeing his penis was the highlight of the movie, rivaled only by his beautiful ass on ample display. He gazed at the camera with all the loaded essence of charm, insolence, and trickery."

After Brass's harangue, he informed O'Toole that he was having lunch with Maria Schneider at the Taverna Flavia, which had enjoyed its heyday during those heady days in the 1950s when Rome was sometimes defined as "Hollywood on the Tiber." Flavia attracted such dignitaries as Frank Sinatra, Mario Lanza, and Elizabeth Taylor.

"I saw Maria—in fact, I saw a lot of her in *Last Tango in Paris* with Brando, who made an ass of himself, literally— and I was impressed with her," O'Toole said.

"Perhaps you'd like to join us," Brass said. "Meet our Drusilla in person."

"How delightful for McDowell," O'Toole said. "That means the lucky bloke will at least get to screw her on screen. Perhaps off-screen as well. Maybe I, too, will get lucky."

"Perhaps, like you said," Brass noted, "But you can't be sure. She's part lezzie, maybe a whole lot lezzie. You don't look like you have any tits."

"Perhaps my charm will win her over," O'Toole said.

He would later recall how Maria

Peter O'Toole became enchanted with Maria Schneider, seen here with Marlon Brando in a scene from their 1972 erotic drama, *Last Tango in Paris*.

O'Toole said, "She was like a little Lolita, only more perverse. In Rome, Maria and I carried out what Brando only started in Paris."

Blood Moon's *Brando Unzipped* was the most revelatory biography ever published about "Stanley Kowalski & The Godfather."

"Marlon Brando understood sexual liberation long before the rest of us," said Danforth Prince, the publisher.

"Here, as interpreted by Darwin Porter, is a portrait of Hollywood's most seductive Bad Boy as you never could have dreamed."

In *Peter O'Toole—Hellraiser, Sexual Outlaw, & Irish Rebel*, Darwin Porter and Danforth Prince depicted Lawrence of Arabia embroiled in enough scandals to fill the Roman Colosseum.

Count on O'Toole for a provocative comment: "Katharine Hepburn called me a pig and a drunk. She even bashed my head a few times with an empty liquor bottle. But I adored her. I told her that one night with me would cure her of her lesbianism."

Schneider entered his world, looking very much like she did when at the age of nineteen she had starred in Bernardo Bertolucci's *Last Tango in Paris* (1972).

When she made her entrance into Flavia, she'd just finished portraying "The Girl" in Michelangelo Antonioni's *The Passenger* (1975), opposite Jack Nicholson.

Introduced to O'Toole, she politely shook his hand. As she sat down to order a Campari, she confessed, "After seeing *Lawrence of Arabia*, I had a dream that very night. I dreamed you were a desert Sheik and I, a virgin in a white dress. In my dream, you kidnap me and ride away with me on this beautiful white stallion. We arrive at this large white tent in the desert, where you take me inside and proceed to perform depraved acts on my ravaged body."

"Perhaps we can make your dream come true," he told her.

ALL THE ACTORS (INCLUDING O'TOOLE'S BODYGUARDS) GET NAKED. ONLY TIBERIUS AND NERVA ARE ALLOWED TOGAS

At Cinecittà, on the first day of one of his scenes as Tiberius, O'Toole met the film's co-producer, Franco Rossellini, a handsome intense young man. Of all the people working in production, he found him the most agreeable, an initial impression that was more or less verified when he accepted his invitation to dinner at his favorite trattoria, Ristorante Rugatino, where the paparazzi often photographed him with his friends, Anthony Franciosa and Shelley Winters, during their marriage.

The son of the famous composer, Renzo Rossellini, he was also the nephew of film director Roberto Rossellini, who had married screen legend Ingrid Bergman after a scandalously adulterous affair that had virtually destroyed (at least temporarily) her Hollywood career.

Franco was often photographed with Bergman's daughter, Jenny Ann Lindström, and there were rumors published in the press about an impending marriage.

Franco revealed that he and Roberto had launched a TV series based on the notorious life of Caligula. However, their finances were low, and it appeared that the series would be the most lavish production since Richard Burton, with Elizabeth Taylor, left town after the filming of the ill-fated *Cleopatra* in 1963.

Franco flew to New York to meet with Bob Guccione at his elegant private home, because he'd expressed interest in being co-producer of the film and putting up the millions needed for production.

"So that's how the *Penthouse* playmates got involved," Franco said. "I don't want anyone to know this, but Roberto, against my wishes, is planning to sue Guccione and Vidal for plagiarizing his material from our doomed TV series.

[Although threatened, based on the advice of his lawyers, Roberto's lawsuit was eventually dropped.]

The next day, O'Toole dined with McDowell, whom he had known in London. McDowell told O'Toole that he had insisted that a provision for script approval be written into his contract, and that consequently, he was personally rewriting each of his lines and scenes from the Vidal script. "I want to get rid of all of Caligula's cruelty and homosexuality," he said. "My Caligula, at least as I am conceiving him, will have the character of an anarchistic *provocateur*."

"Whatever that might be, my good man," O'Toole said, as he was becoming increasingly bewildered by the film he'd contracted to make.

McDowell told O'Toole, "Originally, Tinto Brass was asked by Paramount to direct me in *A Clockwork Orange* (1971).

"He had a scheduling conflict, and that's when Stanley Kubrick stepped in. Critics protested that my *Clockwork Orange* was too strong to stomach. What in hell will they say about *Caligula*?"

During his final days at Cinecittà, Darwin witnessed the backstage frenzies of an epic film in chaos. "Everybody seemed to have adopted the slogan, 'When in Danger, When in Doubt, Run in Circles, Scream and Shout.'"

Guccione flew from New York to Rome to confront Tinto Brass. He'd seen the first rushes and was horrified, claiming that this was not the film that he had instructed his director to shoot.

"I wanted to see the actors actually engaged in intercourse—not all this fake shit," he shouted, with O'Toole listening in. "Don't you think modern audiences are sophisticated enough to know the difference between a real fuck and merely the mock?"

The die was cast. A battle as epic as the film ensued. O'Toole later said, "Thank God I was leaving and flying back to the mere craziness of London, which lacked the insanity of Rome."

On the way out, he said, "I'm not ashamed of having made a shilling or two in a blue movie. Of course, from what I later saw, and that was only a few clips, *Caligula* was boring rubbish, entirely unerotic. Talk about scripts. What bloody script? Gielgud and I were told to improvise our lines as Nerva and Tiberius. I don't know. McDowell may have written his lines or not. All I know is that Guccione didn't get his ultimate wish. Perhaps he didn't even present his request to his star. But he confided to me that his secret desire involved having Malcolm show off his erection in a close-up."

Guccione told O'Toole, "I've hired *Penthouse* Playmates and Pets as extras. Brass seems intent on hiring women with withered bodies. I also want plenty of male nudity, including erections, so we can attract horny women and gay guys. I know what women want. Most of them tell me that they can't really assess the power of a man just by showing them nude. Many men are growers, not showers."

"I hired two queens as my casting directors for the male extras. I instructed them to hire young men with at least nine, preferably ten, inches. Some 200 men showed up at Cinecittà for my casting call. They were told they had to produce erections. Some of them jerked off for the queens, others preferred the queen to volunteer their mouths, which they were only too glad to oblige."

"You should have made an entire movie featuring clips of the casting auditions," O'Toole advised. "I'm sure such a film would have made millions."

Guccione ultimately dismissed Brass, taking over the filming of *Caligula* himself. His intention involved transforming it from a serious political parable into a hard-core porn movie.

As outrageous as *Caligula* was, it was a prayer meeting compared to how the sensationalist Roman press was describing it. The orgies were said to be real, not simulated, and nine-year-old boys and girls who were even younger were rumored to be participating. Some of the female extras were said to be filmed servicing horses.

In one scene, McDowell was falsely rumored to have revived a custom that once was common during the heyday of the Roman Empire. Six comely boys were strung up by their feet and brutally sodomized by Caligula and his guards. All of this was just some reporter's fantasy.

There were calls for the Roman police to raid Cinecittà and to shut down production.

"I'm being defamed," Vidal protested to the press. "I have nothing to do with what's going on there. Blame Tinto Brass. If not him, Bob Guccione. He's the real culprit."

Right before he left, O'Toole was introduced to the Oscar-winning artist, Danilo Donati (famous for the art direction in Fellini's *Satyricon* and *Casanova*). He had been brought in as costume and set designer. In preparation for the filming of *Caligula*, he set about creating a *Felliniesque* fantasy, designing skimpy costumes for all the actors, including in some cases four-foot-long phalluses, held in place with rubber straps and belts, as inspired by the erotic frescoes discovered in the volcanic ruins of Pompeii.

"I was glad to see the project end," O'Toole said. "Everyone except

Malcolm, Helen, John, and me were suing each other. Vidal was among the first to file a suit to have his name taken off the picture. Brass followed."

After he was dismissed, Brass sued both Guccione and Franco Rossellini for "improper dismissal and breach of contract."

He actually won, but never collected any damages, seemingly entrapped in a tangled legal web of complications and counter challenges from *Penthouse* lawyers in the Italian and U.S. courts. The case dragged on seemingly without end. Brass, as reported in the press, finally said, "Tired of the whole thing, I threw up my hands and surrendered. I don't want to speak of *Caligula* ever again."

Based on delays, confusion, ineptitude, and litigation, *Caligula* did not appear in theaters until late in 1979. Franco Rossellini, in the meantime, took advantage of Cinecittà's elaborate sets replicating ancient Rome and made use of them as backdrops for an independent film he was producing based on the scandal and blood-soaked life of Messalina. To Guccione's rage, his movie made it into theaters before Guccione could release *Caligula*, thereby pre-empting some of the fire and passion of *Caligula* with equivalent visuals from a competing film.

Like Gielgud, O'Toole claimed that his scenes as Tiberius were shot before the film mutated into an XXX-rated movie. Even though he had not yet seen the complete finished version, he publicly denounced *Caligula*.

When he heard about O'Toole's denunciations, Guccione told the press, "O'Toole was far too drunk during the shoot to know what he was doing."

Reacting to that, O'Toole threatened a lawsuit, claiming that he had never been drunk on the set, and that he had "gone on the wagon" prior to the debut of filming because of a major health crisis.

Reviews were harsh, Roger Ebert asserting that "*Caligula* is sickening, utterly worthless, shameful trash. People with talent allowed themselves to participate in this vulgar

A syphilitic kiss, a venereal embrace: O'Toole playing up the debauchery of a dying potentate in *Caligula*.

Things ended disastrously for almost everyone involved.

travesty. Disgusted and unspeakably depressed, I walked out of the film after two hours of its 170-minute length."

Acerbic Rex Reed denounced the film as "a trough of rotten swill." Writing for *The Daily Mail*, Jay Scott compared Caligula unfavorably to the Franco-Japanese film *The Realm of the Senses* (1976), describing that movie as a better treatment of extreme sexuality. "*Caligula* doesn't really work on any level. It is a boondoggle of landmark proportions."

David Denby, a New York critic, defined *Caligula* as "an infinitely degraded version of Fellini's *Satyricon*." Another critic, Leslie Halliwell, denounced *Caligula* as "a vile curiosity, of interest chiefly to sado-masochists." *Time Out London* labeled it "a dreary shambles."

Guccione had hoped to make $100 million off *Caligula*, but it grossed only $24 million, a million dollars less than its production costs.

As the 21st Century moves on, *Caligula* remains one of the most infamous cult movies ever released, although dozens of countries around the world still forbid it to be shown. However, so eagerly is *Caligula* sought out that many private viewings of the smuggled video are screened, usually in secretive defiance of local obscenity laws.

"Oh, my God!" O'Toole said, shortly before his death. "In some circles—in rather low-rent parts of town—*Caligula* is my most famous film, even more famous than *Lawrence of Arabia*."

Chapter Sixteen

THE DAY DIANA DIED IN PARIS
BETRAYAL & DEATH OF A PRINCESS

Prince Charles had taken Lady Diana Spencer as his bride, making her the newly designated Princess of Wales. Even though he has his arm around her, he has a skeptical look on his face. She seems not happy and rather concerned, as if asking, "What in hell am I doing here?"

"It was the last day of August in 1997, and Darwin Porter and I were in Paris updating the latest edition of the Frommer guides to that city," said Danforth. "We both were checked into the Hotel de l'Abbaye Saint-Germain, a former convent on the Left Bank. I occupied what used to be the favorite room of the Italian actor, Marcello Mastroianni."

"From a room on the floor below, Darwin phoned me early one morning. I'd gotten in late and was a bit drowsy, but his news shocked me into a state of alert. 'Turn on the TV news,' he said. French radio is broadcasting that Princess Diana has just died. Car accident."

The news stunned millions of people around the world, including Bill and Hillary Clinton on Martha's Vineyard.

"For the rest of the day, I was mesmerized in front of the TV as the news unfolded. In much of the rest of the world, not a lot of work got done that day, except behind the scenes in England and Paris. To compound matters, there was another report that Mother Theresa had also died, but it was the death of Diana that was sucking up all the oxygen in the room."

At the time of her death, Diana was thirty-six years old, and at the peak of her beauty—in fact, she was often called the world's most beautiful woman. She certainly was the most photographed woman on earth. It had been sixteen years since her storybook wedding to Prince Charles.

As the morning moved on, more and more of the details associated with her death were revealed.

Diana had been staying at the exclusive Ritz Hotel (Paris) with her lover, Dodi Fayed. He was the son of the super wealthy Mohamed Al-Fayed, owner of the Paris Ritz and Harrods, the most famous department store in England. He had purchased a luxurious yacht, *Jonikal*, in which Diana, his son, and her sons might want to sail, perhaps getting adjusted to their possible new stepfather. The press had run reports that Diana was pregnant with Dodi's child.

After dinner at the Ritz, Dodi and Diana were going to transfer to his townhouse. They were to be driven there by Henri Paul, head of security at the Ritz. Unfortunately, he was drunk at the time. The other passenger in the car was Diana's bodyguard, Trevor Ress-Jones.

As they set off, a string of paparazzi followed them in speeding cars. Paul stepped on the accelerator just before the entrance to the Pont d'Alma tunnel. Traveling at 65 mph, he lost control of the vehicle and crashed, killing himself and Dodi. The seriously injured bodyguard would survive. Diana was bleeding internally as she was sped to the Pitié-Salpêtrière Hospital in an ambulance with its red dome light flashing.

Diana was rushed into the emergency room, as doctors realized almost from the beginning that she was beyond saving. They nonetheless labored valiantly, trying to sustain her life. She was immediately hooked up to a heart-lung machine. Doctors feared that the CPR she'd been given in the ambulance had only made matters worse. Internally, she was bleeding profusely. At one point, after she'd been cut open, a doctor actually squeezed her heart with his hands to keep it pumping, but to no avail. There was no way to stem the bleeding. Then she suffered cardiac arrest. All efforts to save her life stopped at 3:45AM. She was pronounced dead.

Before that, an aide had phoned Prince Charles at Balmoral Castle in Scotland, where he was staying with his parents and his two sons. He was told that Diana had been seriously injured in a car accident in Paris, and that her companion, Dodi Fayed, was dead.

He was given other details, too, but was informed that doctors were working on Diana to save her life.

In a surprise move, Charles chose not to alert the Queen first, but to call his mistress, Camilla Parker-Bowles, Diana's rival. Both agreed that Diana was a strong woman and would make it through the night.

Charles then called the Queen, and both of them agreed not to awaken Harry and William until morning.

Charles was up for the rest of the night, and even before aides called again, he heard the news of Diana's death on the British Radio 5.

News of her death created shock in some quarters, especially when early risers in Britain turned on their radios or TVs.

On hearing of her death, Charles was said to have become hysterical, and an aide had to inform the Queen. Later that day, Charles had the horrible task of having to tell William and Harry that their mother was dead. The Queen was reluctant to let Charles go, but he told her he was leaving at once to fly to Paris.

The staff reported that Charles left "in a broken face," but that the Queen and Prince Philip that morning were rather stone-faced. Philip, of course, had never tried to conceal his contempt for Diana.

That day in Paris, and during the days to come, Diana's death provoked conspiracy theories around the world—and a lot of fake news. One bystander told French Radio that he had seen Diana walk away from the car seemingly uninjured.

One report claimed that a diamond and ruby necklace, once owned by Queen Victoria, had been stolen from her neck during the ambulance ride to the hospital. Another reported that a bag of cocaine had been removed from the wreckage of the car.

The most outrageous theories were being broadcast from the Arab world, at least some of them originating in Cairo. The Egyptians had been proud that their native son, Dodi Fayed, was dating the Royal Princess of England, the mother of a future king. The charge was that British Intelligence had "arranged" Diana's death because they did not want the mother of the future King of England converting to Islam.

In Libya, Moammar Gadhafi blamed her death on both British and French Intelligence.

More revelations were on the way, including an exposé of her affair with John F. Kenney, Jr., in Manhattan. Various sources came forth, alleging that she thought he might become President of the United States in the future and that, if married to him, she could reign as First Lady in the White House. She was said to have talked to friends, telling them she wanted to be "The New Jackie."

It was also revealed that the real estate tycoon in New York, Donald Trump, had proposed marriage to Diana after her divorce from Charles.

She told her secretary, "I think Trump is a creep." His offer was rejected.

Another theory was floated that the F.B.I. and/or the C.I.A. had engineered her death.

Dodi's violently angered father was blaming Buckingham Palace as responsible for the deaths, and called Prince Philip, "the most wicked man on Earth."

It was also reported that Diana lived in fear that Charles would order an aide to tamper with the brakes of her car.

"Later in the afternoon of the day of her death, I strolled over to the Pont d'Alma where the crash had occurred," Danforth said. "A large crowd had gathered. It was a sad, sad day in Paris."

In one of the great royal weddings in British history, Lady Diana Spencer and Prince Charles were married. He was now the Prince of Wales, she his Princess.

But the bride and groom seemed to be looking in different directions.

Buckingham Palace insiders wondered if Charles would be able to tear himself away from his mistress and do his duty, fathering an heir to the throne.

Tens of thousands of people would remember where they were when they heard the news of her death. *[Depending on what generation you belong to, the days of certain deaths stick in your mind forever: December 1, 1941, the Japanese attack on Pearl Harbor. The death of Marilyn Monroe; the day John F. Kennedy was assassinated in Dallas.]*

For a grand funeral and days of mourning, Diana devotees were remembering "The People's Princess," and "The Queen of Hearts."

She had confided to friends that she wanted to live to see Prince William crowned as King of England.

"As a final word," Danforth said, "I'd say that the Princess didn't marry Prince Charming and live happily ever after, like in those fairytales someone read to us as children."

How a Dashing English Cavalry Officer, the Ex-Lover of Princess Diana, Opened a Chic Bar in Marbella

When she was at the peak of her beauty and sexuality, after Prince Charles turned out to be a dud of a husband, spending his nights with his mistress, Diana went looking for love elsewhere.

It was 1986, two years after the birth of Prince Harry. One afternoon, while watching a polo game, she found the man she'd later fall in love with. James Hewitt, born in Derry, North Ireland, in April of 1958, was a handsome, red-haired, strapping young cavalry officer in the British Army.

From afar, he had always adored her. And, as numerous biographies have revealed, she was sexually attracted to him from the moment of her introduction. Soon, their affair was in full swing, though they had to keep it under the radar screen.

What was going on at the time was later revealed in the biography *Diana, The Last Word*, by Simone Simmons, published in 2003. Ms. Simmons was a healer and a clairvoyant, who, during the last five years of Diana's life, became her confidante. This book revealed that with Hewitt, Diana experienced oral sex for the first time, as well as her first orgasm.

Diana revealed that "Jimmy treats me like a sex slave," later admitting that she loved it. She lavished gifts on him, including a diamond tie pin, and she even purchased form-fitting underwear for him "to show off his best hidden assets."

She opened charge accounts in his name, later admitting, "He was bloody expensive."

For five years, their love affair flourished, although she had to admit that out of the boudoir they had little in common, finding him as interesting as a knitting pattern. "His head was in his trousers," she told Simmons.

She confessed to being nosy and began to suspect he was having affairs outside their boudoir in Kensington Palace. One night, she searched the pockets of his trousers and found the phone number of a woman who turned out to be one of his mistresses. She confronted him with that accusation that night, and he angrily denied it. "How could I make love to you so forcefully, and for such extended periods, if I'm wasting my seed elsewhere?" he was rumored to have said in his defense at the time.

She hired detectives to follow him, and indeed, one of the men she employed turned up with some incriminating evidence, some of which was photographic proof.

One of the detectives bluntly said, "Ma'am, I just don't understand. He's the luckiest man on the planet, and he turns elsewhere."

She knew that the time had come for her to move on, and she told him she could no longer see him.

Hewitt later revealed that after Diana said farewell, he contemplated suicide. "I got into my car and loaded a few things," he said, "and then took the ferry across the Channel to France. I planned to shoot myself in transit. But at the last minute, my mother insisted on going along, too, and she just may have saved my life."

During their relationship when he was away for any extended period, Diana wrote him passionate love letters. She later admitted to Simmons, "They were red hot, even pornographic, praising his lovemaking."

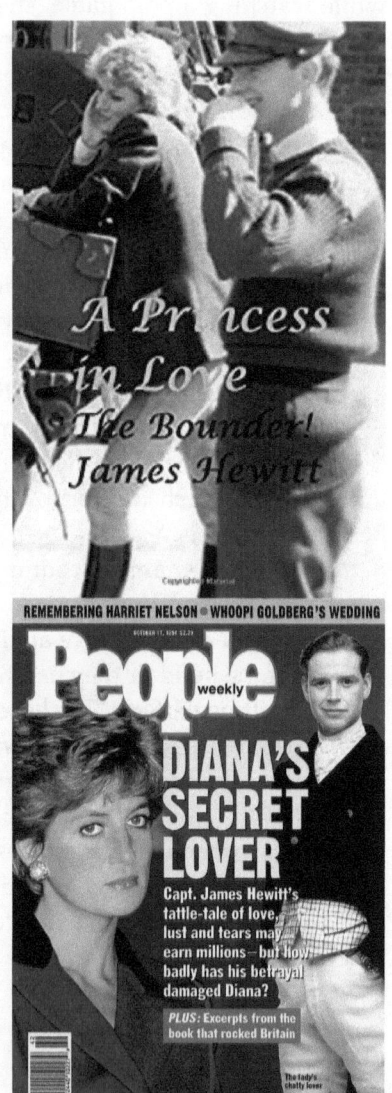

Later, she heard he was going to sell her letters to the highest bidder, and she knew at once she had to buy them herself. In a call to him, she learned that he wanted £250,000 for them, later doubling that price. She felt she had to pay it.

He wanted the cash-only transaction to take place in the resort of Benidorm on the eastern coast of Spain. With the banknotes stuffed in a large purse, she flew to Spain, wearing a wig and dark glasses. However, someone—perhaps Hewitt—alerted the press and paparazzi, and she was mobbed. She returned on the next plane to London.

Much more information about these love letters later appeared in a tell-all book about Hewitt's affair with Diana. Published in 1994, it was entitled *Princess in Love* and written by Ann Pasternak, a relative of the early 20th-Century Russian writer Boris Pasternak, who had written the highly acclaimed novel, *Doctor Zhivago*, which was adapted into a film, and a box-office hit, in 1965.

After reading *Princess in Love,* Diana gave her own review: "I hope his cock shrivels up."

Diana read the book with heartbreak and in tears. According to those close to her, she felt a sense of the most awful betrayal—first with her husband, Charles, and now with her years-long lover, Hewitt.

She also had to face rumors that Hewitt and Prince Harry looked alike, especially with their red hair. A tabloid published a picture of Harry, age 11, and Hewitt, age 11. They looked like identical twins.

Diana denied that Hewitt was the father of Harry, saying he had been born two years before the debut of her affair with him. She said that the red color of Harry's hair came from her own family, the Spencers. In fact, she sometimes referred to her growing boy as "My Little Spencer." *[She was Diana Spencer before she married Charles.]*

When Bill Clinton, as President, got into all his trouble, even an impeachment, in part because of his affair with Monica Lewinsky, she wrote him a long letter, sharing his grief. She called the two of them "fellow sufferers."

She gossiped with Simmons about the U.S. President: "I don't find him sexy at all. Perhaps that awful girl Monica did. I wonder what the presidential willy looks like."

A reporter for the *New York Daily News* wrote: "Diana's former lover, James Hewitt, wrote a kiss-and-tell bio of her. But he has suffered bad Karma ever since. His riding school has failed, and he was busted for alleged drug possession and tax evasion."

In 2009, after describing his affair with Diana in an ongoing stream of Reality TV shows, he opened a bar in Spain.

It was was in Marbella, the chic resort along the Costa del Sol, that southern strip of Andalusia that looks southward toward the coast of North Africa.

Dedicated to his favorite sport, Hewitt named his bar *The Polo Club*.

Marbella had been a chic resort long before Hewitt discovered it. In 1954, the Marbella Club opened, catering to an international coterie of movie stars, business tycoons, famous athletes, and aristocrats, many with titles. Famous names like Bismarck, Rothschild, Thurn und Taxis, and Metternich checked in.

At one point, the club was run by Princess Marie-Louise of Prussia, the great-granddaughter of Kaiser Wilhelm II.

Prince Rainier and Princess Grace were among the visitors, as was King Fahd of Saudi Arabia. *[He spent up to five million Euros a day here.]*

Everyone from the Aga Khan IV to Julio Iglesias followed, as did exiled Cuban dictator Fulgencio Batista, who had escaped from Cuba with $300 million.

"Assigned to update *Frommer's Spain*, Darwin and I headed at once to Hewitt's bar on our first night in town," Danforth said. "We would visit it annually until it shut down in 2013."

Darwin referred to Hewitt as "a babe magnet." Sometimes, the ladies clustered around him, wondering which of them he would choose for that night.

"When I first met him," Darwin said, "I found him a real English gentleman, full of charm and grace. The kind of man a young woman could take home to meet her parents. It was obvious to me why Diana found him so appealing after those dull nights with Charles before he moved on and into a separate bedroom."

Hewitt admitted that he'd been dazzled by Diana's beauty and charm, but at first could hardly imagine that he, a commoner, had a chance to bed the Princess of Wales.

"It seemed too good to be true. But sometimes dreams come true, though not often."

He seemed filled with a sense of male pride, secure in his appeal, his charm, and his masculinity. He once told friends that he had enough self-assurance to walk nude through a room filled with people.

He admitted he still has nightmares about Diana's tragic death in Paris. "But all in all, I can't complain. I was given five years with the most desirable woman on the planet."

In May of 2017, Hewitt, by now back in England, suffered a heart attack and a stroke.

He survived and was released from the hospital after undergoing extensive treatments. He may be living now with his mother in a two-bedroom flat in a former country house near Exeter.

James Hewitt and Prince Harry.
Embarrassing Physical Similarities, Mortifying Publicity

Chapter Seventeen

ONCE THE WICKEDEST CITY ON EARTH,

TANGIER

ATTRACTED CELEBRITY BOHEMIANS IN ALL HUES

In the latter half of the 1950s, the city of Tangier, lying on the northern coast of Morocco, across the channel from Spain, attracted debauched expatriates from America and Europe. "Many came here in search of drugs and boys," said Truman Capote.

Capote joined the *literati* who had already arrived: Tennessee Williams, Gore Vidal, Jack Kerouac, Allen Ginsberg, and William Burroughs, who wrote *Naked Lunch* in Tangier between shots of heroin.

Darwin Porter would spend most of his life traveling through Europe and the Caribbean for the Frommer guides. But his first trip abroad, when he was eighteen years old, was to North Africa, beginning in Tangier and ending in Cairo.

Little did he know at the time that for decades, he'd be covering Morocco for the Frommer guides, even living there on and off, using it as a base to explore parts of Africa, including Upper Volta (now Burkina Faso) and what used to be Spanish Morocco.

For months, he wanted to write a book about his experiences there—

some of them fabulous, others horrendous.

What follows are some impressions from his diary, each of them focusing on the mysterious city of Tangier and some of the legendary eccentrics he encountered there.

***

The dazzling white city of Tangier is fickle, winking at the Mediterranean with one eye while casting a flirtatious glance at the Atlantic with the other. A sandy 2½-mile beach runs across its seafront.

If you arrive aboard the ferry from Alcegiras (Spain) during daylight hours, Tangier doesn't look mysterious at all, but bright and airy with palm-lined boulevards. However, once you've penetrated into the Casbah, your initial impression changes.

Tangier is a city of glaring contrasts. Whereas hundreds of women in white *haiks* stroll along ancient streets, the way their great-grandmothers did, other Moroccan women may wear a dark *djellaba*, peering out at you over their veils. Yet there are also modern, Europeanized women attired in blue jeans and high heels. At nighttime cabarets—at least during the city's pinnacle of decadence—many of the belly dancers didn't even wear a diamond in their navels.

Vivid contrasts are seen in the men as well. Old bearded relics of yesterday hobble down the alley-like streets with their weary donkeys burdened with cargoes, looking like residents of Jerusalem before the birth of Christ. More modern men pay homage to Muslim traditions by wearing camel-hair robes. Hundreds of others, in total disregard for the customs of their ancestors, especially during cooler months, appear in blue jeans and leather jackets, a wardrobe that might fit easily into the Bronx.

Between 1906 and 1957, Tangier was an international city, much of it under the control of Spain or France before the government of Morocco took over.

Actually, during its international days, there was little governing at all. The word was out: When you had been kicked out of every other city in the world, Tangier would welcome you. It was a city where any variation of decadence and "sin" was tolerated—some said "welcomed"— and that meant *everything*.

During its post-war heyday, Tangier was a sun-bleached, sybaritic Eden set against a backdrop of verdant hills. It became a notorious rendezvous for celebrities with decadent desires, perhaps the most ever assembled in one outpost in Africa: artists, heiresses, writers, drug addicts, deposed royalty, pretend counts, hustlers around every corner, con men, thieves, movie stars like Marlene Dietrich and Errol Flynn, depraved playboys, clients of bordellos staffed with males and females of all conceivable ages, smugglers, gun runners, desperados fleeing criminal charges, ex-Nazis, literary renegades, and boatloads of pederasts preferring the "under twelve" set.

Tangier was tantalizingly exotic, but also sinister, and it could be outright dangerous at night if you turned down the wrong alley in the Medina.

The polyglot cast roaming the street consisted of some of the world's most notorious men (or, in some cases, most notorious women). Most were hellraisers and sexual outlaws and included a coterie of madmen who'd been certified as insane in their native lands.

Whatever the nature of the offense, foreigners were almost never arrested. The two official charges that could get you into trouble were rape or murder. But when the authorities pursued malfeasance, their charges often combined both rape *and* murder.

If you rustled up enough *dirham*, you could usually get off, although after paying their bribe, murderers were put on the exit ferry back to Algeciras. Rapists, however, were usually allowed to stay on.

A bribed officer told a Sicilian nobleman who had strangled a twelve-year-old girl to death in a brothel, "You look like a kind man—and certainly one who's generous with *dirhams*—and I know in your heart that you didn't mean to kill her. I'm a man of the world. Sometimes, it's necessary for a man to take desperate measures to achieve orgasm, especially as one ages. And after all, women were put on this earth to service their masters."

Author William Burroughs said you could go into any pharmacy and order any drug without prescriptions. The most popular item at any pharmacy was *majoun,* a cannabis jam, very potent.

William Burroughs
Deceptively conservative-looking.

A wicked devil, Sultan Ben Youssef, would routinely order a particularly mysterious concoction from a hideaway pharmacy in the Casbah. In the basement of his villa, he would feed it to a hustler who he had picked up on the street. When the boy became unconscious, he would castrate him. After that, Youssef's servants would drive the unconscious boy somewhere into the desert and dump him. When he came out of his coma, he'd discover that he'd been mutilated.

One night the Sultan made a mistake.

The boy he kidnapped, drugged, and castrated was one of the fifteen sons of Tangier's police chief. All of the Sultan's money and all his possessions were seized. The Sultan was put on a plane to Cairo with his two wives and eight concubines.

A burly Corsican, known as "Jacques," looked like a French version of that old-time movie star, Wallace Beery. For the equivalent of $500, he could rid you of any enemy. After stabbing his victim, he would haul the corpse to a remote corner of the Sahara and dump it. The hot sun would quickly "cremate" whatever remained, but only after the vultures had their dinner.

In 1946, many Nazis, some of them former members of the Gestapo, fled to Tangier after the collapse of Berlin. They found the lifestyles of Tangier so *laissez-faire* that they opened a bar called the Toppkeller, named after a notorious tavern that had once thrived in Weimar, Germany, attracting artists and models.

Many of these Nazis boasted openly about how many Jews they had sent to the gas chamber, having concluded that it was a safe subject to talk about in a country where Jews were treated like a despised minority.

Behind the Toppkeller's bar, a swastika was prominently on view. Otto Skorzeny held court in front of it nightly, boasting about how he, as an agent of the Gestapo, had kidnapped Mussolini. Another client of the Toppkeller, Heinz Müller

Otto Skorzeny maintained the dubious claim that he had kidnapped Mussolini.

When word reached Hitler in his bunker that partisans had executed the Italian dictator and his mistress, Clara Petacci, the Führer told his aides, "His fate is of no concern to me now."

The great artist, Henri Matisse, depicted above in 1913, visited Tangier.

"I came to paint and to do other things," he said, enigmatically.

had pursued a most bizarre career. In 1943, partly as a medical experiment, the Gestapo had assigned him the task of surgically removing the skins of very handsome Jewish boys.

"I always did it very slowly," he claimed, "so that I could enjoy it more. Before I carried out my assignment, I ran my fingers through the hair of the boy and patted his cheeks. He was strapped to an operating table. I have never seen such fear in anyone, as I did in the eyes of those young boys about to be sacrificed. I didn't want those haunting eyes to distract me, so I used my sharpened fingernails to gouge out their eyes before I began. Never have I heard such screams."

Fortunately, the Toppkeller had a short lifespan. By 1947, most of its clientele had emigrated to Argentina or Paraguay.

Most of the city's most inhumane devils left in the years that followed, leaving their more benign outlaws more or less comfortably ensconced Once, in the early 1960s, Darwin encountered a Scottish landowner who employed a staff consisting entirely of dwarves—about a dozen of them—within his home in the Casbah.

Long before Darwin's discovery of Tangier, many famous people

Jack Kerouac, an American expat in Tangier, was the most visible literary icon of the 1950s Beat Generation.

In 2003, author Gore Vidal was interviewed in Hollywood by a reporter. His first question was, "What was it like fucking Jack Kerouac?"

Gertrude Stein (left) and Alice B. Toklas were early members of the literati to discover the charm of Old Tangier, as it existed back in the 1920s.

"Considering their looks, Gertrude and Alice were lucky to find love at all," said Ernest Hemingway. "I think Gertrude's breasts might have weighed ten pounds each. She had the strong face of a German Jew."

had preceded him, notably Gertrude Stein and her lover, Alice B. Toklas, who had spent three summers in a row here in the 1920s. Mark Twain put it simply: "That African perdition called Tangier." Composer Aaron Copland called it "a madhouse." Errol Flynn said, "Tangier is a boiling cauldron of estranged people seeking kinky kicks."

David Herbert, the second son of the Earl of Pembroke, purchased a former harem and continued the tradition of its builders. But instead of beautiful women, he populated it with boys. His agents scouted England, France, Denmark, Norway, Germany, Italy, Spain, and Portugal for its occupants. Once enticed to emigrate to Morocco, the boys found themselves locked away under 24-hour guard. In spite of all that, the Earl, a widely acknowledged cross-dresser and drag queen, rose in prominence among the elite and was eventually acknowledged as the uncrowned "King of Tangier."

The artist, Henri Matisse, said, "Oh, Tangier, Tangier. I wish I had the courage to get the hell out."

Tennessee Williams used to say at the Hotel El Farhar. He wrote, "It rhymes with horror—spectacular view, every discomfort." Even so, he recommended it to his visiting friend, Truman Capote, and his lover, Jack Dunphy.

Author Robert Ruark in 1950 expressed his opinion: "Sodom was a church picnic, and Gomorrah a convention of Girl Scouts compared to Tangier, which contains more thieves, black marketeers, spies, thugs, phonies, beachcombers, expatriates, degenerates, crooked operators, bandits, bums, pimps, tramps (male and female), vile politicians, and charlatans than any place I ever visited."

The Honorable David Herbert, second son of the England's Earl of Pembroke, was the uncrowned "Queen of Tangier." He owned the largest collection of designer clothes for women in all of Morocco.

An invitation to one of his lavish parties was highly sought after. His guests were likely to include Ian Fleming, the creator of James Bond, and Barbara Hutton, the Woolworth heiress.

"Before coming to Tangier," Capote wrote, "you should do three things: Inoculate yourself for typhoid, withdraw your savings from the bank, and say goodbye to your friends—heaven knows when you will ever see them again. Because Tangier is a basin that holds you."

Nights in Tangier were laden with the scent of jasmine and the heady smell of *kif* (a combination of marijuana and tobacco). The wind also carried the scent of mint, eucalyptus, mutton grease, and dung.

The haunting echoes of the *muezzins* cut through the night.

Literary renegades like William Burroughs and Jack Kerouac were eager to record their own versions of these Arabian nights.

Darwin's favorite retreat was the bar at El Minzah Hotel, built by Lord Bute in 1930. Once, Errol Flynn hosted his parties here, with a pianist murdering Cole Porter tunes. Flynn was long gone when Mick Jagger and the Rolling Stones arrived to wake up sleepy Tangier.

By then, most movie stars had departed for other climes. But perhaps not. Wasn't that Catherine Deneuve you spotted shopping in a Souk for something exotic?

In the 1980s, Malcolm Forbes, the billionaire publisher, tried to resurrect the glory days of Tangier, even importing a movie star who represented beauty and glamour around the globe—none other than Elizabeth Taylor. They were rumored to have been lovers, but everybody in Tangier knew that Forbes was gay, often entertaining strings of young Arab boys.

Elizabeth and Forbes had been platonic friends since September of 1987. She had sailed with him aboard his yacht, the *Highlander*, and gone hot-air ballooning and motorcycle riding with him.

For several days in August, Elizabeth was a guest at Forbes' lavish 70th birthday bash in Tangier. The venue was his 19th-century palace, once inhabited by a Sultan.

For this event, which was covered by the world press, Forbes invited six hundred of the world's elite. At the palace, the smell of marijuana and

Left to right, Emilio Sanz, Pepe Carleton, Truman Capote, Jane Bowles, and Paul Bowles, near the beach in Tangier.

According to Capote, Tangier was "a basin holding you, a timeless place, where days were sliding by less noticed than foam in a waterfall."

Billionaire Malcolm Forbes with Elizabeth Taylor in 1987, presiding over the "Birthday Party of the Century," his 70th. There were those who described it as love, but insiders knew that theirs was a *faux* romance.

When his 600 party guests departed, Forbes became the self-styled "Sultan of Morocco," accessorized with a harem of beautiful boys imported from around the world.

hashish was so powerful that dozens of air purifiers were installed.

Talk about name dropping: They included Henry Kissinger, Walter Cronkite, Barbara Walters, and Beverly Sills, who was hired to sing "Happy Birthday." He also invited 300 CEOs of *Fortune 500* companies. Headlines referred to it as the Birthday Party of the Century.

The day after the party, Forbes took Elizabeth diamond shopping, with him picking up the tab. "I was too generous," he told an aide. "What a greedy bitch."

The late Doris Lilly commented on the party. "Everyone knew that darling Malcolm had a fetish for young, olive-skinned Moroccan boys. That taste could certainly be satisfied in Tangier. He also entertained six to eight boys in a leather gang, which satisfied his sadomasochism. It was sad that he lacked the courage to come out of the closet; in fact, the hoax of a *faux* romance that he and Elizabeth tried to pull off seemed a bit ugly to me. They were never lovers—perish the thought. They used each other to enhance their public images."

As it turned out, this lavish celebration in Tangier might be called Forbes' end-of-life party. Within about six months, he died in his sleep of a heart attack on February 24, 1990.

***

Paul Bowles adopted and embraced Moroccan culture more deeply than any other expat. He entertained guests by playing Indian music and rolling "huge bombers."

Here are some thumbnail sketches from Darwin's diaries of the famous people of yesterday who came to Tangier to partake of its forbidden fruit.

The Last of the Bohemians
PAUL & JANE BOWLES
Literary Renegades In Tangier

At the Parade Bar, during his first visit to Tangier in the early 1960s, Darwin was introduced to the expatriate composer and author, Paul Bowles. "To me, he was Mr. Tangier himself, and we bonded at once and became friends for years."

After emigrating to Tangier in 1947, this New Yorker became the most famous "American male in residence," living there for the next 52 years. "He knew everything that was going on, and I was eager to learn," Darwin said.

In college, he had read his 1949 novel, *The Sheltering Sky*.

Tennessee Williams had praised it for its "interior flashes of fire."

A saga of alienation and existentialist despair, it was the story of Port Moresby and his wife, Kit, as they travel in the North African desert. *[Its two lead characters were clearly based on Paul and his wife, Jane Bowles. Modern Library ranked it as among the 100 best novels of the 20th Century.]*

In 1990, Bernardo Bertolucci adapted it for the screen in a film that starred Debra Winger and John Malkovich.

Paul was born in Jamaica, Queens (NYC), in the winter of 1910. His father, Claude Bowles, a dentist, didn't want a son. During the first winter of his infant son's life, he tried to kill his newborn by leaving him exposed on a ledge near an open window during a snowstorm. Paul was rescued in time. Extraordinarily precocious, he could read at age three and was writing stories when he was only four.

As a young man, Bowles was escorted to Paris by the celebrated composer, Aaron Copland, who became his lover and life-long friend. Once in Paris, Bowles became part of the literary circle of Gertrude Stein, who introduced him to Picasso, Ernest Hemingway, and F. Scott Fitzgerald. In 1931, Copeland took Bowles to Tangier, where he fell in love with the city and in time made it his home for life.

Composer Aaron Copland and Paul Bowles were more than just good friends.

[Bowles also spent time in pre-war Berlin, where he fell under the spell of the English novelist, Christopher Isherwood, at the time compiling background for his The Berlin Stories (1935-39).

In 1972, Bob Fosse adapted one of Isherwood's stories and made Cabaret, starring Liza Minnelli in her best-known film. Her

Paul Bowles in Morocco

character of Sally Bowles became a household name.

What most movie fans didn't know was that Sally's name was inspired by that of Paul Bowles.]

In the late 1930s and throughout the war, Paul established a reputation as a composer, collaborating with such towering figures as Orson Welles and Tennessee Williams.

Success finally came, and Bowles was soon working with music critic Virgil Thomson, conductor Leonard Bernstein, choreographer Merce Cunningham, director John Huston, and French author Jean-Paul Sartre.

It was through Paul Bowles and his introduction to the glories of Tangier that Darwin, in the 1960s, rented a former harem. "It rose six floors of tiny, one-room cells" and stood in the old Casbah. The rent was fifty dollars a month."

"Paul's many friends, including me, looked on with disappointment and regret as he gave his heart to a relatively heartless stream of young Moroccan boys—with names like Hamri, Mrabet, or Yacoubi—exploited him."

"I remember meeting one young man, Aziz Jaouhari, who was born in the Imperial City of Fez, Morocco. He was a painter, using as his subject evocative views of the Casbah. Paul, among others, had taught him English."

He was very frank with Darwin, admitting that Paul was in love with him, even though he preferred women. "I tolerate Paul for the *dirhams* he gives me. My goal is to become what you Americans call a gigolo. Many rich women come to Morocco, and I want one of them to adopt me."

"I'm a great lover, straight out of a lusty saga from *Arabian Nights*. In old days, if exhibited nude at a sex slave auction, I would have commanded the highest price."

"When I was nine years old, I worked in a Spanish-owned boy bordello which used to stand a few blocks from here. The owner catered mostly to English or American pederasts. He told these old farts I could fulfill the most exotic of requests."

***

During Darwin's second week in Tangier, Paul introduced him to his wife, Jane Bowles.

"Although I was acquainted with Jane for many years, I never got to know her," Darwin said. "I don't think Jane knew who Jane was. I found her fascinating, among the most wondrous of the wonderful women who have come and gone from my life. But what Jane cared about, no one knew."

Born to a Jewish family in New York in 1917, she had led a short, tragic life during her career as a writer. She seemed to have nothing to hide, saying, "I'm a Jew, lesbian, alcoholic, communist, and I'm a cripple" *[She was not a cripple, but walked with a limp.]*

"I'm married to Paul Bowles, a homosexual," she said, "and we have an open marriage among these sybaritic expatriates who flock to Tangier to fulfill their secret, often illegal, desires."

One night at the Café de Paris, Jane discussed the honeymoon she'd shared with Paul, whom she'd married in 1938. "He took me to Costa Rica. Then we went to Paris where I spent my nights in lesbian bars. He became a regular patron of a boy bordello once frequented by Marcel Proust. We were not ashamed of our sexuality."

On another night, sitting in Tangier at the Café de Paris, she was approached by two female American college students. "Are you THE Jane Bowles?" one of them asked.

"One and the same," she answered. "Just call me a kike dyke."

Her literary output was tiny: One novel, a full-length play, and seven short stories. Even so, she lives on as a cult figure, a rare literary female renegade.

Tennessee defined her novel, *Two Serious Ladies*, first published in 1943, as his favorite book. It became a cult classic and made her the darling of the *avant-garde*.

Critics wrote of its plot that encompassed a seedy world of bars and bordellos, the depredations of deadbeat odysseys, characters of a sphinx-like opacity, set in a Panamanian port peopled with nothing but half-breeds and monkeys in passionate pursuit of elusive happiness.

"In Paris, at the Monocle, a lesbian bar, Henry Miller of all people, picked me up and took me back to his dingy garret and banged me all night," Jane said.

The author of the controversial *Tropic of Cancer* told her, "I get off screwing lesbians."

"I occasionally make it with a man, but they have no mystery," Bowles said. "Women, on the other hand, are profound, mysterious,

Jane Bowles, a self-described "kike dyke," depicted here with her young Moroccan lover, Cherifa, a grainseller in the souk. At night, her veil came off for Jane.

and very, very obscene."

Her only full-length play, *In the Summer House*, debuted in New York in 1953 and closed three weeks later. With bitterness, she said, "What's the damn point of writing about a play for five hundred of your gooney friends?"

Her play was an odd-duck drama about errant mothers and daughters. It opens with an actress wearing a flaming red wig and delivering a monologue in a Judy Holliday voice. The set was compared to "a Salvador Dalí landscape bathed in Georgia O'Keefe's light."

Over the years, various productions of Jane's play starred such formidable actresses as Miriam Hopkins, Judith Anderson, Mildred Dunnock, and Anne Jackson.

One hot afternoon, Jane invited Darwin to stroll with her into the souks of the Medina. "There, you can meet the love of my life, a young Moroccan woman," she said. "I have bought this beautiful gift for her, an elegant scarf from Paris."

The Grand Socco needed a Van Gogh to capture its color and tawdry glamour.

Stall after stall was filled with locally produced foodstuffs: figs and almonds, wild artichokes and purple sweet peppers. Stalls of narcissi competed with African daisies.

The Medina had ample amounts of human drama, too. "When mothers with small babies saw us coming, they pinched their infants to make them cry, hoping we would give them *dirhams*," Darwin said. "A Berber tribesman passed by wheeling an old baby carriage. Inside it was an injured sheep he was selling."

"Unsure of our sexual preferences, Moroccan boys, some no more than twelve, offered their bodies for sale. When we showed no interest, they offered (for a price) to take us to a bordello filled with a harem of beautiful girls from many different countries," Darwin said.

At last, we came upon Jane's beloved, Cherifa, a young, good-looking Moroccan grain seller surrounded by sacks of oats, barley, and wheat. She was attired in blue jeans and a blouse, with a wool blanket in peppermint stripes around her shoulders. She looked not at Jane, but at the gift she had brought.

Jane explained that a shipload of Moroccan sailors would soon arrive in port, and that Cherifa carried a switchblade in her jeans in case some of them tried to haul her away for a gang rape, which they often did to young girls when they were in port.

That night, with Jane off with Cherifa, Darwin dined with Paul at the Parade Bar.

Paul gossiped about Cherifa, asserting, "I don't know what the attraction is for Jane. To me, the girl is a complete bore, and she is out to see what she can get from Jane. She's a wild girl, always coming up with an odd request. The other day, she wanted my wife to buy her a sheep."

"She is a bit eccentric, carrying around this certificate from the police, stating that she is a virgin. Let's face it—Jane's love for Cherifa is hardly an *affaire du coeur*."

"That Cherifa, whom I have come to detest, is a real eccentric," Paul continued. "She decorated Jane's small apartment by applying menstrual blood in big smears across the walls, and by thumb-tacking plastic packets of her pubic hair to the walls."

"She bottles goat entrails in alcohol. She also places on the tables clear jars of the grains she sells in the Souks, but only after she wets them down with her urine. She keeps jars of her feces, onto which she labels the dates of their collection, in her closet. I think she's a witch who has cast a spell over Jane."

In the years ahead, Darwin watched sadly as Jane—a life-long alcoholic—descended more deeply into madness. In 1957, at the age of 40, she suffered a stroke. Writing—always a struggle for her—eventually became impossible. She complained that "Paul steals my creative ideas and then gets all the literary glory."

Suffering bouts of depression and bordering on suicide and/or insanity, she moved in and out of mental institutions in both Spain and America. She experienced frequent epileptic fits and what she called "the darkest of the darkest nights in the vastness of the Sahara, where I am a helpless young girl tied to the ground as forty Moroccan tribesmen prepare to gang rape me."

By then, a legend had built up around her. Members of her cult compared her to Zelda Fitzgerald, Vita Sackville-West, and to Louise Bryant. Despite her rather minor literary output, some critics compared her to Colette or Doris Lessing.

Tennessee said, "Jane and Paul are The Last of the Bohemians who had once flourished in Greenwich Village."

Through it all, Jane and Paul remained dedicated to each other in their unconventional marriage. "Love comes in many forms," Darwin said, "and that is so the world over. Paul's devotion to Jane was an exotic bouquet of Venus's Flytraps tied with a rainbow-hued silk ribbon."

According to Tennessee, "That duo, wherever they're headed, will always be more intriguing than any place they inhabit."

After far too short a life, Jane Bowles died on May 4, 1973 in a mental asylum in Málaga, Spain.

As stated by Darwin, "During my last visit to call on Jane, more than a decade after her death, my co-author, Danforth Prince, and I were in Málaga researching *Frommer's Andalusia*. We carried red roses to a cemetery (*Cementario de San Miguel*) on an isolated hillside at the edge of town."

"There, we found her grave, a faded bunch of plastic flowers at the base of her tombstone, perhaps placed there by some long-departed fan."

The clouds looked ominous that afternoon, and a fierce storm seemed to be brewing. Before rushing off, Darwin spoke to the grave.

"Jane, you were one hell of a woman. What a privilege to have known you in a better day."

That night over dinner, he said, "So, that's how a literary legend ends up: On some weed-infested, god-forsaken hill near a bouquet of red roses that will soon wilt and die like Jane herself."

Royal Photographer
CECIL BEATON
"Basking in the Glory of My Own Genius"

Cecil Beaton was one of the first celebrities Darwin was introduced to in Tangier. The setting was the bar of El Minzah Hotel. Darwin was having a drink with the manager of the hotel, getting an update on its facilities for the *Frommer Guides*.

Beaton entered the room, and the manager invited him over. After a few minutes, the manager was called to the front desk, leaving Darwin along with Beaton.

He had long admired this English fashion designer, winner of two Oscars for the Lerner & Lowe musicals, *My Fair Lady* in 1956 and *Gigi* in 1958.

He was a world-class photographer, diarist, and painter, as well

Cecil Beaton with author Anita Loos
(Los Angeles, 1929)

"Absolutely, everything about him was an aesthete," as Cyril Connolly remembered their time together at the repugnant St. Cyprian's School in Eastbourne. "He lived for his feelings and his response to art."

as an interior designer and the official photographer of Queen Elizabeth and the Queen Mother. He had taken the wedding pictures of the Duke and Duchess of Windsor after the Duke had abdicated the throne of England "for the woman I love."

Beaton was also a world-class seducer, said to have bedded both stars of the 1930 film, *Morocco*, Gary Cooper and Marlene Dietrich.

Other seductions had included both Greta Garbo and Rudolph Nureyev.

Arch, with more than a touch of cattiness, even bitchery, he seemed to be the world's second-most-spellbinding *raconteur*, beat out only by Noël Coward.

"Perhaps the worst thing in the world is being bored," Beaton said. "The first worst thing is being a bore."

"Even though we've maintained a surface kiss-kiss friendship, Noël was a dedicated critic of mine. He once told me my sleeves were too tight and my voice too high and precise. Oh, that Noël—what a bitch she is!"

"My beloved Greta (Garbo) bolstered my confidence."

"Some people," she said, "when you were very young, and effeminate, may have found you most obnoxious to begin with, but you worked and proved yourself useful, if for no other reason than to be selected by Queen Elizabeth as her official portrait photographer."

"All the great ladies find me charming—and that I am—but I have a certain 'attitude' about women. I adore dancing with them. I like to take them to the theatre and parties. I like to talk about gowns with them and gossip about other women. But I'm really much more fond of men. In *My Fair Lady*, I would much more have preferred to seduce Rex Harrison instead of Audrey Hepburn."

"I just heard that Truman Capote is in town," Darwin said. "I first met him at Anaïs Nin's literary salon in Greenwich Village."

"Well, I owe him a favor," Beaton said. "When I was in Honolulu and had taken two 'rough trade' sailors back to my suite, after I'd fellated them, they tried to steal my most valuable camera. Guess what? To my rescue came Mighty Mouse Capote, and he chased the navymen out the door. My camera was saved."

Beaton suggested he have the manager call Capote to come and join Darwin and him at the bar.

"Truman will mince down the mountaintop where he is lodged," Beaton said. "I can see him now, this exaggerated little figure with a shopping basket filled with a bottle of Listerine, white chocolate, tins of butter, candies, and books from the American Library here."

Within a reasonable amount of time, Capote arrived, fluttering about the bar before landing at our table. He turned to Beaton "Wouldn't you know it. Here we are, two iron-winged butterflies finding ourselves on the same hollyhock."

He had discovered Tangier during his first visit in the summer of 1949.

Darwin was convinced that Capote was both a challenge and something of a threat to Beaton as a raconteur.

Capote could always be counted on to relay an outrageous tale, whether it was true and accurate or not. He once said, "Southerners like this Alabama boy you see before you will never let the truth intrude into a good story."

Both Beaton and Darwin had already heard his famous tale about how he'd learned that Eleanor Roosevelt had seduced Katharine Hepburn.

Virtually anyone who had ever come into contact with Capote knew that he claimed to have seduced both John Garfield and Errol Flynn, finding neither actor suitable to his taste.

That afternoon in Tangier, he talked about how he had discovered sex: "When I was twelve, I was forced to attend St. John's Military Academy in Ossining, New York. During the day, the boys in my dormitory mocked me for being a sissy. But at night, they forced me into one bunk after another. Before dawn, I'd done all eight of my fellow dorm mates. I repeated that scenario again and again until I eventually graduated from military school with flying colors."

He then relayed yet another outrageous tale. Since then, it has been widely distributed in printed form within several respected biographies, including Darwin's *Humphrey Bogart, The Making of a Legend*, published in 2010.

For the 1954 release of *Beat the Devil*, John Huston turned to Capote to craft a script that would flatteringly feature his stars—Bogart, Jennifer Jones, and Gina Lollobrigida.

According to Capote, one night on location in Italy, he challenged a drunken Bogie to an arm-wrestling contest. If he won, his requested prize was to fellate Bogie.

Assuming (incorrectly) that he would easily beat "this short, limp-wristed guy," Bogie agreed, but on one condition. In the highly unlikely event that he lost: "I'll go through with it, but you can't swallow."

Capote won and took his prize, but didn't follow through on his commitment not to swallow.

The other surprise was that throughout most of the remainder of the shoot, Huston moved Capote into his bed every night, telling the crew, "We often work on the script until the wee hours."

Capote told Beaton, "I know you've seduced both Garbo and Dietrich, but I could have had them too. Each of them would be only too willing to go to bed with me. But I can't understand why anyone would want to go to bed with a woman…boring, boring, boring."

He also proclaimed, loud enough for everyone at the bar to hear, and perhaps as a means of further provoking Beaton, "I'm an alcoholic. I'm a drug addict. I'm a homosexual. And I'm a genius!"

Three days later, Beaton and Capote each departed for Paris, where Beaton proposed marriage to Garbo. According to what he later reported, Garbo answered, "What a brutal question."

Reportedly, she was not impressed with Capote. She said, "He is not first class, but ridiculous and silly. He should not criticize people for their private lives. That's each individual's own business. It's offensive to do so."

However, as both Beaton and Darwin knew, that criticism would not stop Capote. When he published excerpts from his unfinished novel, *Answered Prayers* in ways that embarrassed its members, the social circle which had once cherished him abruptly and coldly dropped him forever.

***

JEAN GENET
An Eccentric, Occasionally Criminal Genius whose All-Black Accessories Included a Beret and High Heels

Jean Genet in 1927, age sixteen.

In 1948, Genet sent this photo to Violette Leduc, author of *La Bâtarde:* "To my dear Violette, with all my kindness and the tenderness of my sixteen years, Jean."

In 1968, Darwin learned that the author, Jean Genet, that most controversial of all French writers other than the Marquis de Sade, had migrated to Tangier for the remainder of spring.

Consequently, Darwin timed the on-site research for his update of *Frommer's Morocco* to coincide with Genet's time there. Genet, a former vagabond, prostitute, petty criminal, novelist, dramatist, political activist, poet, and philosopher vastly intrigued him.

As a playwright in the Theatre of the Absurd, Genet's subjects embraced existentialism, sadomasochism, homosexuality, and criminality.

Born to a prostitute in Paris in 1910, he had recounted his incredible life in *The Thief's Journal* in 1949. A great deal of his young life had been spent in and out of prison, sometimes on a charge of lewd acts.

Darwin had read his provocative first novel, *Notre-Dame-des-Fleurs (Our Lady of the Flowers; 1944)* three times. The memoir of a young man's immersion into the Parisian underworld, it had also been a favorite of Picasso, Jean-Paul Sartre, and Jean Cocteau.

Darwin had expected to try to find Genet staying at some seedy hotel in the Medina or patronizing a café heady with the smoke of *kif*. Not so. He was staying at the ritzy Hotel El Minzah, where Darwin's friend, the manager, agreed to introduce him. That meeting occurred in the hotel's bar, where Genet had arrived with three friends. Their table reverberated with a polyglot of languages—French, Arabic, and English.

After Darwin was introduced and seated, Genet turned to him: "I detest middle-class Americans," he said in French, which did not need translation. For the next two hours, Genet spoke candidly to his three guests, but pointedly ignored Darwin, who understood only some of the French, none of the Arabic, and all of the English-language comments.

Much of what he heard from Genet was provocative. "I do not like men in powerful positions," he said. "I once sat at table with Geôrges Pompidou. He may have presided over France, but I thought him a pompous ass. Get it? Pompidou as in 'pompous.' I am friends with Fidel Castro, even though he refuses to let me suck his cock. Except for Castro, I feel all heads of government should be assassinated."

"Could you imagine spending an evening with Richard Nixon? I bet he's hung like a church mouse."

"Instead of Nixon, I would have preferred to have spent time with Josef Stalin, even though he banned all my works from the Soviet Union."

"I didn't like Hitler, of course, but I adored those Nazi soldiers, especially the blonde, well-built studs who invaded Paris and screwed us every night. One night, I took on eight men from the Master Race in all their uncut glory."

To Darwin's amazement, he learned that as a journalist, Genet had covered the bloody and riot-soaked Democratic Convention (1968) in Chicago, where Hubert Humphrey was nominated as the Democratic Party's candidate for President. Outside the convention hall, police were clubbing rioters. Genet was censored in the United States and later expelled when the government refused to give him a visa. "But not before I got to meet Jane Fonda."

"I really don't care a rat's turd about America and its so-called democracy. It's not democratic at all. It tries to control what women do with their bodies or where men place their cocks. Some democracy! They sent their mighty warriors to liberate France. I later learned that General Eisenhower was impotent. After the war, we also learned that Hitler had only a small, deformed penis and a testicle that had never descended."

Genet felt he had to explain why such an advocate of the poor and underprivileged stayed at the most expensive hotel in Tangier. "Because I'm a dirty dog. I stay here because I like to see elegant people cater to a filthy cur like me."

Someone asked him if he believed in God. "I don't know," Genet said. "I do know that the world exists. But only God, if there is such a creature, knows if he exists."

"At last I got to sit opposite Jean Genet," Darwin said. "Okay, so he was a bit hostile. Jean-Paul Sartre would write a book *Saint Genet* about him. And Sartre's lover, Simone de Beauvoir, called Genet 'a thug of a genius.'"

That night, Genet attacked the writings of Tennessee Williams, despite his admission that he had never seen one of his plays or read any of his fiction. "He once phoned me in Paris and tried to set up a rendezvous, but I rejected him. From what I heard about him, I don't think anything he wrote would interest me. All those depraved Southern Magnolias. I heard he was a virgin until he was twenty-six. Why would a man who discovered sex so late write anything of value? I was nine when I wandered into bed with a piece of flesh who devoured me."

The most remarkable tale Genet spun that night was that he'd met the love of his life, a boy named Azedine, when he was just two months old. "He smiled the smile of smiles at me, and I took care of him for the rest of his life. I bought him his first bicycle. I sent him to good schools. I even built a house for him and his bride. It was a great love."

Genet had once posed for a nude sculpture by the great Giacometti. But on his last day of posing, he robbed him.

His plays, such as *The Maids* (1947) and *The Balcony* (1956), had been presented in avant-garde theaters across America and Europe. He became a spokesman for both the Black Panthers in America and for the struggling people of Palestine in the Middle East.

At El Minzah that afternoon, he never removed the black beret that covered his bald head, but it was only when he rose to leave that Darwin noted that he was also wearing towering black high heels.

Two nights later, still in Tangier, Darwin made a dinner reservation at the Brasserie de France. When he got there, he encountered Genet again, dining with two Moroccans. He beckoned Darwin to come and sit at his table. His invitation, delivered in French through an intermediary, was translated as: "Tell the American boy that he can join us, providing he doesn't say anything, listens politely, and then pays the bill at the end."

A Writer's Sepulchre

Genet's grave in Larache, Morocco. Lonely in death, as in life.

Darwin accepted this dubious invitation solely as a means of temporarily positioning himself in Genet's legendary orbit.

Throughout the course of dinner, Genet had been paying excessive attention to the handsome young Moroccan waiter. At one point, near the end of the meal, he whispered something in his ear.

Finally, when everyone had finished, Genet turned to Darwin and said something in French, words which were translated to him as: "Tell the American boy that he should not only pay for our dinner, but I want him to give the waiter the equivalent of fifty U.S. dollars, in exchange for which I plan to spent the night with him."

***

Genet eventually developed throat cancer and, in a seedy hotel room in Paris, he was found dead on April 15, 1986. He died a day after Simone de Beauvoir also died. But whereas she received a state funeral, Genet was buried in an obscure Spanish Cemetery in Larache, Morocco.

"During his visit to Morocco the following year, Darwin visited the site with me," said Danforth. "We noted that his grave overlooked a former Spanish bordello, one which had once catered to soldiers. Genet would have liked that."

An old Moroccan woman tended to the cemetery, living in a little shanty on the grounds. Weeds had grown up on Genet's grave, and a tired-looking goat was munching on them.

BARBARA HUTTON
The Woolworth Heiress
Poor Little Rich Girl

The most illustrious resident of Tangier—and certainly the richest—was the much-married Barbara Hutton. For three decades in the post-war era, she called this Moroccan city her home.

She was the daughter of the Five-and-Dime Woolworth tycoon, Frank Winfield Woolworth.

Here on hot Moroccan moonlit nights, she hosted the most lavish parties in the history of modern North Africa. In addition to spectacular food and drinks, they featured camels, snake charmers, belly dancers, and entire tribes of dancing, singing "Blue Men" from the Atlas Mountains.

After her divorce from her third husband, actor Cary Grant, Barbara had flown to Tangier when she heard that the sprawling palace of Sidi Hosni had come on the market. In the medieval core of Tangier's Casbah, it consisted of seven separate houses joined together. It had fallen on bad days which had included a recent stint as a debtor's prison.

In preparation for its acquisition, she checked into El Minzah and was escorted to an inspection of the property the following morning. The dictator of Spain, General Franco, had already bid $50,000 for the palace, but after her visit, she doubled his bid, angering Franco so much that he threatened to have her permanently banned from Spain.

After its acquisition, she imported craftsmen from all over Morocco, especially Fez, to decorate it. Precious antiques and artwork were shipped in from Europe, including paintings by El Greco, Salvador Dalí, Fragonard, Braque, Manet, Klee—even Grandma Moses.

Her most precious possession was called "The Million

Barbara Hutton, in her Moroccan Palace. She ruled like an empress. Her favorite saying was, "Money can buy you sex, but never love."

Dollar Tapestry," a 15th-Century wall hanging studded with precious stones that included pearls, diamonds, and rubies. Dozens of matching, jewel-studded floor cushions came with it. During her parties, she had to hire security guards to protect both the tapestry and the cushions from guests who might otherwise have ripped out (and stolen) the jewels.

Dressed in a glittering caftan and seated on a throne, and in some instances, not completely coherent, Barbara, as the unofficial "Queen of the Casbah," received each guest.

To her palace, she welcomed guests who included the film star, Claudette Colbert, and of course, the globe-trotting Greta Garbo with Cecil Beaton.

Marlene Dietrich showed up, as did Aristotle Onassis with his opera diva, Maria Callas. Charlie Chaplin arrived with Oona O'Neill, the daughter of playwright Eugene O'Neill. Chaplin told Barbara, "The most beautiful form of life is a very young girl just starting to bloom."

In between lovers who included Howard Hughes, James Dean (that is not a typo) and Michael Wilding (later Mr. Elizabeth Taylor), Barbara at the time was husband hunting.

She said, "American men don't understand me. European men are more sophisticated, more mature. I won't say that my husbands thought only of my money, but it had a certain fascination for them."

"I don't think I'll get involved with movie stars, either American or British again." She related her experience with Michael Rennie, a Yorkshire-born, smoothly handsome star who is known today mainly for his cult classic sci-fi film, *The Day the Earth Stood Still* (1951).

She claimed, "Michael came out of the bathroom wearing a rubber diving suit. In one hand, he had a bullwhip; in the other a jar of Vaseline." Her anecdote abruptly ended there. Her guests never learned what happened next.

"Mostly, I go for men with titles," she told Dietrich. "But I did seduce one of my security guards. He left me black and blue, torn and tattered, and with this awful stickiness."

"Jimmy Dean, however, whom I picked up one night in Hollywood, was so young and tender, so very sweet, so unlike Errol Flynn's pal, David Niven. When David pulled off his shoes and stockings, I was disappointed. I swear he had the smallest feet I'd ever seen on a grown man. But when he stripped down, he lived up to his reputation of 'beer can.'"

In 1947, a year after settling into her palace in the Casbah, she married Prince Igor Nikolayevich Troubetzkoy. A French-speaking aristocrat of Russian lineage, he was a world-class auto racer.

When Barbara met him, he'd been running a black market operation in Paris in collaboration with Errol Flynn and the notorious Freddy McEvoy, selling U.S. Army surplus goods. Both of these men had previously been lovers of Barbara.

"Freddy virtually sold Prince Igor to Barbara, who was willing to pay the price of $100,000," said tobacco heiress Doris Duke, Barbara's "frenemy" since childhood. "I know because he was offered to me first. Errol, my former lover, made the offer himself."

Biographer C. David Heymann described Prince Igor as "having the sleek body of an athlete and the cherubic face of a choir boy. He had dimples, a high forehead, twinkling green eyes, butterscotch hair, and a delicately formed mouth."

Against all expectations, the marriage lasted until 1951.

Fashion designer Oleg Cassini said, "Men were the chief stimulus in Barbara's life. She buys them, sells them, barters them, or replaces them in much the same way a stockbroker operates on the Exchange. Sometimes, she even marries one of them."

After dumping her nobleman, Barbara married Porfirio Rubirosa, the Dominican playboy who had briefly been wed to Doris Duke.

"I married him because Doris told me he had the most magnificent penis in the world. But I found it a frightening appendage and actually screamed when he first stripped for me. I agreed with Jerome Zerbe, the society photographer, who claimed, 'It looks like Yul Brynner in a black turtleneck.'"

Darwin first visited Barbara's palace in Tangier in the 1960s with his newly minted friend, Paul Bowles. "She did not like my novel, *The Sheltering Sky*," he said.

She had appraised Bowles' masterpiece to him like this: "It's full of violence and cruelty. All the Moroccan characters in the book are *outré* or abandoned or decadent. It presents a distorted view of Morocco."

"She always invites me to her parties, but she doesn't really like me," Bowles said.

Darwin always remembered being introduced to the heiress. Partially inebriated and not completely coherent, she was sitting on her throne wearing a diamond-and-emerald tiara that had once belonged to Catherine the Great of Russia.

"She did not look well," he said. "She was hideously underweight, her arms like toothpicks, and she had this deathly pallor."

"Barbara," Bowles said. "You should let me come tomorrow and take you for a little walk in the Casbah. You need some sun."

"No, I can't face the fierce sun," she said. "As for walking, I no longer do that. If I have to go somewhere, I have two of my security guards carry me."

After his encounter with her, Darwin wandered around the premises, mingling with the other guests. Her palace and grounds had been compared to a Garden of Eden, where nightingales sang and fountains splashed.

Bowles asserted, "It was like living in one of those crystal balls you shake and it snows inside."

In 1975, Barbara paid her last visit to the Casbah. She did not look well. Her sixth husband (1955-59) had been Baron Gottfried von Cramm, a German nobleman and noteworthy tennis player.

It was in Tangier that she met her seventh and final husband, a Vietnamese "Prince," Raymond Doan Vinh na Champassak. That marriage was a disaster, her shortest union.

On May 11, 1979, Barbara had more or less permanently returned to Los Angeles, where she suffered a stroke and died. Among her final words were, "Money can't buy you happiness."

***

"During our final research trip to Tangier, Darwin and I stood on the pier waiting for the ferryboat to haul us back to Algeciras," Danforth said.

"The days of Tangier's tawdry glory are over," he said. "Day trippers from Spain will soon arrive, with concealed money belts tied around their waists, Many of them will be waving our guidebook to Morocco."

As we sailed away from North Africa and back toward Europe, Darwin looked back at Tangier, a city with so many memories. "There's a lot still going on in this tired old relic," he said. "But today, you can't really know what that means unless you gain entrance to what's behind all those locked doors."

***

That night in Spain, Darwin recorded some of his memories of Tangier from long ago.

He recalled the night when Jane Bowles stripped and danced nude in

Marlene Dietrich..."God had a talent for creating exceptional women."

Guitta's, a lesbian bar that she used to frequent most nights. "Today," he wrote, "it's a French bank."

He would always remember the first of many encounters he had with Marlene Dietrich, that *femme fatale* of yesterday. Jay Hazelwood, the owner of the Parade Bar, introduced Darwin to the great diva: "And what do you do, young man?" she asked him.

Not wanting to admit that he was a travel writer—"too mundane"—he described a novel he was working on entitled *The Delinquent Heart*.

She smiled. "I adore the title: The story of my life."

Since then, "the most wicked city in the world" has faded into a blander relic from yesterday. When the King of Morocco seized what had formerly been an international zone, he set about "cleaning it up," closing the bordellos and arresting and/or deporting known murderers and rapists.

In time, all the legendary characters were gone, including swashbuckling Errol Flynn, hellraiser Peter O'Toole, and the iconoclast author, Henry Miller, who'd achieved worldwide notoriety after the publication of his highly sexual novel, *Tropic of Cancer*, in Paris in 1934.

A major figure of the Beat Generation, William S. Burroughs, born in 1914 to a wealthy family in St. Louis, was a heroin addict who came to live in Tangier. His fellow beatnik and author, Jack Kerouac, labeled him "the greatest satirical writer since Jonathan Swift."

Burrough's celebrated novel, *The Naked Lunch*, was eventually appraised and listed among the greatest 100 novels of all time, even though it depicts such horrors as child murder and acts of pedophilia.

[In 1951, Burroughs had killed his second wife, Joan Vollmer, in Mexico while drunkenly acting out a stunt inspired by the legend of William Tell.]

Norman Mailer declared that "Except for myself, Burroughs may be the only American writer possessed by genius."

Darwin didn't know what to expect when he was first introduced to him at the Parade Bar. Afterwards, he agreed with Gore Vidal's description: "He looked like a traveling salesman who had gone too far in a wrinkled gray suit."

"Of all the writers I've met in my life, Burroughs terrified me as a real literary outlaw," Darwin said.

A Pulitzer Prize-winning author, Ted Morgan, had already authored biographies of Sir Winston Churchill, Franklin D. Roosevelt, and W. Somerset Maugham. In reference to Burroughs, he said, "Burroughs was a junkie forced to live much of his life in exile, his books banned, his homosexuality outlawed in most places. His life reads like a counterculture adventure story—his quest for the ultimate hallucinogenic drug in the jungles of South America, and his out-of-body experiences in the famous Beat Hotel in Paris, and finally, his induction into the staid Institute of Arts and Letters, and his adulation by the young everywhere."

Jack Kerouac, the high priest of the Beat Generation, was a friend of Burroughs. He developed a cult following among the Beatniks when he wrote *On the Road*. Author Dennis McNally nailed him: "He was an enigmatic American figure, the 'King of the Beats,' who prefigured the turned-on, dropped out, ecstatic wandering hero of the 1960s. He was a catalyst for the enormous post-war shift in American literature and culture."

One night at the Parade Bar, Darwin heard Kerouac attacking such homosexual writers as Tennessee Williams, Paul Bowles, Gore Vidal, and Carson McCullers, author of *The Heart is a Lonely Hunter*, one of the greatest of American novels.

When Vidal heard of his tirade, he spread his own story about Kerouac, loudly asserting that Kerouac had picked him up years ago in the San Remo Bar in Greenwich Village, and that the two of them had returned together to the Chelsea Hotel.

"When he dropped his pants, I felt I'd need a tweezer to find it. He gave me a blow-job and I turned him over and sodomized him. Drugged, he spent the rest of the night sleeping it off in my bathtub. He was impotent."

On another night, over drinks in Tangier at the Café de Paris, Kerouac told Darwin, "Sometimes I feel as bad as Allen (Ginsberg). He's often haunted by dreams of snakes wiggling after him, emerging from his own vomit. Sometimes, like Allen, I think I'm going out of my mind, too. To save myself, I think of Emerson's dictums in *Self-Reliance*: 'Listen to the sea, cherish the butterflies, and feed the raccoons, birds, and mice.'"

TENNESSEE WILLIAMS:
"Tonight, I'm Committing Suicide."

Thanks to his diary, Darwin would forever remember the summer of 1962 in Tangier. He was invited to stay with Tennessee Williams and his new companion, a young poet named Frederick Nicklaus, a cousin of the golf pro, Jack Nicklaus. At the time, he was working on an anthology of poetry entitled *The Man Who Bit the Sun*.

Tennessee had rented a small, sparsely furnished villa, a three-minute walk from Tangier's beachfront.

He had recently dumped his long-time lover, Frank Merlo. *[Merlo had been the inspiration for the fictional character of Stanley Kowalski in* A Streetcar Named Desire. *On Broadway and on the screen, Marlon Brando had portrayed Stanley as "a walking streak of sex."]*

Tennessee was reworking his latest play, the murky *The Milk Train Doesn't Stop Here Any More*. It would in time reach its second attempt on Broadway with the odd couple, Tallulah Bankhead devouring poor Tab Hunter. Elizabeth Taylor and Richard Burton would turn the play into a film entitled *Boom!* (1968). To Williams, the title was a reference to "the sound of shock felt by people each moment of still being alive."

The playwright told Darwin that, "Freddie Niklaus is my new angel who's come to rescue me from the demons who descend on me after midnight, trying to rip out my soul and devour it. But we can only communicate in bed."

"My days with Frankie ended badly," he confessed. "The Sicilian bitch locked me out of my own house."

During his stay in Tangier, Tennessee was either popping what he called 'crazy pills,' or else ordering Darwin to mix him another double martini.

"Like my heroine in *The Roman Spring of Mrs. Stone*, I am drifting this summer." *[Shot in Rome and released in 1961, it starred Vivien Leigh as Mrs. Stone, a recently widowed former actress, and Warren Beatty as her gigolo lover.]*

"You were wonderful in Rome to Viv and me," Tennessee told Darwin. "Both of us were two lost souls wandering about, each of us reeling from the heartbreak that Warren bestowed on us. He has the sex appeal to make man or woman fall in love with him, and then he abruptly departs for his next conquest."

"It was difficult to get Tennessee to leave his (rented) house," Darwin said, "or even to walk to the beach."

On some nights the playwright would ostentatiously announce, "Tonight is the night I'll commit suicide. My glory days are behind me."

Darwin attempted to convince him that his best days as a playwright lay in his future. "You'll even top *The Glass Menagerie* and *A Streetcar*

Tennessee Williams and the Italian diva, Anna Magnani, were kindred spirits. "We each had the same taste in men," Magnani said..."Namely, Marlon Brando."

Named Desire."

"What a charming liar you are," Tennessee retorted. "For all I know, each of my future plays will be obscure failures, performed, if at all, as curiosities Off-Off Broadway."

Sometimes, Darwin would lure Tennessee and his young poet (his new companion) to the Parade Bar or else to Dean's Bar, a snug little nest just downhill from El Minzah Hotel. It was the domain of a dark-skinned gigolo owner, Joseph Dean. He candidly admitted, "I cater to both men and women, whoever can pay my price, be it Barbara Hutton or the late Errol Flynn."

His bar attracted the *haut monde* visiting Tangier, not only Hutton, Garbo, and Flynn, but Ian Fleming working on his next James Bond thriller, and the English painter, Francis Bacon, searching inspiration for his next painting.

One night, they were joined at table by the prolific English writer, Rupert Croft-Cooke, who had migrated to Tangier after serving a prison sentence for pederasty.

Darwin included himself as one of the scandal-hungry journalists who patronized Dean's, along with disgraced diplomats, nymphomaniacal heiresses, Mafia men on the run, and caftaned drag queens from Paris and Berlin.

Darwin suggested that author James Ellroy's description of Los Angeles might also be applied to Tangiers. He might have defined the clientele at Dean's as "every third person being a peeper, a prowler, a poon stalker, a panty sniffer, a prostitute, a pillhead, a pothead, a pimp, a pederast, or a hustler."

Or, put another way, Tangier might have been summed up as having a seismic dislocation that skewed the wicked old city eight degrees off the control axis of the Planet Earth, making it a netherworld cesspool orbiting a dark star.

TANGIER: THE CASBAH

It looked harmless during the day, but at night, "denizens of desire" emerged.

Epilogue

MAGNOLIA MAGIC

"THE PAST IS A MEMORY, AND THE FUTURE IS ONLY A DREAM, BUT PRESS ON MY DAHLING, FOR TOMORROW IS ANOTHER DAY."

—Tallulah Bankhead
("or what's left of her, dahling"),
over drinks with Darwin

Access from Manhattan to the creatively fertile context of Magnolia House was and is fast and frequent and easy. Because of a complicated roster of circumstances, needs, and incentives, celebrity sightings here were frequent.

Darwin Porter began his career as a cub reporter for *The Miami Herald*, later becoming that newspaper's bureau chief in Key West. In time, he wrote an entertainment column and more than fifty celebrity biographies—more than any other writer in history.

Over the decades, he got to know an array of the most iconic cultural figures of the second half of the 20th Century. He entertained some of them at Magnolia House on St. Marks Place in Staten Island.

Darwin claimed, "As an interviewer, I started at the top rung of the ladder and worked my way down."

He was referring to Eleanor Roosevelt, whom he had interviewed at the Fontainebleau Hotel on Miami Beach, or to Harry S Truman, whom he joined for morning walks during the former President's final visit to Key West.

During Truman's presidency, it had been his vacation retreat from the White House.

Or perhaps he meant Senator John F. Kennedy in Palm Beach. Another senator, JFK's best friend, George Smathers, introduced Darwin *[Editor-in-Chief of the University of Miami's student newspaper, and something of a power broker on campus, with strong editorial links to and a bright-looking future with* The Miami Herald*]* to the future U.S. President and Future First Lady, Jacqueline.

According to Darwin, "Both of them were wearing pink pants, and I adored them, but thought they were too sophisticated to ever make it to the White House. After all, I was used to Harry and Bess or Ike and Mamie. What did I know?"

"Both George and JFK were 'babe magnets' before the term was invented," Darwin said.

In the cool, cool of the evening, after a hot day, JFK, George, and I went for a nude swim in the Kennedy pool. I kept looking back at the house for Jackie to emerge. She discreetly opted not to join us.

"The First Lady of the World," Eleanor Roosevelt, listens to a tirade from the Soviet delegation at the United Nations,

In 1948, Harry S Truman holds up a copy of the *Chicago Daily Tribune*, which had printed a "Second Coming" headline that was "fake news,"

Truman said of his rival, Thomas Dewey: "He always evoked that little man on the top of a wedding cake."

***

In his capacity as an entertainment columnist, Darwin also met and interviewed a rising young rock star, Elvis Presley.

Five reporters appeared at the designated time and place to interview this future superstar. Whereas Darwin represented the teenage viewpoint; another writer—a colleague from *The Herald's* sports pages—thought Elvis was a "faggot." Yet another colleague—from the women's pages—insisted that his act should be censored by the morals authorities; and yet another (this one from the Arts & Entertainment page) predicted he'd rise quickly and then collapse as a singer and disappear.

Of the five writers, Elvis got his biggest rave from Darwin, who anticipated his meteoric rise. "This hottie is here to stay," Darwin wrote in his news story, "the firstest with the mostest. Move over Sinatra, Pat Boone, Paul Anka, Eddie Fisher, Vic Damone."

As editor-in-chief of the newspaper associated with his University (the University of Miami), Darwin invited the two biggest stars in America at the time to visit the campus as "Celebrity Honorees." He was surprised when they each accepted: Lucille Ball and Desi Arnaz made their appearance, as choreographed and formally presented by Darwin, to hundreds of excited students.

According to Darwin, "On camera, and surrounded by crowds, they were Lucy and Ricky Ricardo from the highest-rated show on TV. But off-camera, a different duo emerged. Very very loudly, she was giving Desi hell for having run off with two showgirls on Miami Beach the night before."

Later, as Desi stood at the urinal in the Student Union's men's room beside Darwin, the star told him, "I don't take out other broads—I take out

JFK and his best friend, Senator George Smathers (D-FL, aka "Gorgeous George") relax before discarding their bathing suits for a nude swim. "They liked Florida beauty queens," Darwin said.	In the 1950s, Desi Arnaz and Lucille Ball became the most popular comedy show on TV. They were the ever-loving Ricky and Lucy Ricardo. But behind the scenes they were anything but loving.

hookers. Your wife is your wife. Your fooling around can in no way affect your love for her, like my love for Lucy. A man's relationship with his wife is sacred, and a few pecadilloes on the side are meaningless. The world is my oyster," Desi continued. "I just snap my fingers, and Lana Turner, Ginger Rogers, or Betty Grable come running for a chance at my Cuban salami...So do Lorenz Hart and Cesar Romero."

***

As he was growing up on Miami Beach, Darwin became fascinated by show business personal-

One of the "important women" in Darwin Porter's early life was Sophie Tucker, his mother's employer and *The Last of the Red Hot Mommas*. She was Ronald Reagan's favorite singer.

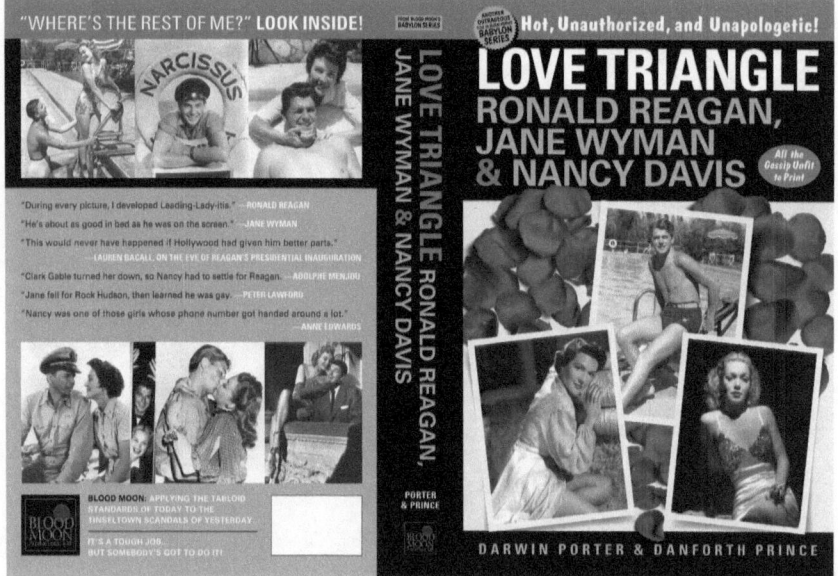

No other book ever laid out Ronald Reagan's marital messes and cinematic dramas in such abrupt detail. It was written at Magnolia House based partly on Darwin Porter's early exposure, on Miami Beach and in Hollywood, to Ronald Reagan's romantic and sexual indiscretions.

ities. Many of them became familiar to him after his attractive, recently-widowed mother became the wardrobe mistress and general "Girl Friday" to the legendary and occasionally bawdy Sophie Tucker, who moved her "entertainment empire" and her entourage to Miami Beach every winter.

As a young boy, Darwin lived in her home, cosseted and pampered as an impressionable fan and the son of "Miss Sophie's" assistant. Witty and occasionally lewd, with a raunchy humor that made liberated listeners guffaw. *Zaftig*, loud, and earthy, Sophie was known and lavishly marketed as "The Last of the Red Hot Mommas." Every visiting celebrity, from Jackie Gleason to Debbie Reynolds, called on "The Queen of Miami Beach."

A star-struck Darwin rushed home from school every afternoon to see which star might be visiting on any given day.

One encounter at Miss Sophie's was with a B-list actor whose career didn't seem headed for any particular glory at the time. It was Ronald Reagan, a devoted fan. Although he'd been dating Doris Day on and off for a while, he didn't seem particularly significant or memorable at the time.

The blonde Reagan escorted to Miami Beach was a Norma Jeane Baker, a then-minor starlet who'd recently been renamed "Marilyn Monroe."

Decades later, a cozy, laughing picture of Reagan with Monroe appeared on the cover of Darwin's seminal "anthology of scandal," *Hollywood Babylon, It's Back* (2008), co-authored with Danforth Prince. Immediately beside it was a photo of Tom Cruise in a strait jacket and a semi-nude Tony Curtis spending quality time with Lord Laurence Olivier in a Roman bath.

Reagan was between marriages, his Oscar-winning wife (Jane Wyman) having dumped him for Lew Ayres, her co-star in *Johnny Belinda* (1948) in which she'd played a deaf-mute who had been raped.

Although Reagan had been planning to ask for Doris Day's hand in marriage, he was also slipping around and dating Nancy Davis, a minor MGM starlet known in insider Hollywood circles as "The Queen of Fellatio."

One night, Nancy told

Margaret O'Brien as she appeared with Judy Garland in *Meet Me in St. Louise* (1944). Darwin recalls his first meeting with his favorite singer: "Memories are Made of This."

Ronald that she was pregnant. Soon after, he dropped Doris and married Nancy "to make an honest women of her." The result? The (unplanned) birth of a daughter, Patti, who later didn't want to be known or publicly associated with her father. When she was older, she officially changed her name to Patti Davis in honor of her mother's maiden name.

Darwin, by now something of an authority on the Hollywood career of Ronald Reagan, eventually wrote a biography about the show-biz embroglios of Reagan and his wifes. Co-authored with Danforth, and entitled *Love Triangle* (2014), it examined the tumultuous and often murky Hollywood interactions of superstar Jane Wyman, B-picture actor Ronald Reagan, and starlet Nancy Davis.

***

During his early formative years, young Darwin's favorite movie was *The Wizard of Oz* (1939), starring Judy Garland as Dorothy. Imagine the delight of the young adolescent when he rushed into Sophie's house and found Judy during one of her social calls to Miss Sophie?

When she was gushingly informed of young Darwin's devotion to her singing, she sang "Over the Rainbow" just for him.

"Now, that's a memory you carry with you for the rest of your life," Darwin said, years later. "Maybe I'll hear her singing that on my death bed when I'm coming to join you, Judy."

Sinatra, syncopating on a sound stage...or buying off a nine-year-old with a ten-dollar bill.

***

One night, Sophie arranged a date between Frank Sinatra and Darwin's vivacious, attractive, and recently widowed mother. When nine-year-old Darwin inconveniently roared into the room where they were bonding, Ol' Blue Eyes pulled out a ten-dollar bill and handed it to Darwin with the instruction to "get

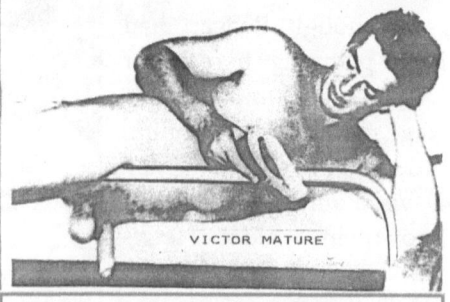

Gore Vidal: "Victor Mature is America's Secret Weapon"

lost, kid."

To some degree inspired by that (very) early encounter, Darwin later wrote a biography dentitled *Frank Sinatra: The Boudoir Singer* (2011).

***

Knowing how star struck Darwin's mother was, Sophie lined up other dates for her with Hollywood men briefly visiting Miami as part of temporary, sometimes "off-the-record" getaways from their problems (or wives), or whatever.

With the exception of Sinatra, most of those movie star beaux are relatively unknown today unless you subscribe to Turner Movie Classics.

One of them was that handsome hunk, Victor Mature, who had recently starred in the 1949 Cecil B. DeMille epic, *Samson & Delilah* (1949) opposite Hedy Lamarr.

In the Forties, Mature had made love to such fabled stars as Rita Hayworth, Alice Faye, Betty Grable, Betty Hutton, Veronica Lake, Lana Turner, Gene Tierney, and Elizabeth Taylor.

Author Gore Vidal claimed that if that nude picture of Mature, snapped when he was lying on his bunk during his service in the U.S. Coast Guard during World War II had been seen by the Nazis, they would have surrendered earlier.

Other of his mother's dates included Richard Widmark, suntanned, laconic, adept at playing demonic characters. He'd been the leading man opposite such diverse blondes as Marilyn Monroe and Doris Day.

Darwin's mother also dated Wendell Corey, who talked about a possible marriage with her. "Wendell who?" you might have asked. In Corey's heyday [the late 1940s and 50s] he was the leading man opposite such legendary ladies of

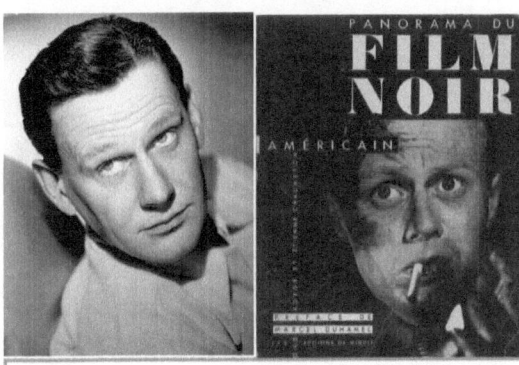

Look who Mamma's dating now, and will either of them become a stepdad?
Movie stars Wendell Corey (left) and Richard Widmark (right) as he appeared on the cover of a seminal French-language overview of American *Film Noir*.

Young Darwin's available, attractive, vivacious, and recently widowed mother, Hazel, dated both of them (and Frank Sinatra, too) based on assignations to some degree arranged by her employer, Sophie Tucker.

the screen as Grace Kelly, Barbara Stanwyck, and Joan Crawford. He'd also appeared in pictures with Kirk Douglas, Monty Clift, Burt Lancaster, and James Stewart.

As a university student, Darwin even dated a future U.S. Attorney General—a female that is—Janet Reno, Attorney General during the Presidency of Bill Clinton. Darwin worked with both of her parents, each a reporter on *The Miami Herald*.

Darwin's one-time girlfriend, Attorney General Janet Reno with her boss, Bill Clinton

In addition to becoming a leading travel writer, Darwin evolved into a celebrity journalist, writing not only a column, but more Hollywood biographies than any other author, as well as six books on U.S. Presidents and their First Ladies.

"It was all about networking, as we call it today," he said. "If you could bond with one celebrity and establish some sort of friendship, you got to meet their friends, often fellow celebrities. That was best represented by Tennessee Williams, my neighbor in Key West."

That eccentric playwright eventually introduced Darwin to such stars as Marlon Brando, Elizabeth Taylor, Bette Davis, Ava Gardner, and Paul Newman.

Darwin would later write biographies of some of these personalities. Through Tennessee, he even met the elusive Greta Garbo and the aging goddess of sex, the indomitable Mae West.

"Gore Vidal, Anaïs Nin, and Truman Capote also brought a whole new cast of characters into my life," Darwin said. "But other than Tennessee, no one introduced me to more stars than what I called 'The Two Jimmies.'"

[He was referring to James Kirkwood and James Leo Herlihy, both novelists and playwrights. Whereas Kirkwood took home the Pulitzer Prize for the hit Broadway musical, A Chorus Line. *Herlihy's best-known work is* Midnight Cowboy, *which won the Oscar for Best Picture of the Year in 1969. According to Darwin, "My Halloween treat back in 1959 was a play that Herlihy had written,* Crazy October. *It was the last theatrical piece that Tallulah Bankhead ever toured in. Thanks to the people I met and the opportunities they led me to, I didn't know at the time that it would change my life."]*

BOOKREADER NEWS
from Danforth Prince

Soon, we'll release another installation of the Magnolia House Series, glitzier and more "show-bizzy" than the one you're reading now.

Based on additional excerpts from the writings and diaries of Darwin Porter, it will address the famous and infamous personalities who preened, shimmered, and rehearsed their till-now-secretive *spiels* within the portals of this house. With the understanding that things might change *[as they so often do, in life, I'm sure you'll agree]* we've tentatively assigned it the following title:

HISTORIC MAGNOLIA HOUSE, VOLUME II
GLAMOUR, GLITZ, & CELEBRITY GOSSIP

WINING, DINING, OR WHATEVER,
WITH THE SELF-ENCHANTED

We envision it as yet another forum for the Celebrity Secrets of Magnolia House. Cheers and xxx with best wishes from all of us.

Stay with Us! Learn more about "Celebrity-Centric Sleepovers" at Blood Moon's **Magnolia House,** a historic and moderately priced "Airbnb" in New York City.

ENTERTAINMENT NEWS

BLOOD MOON PRODUCTIONS,
IN COLLABORATION WITH
HISTORIC MAGNOLIA HOUSE & THE AIRBNB "EXPERIENCES" TEAM

PROUDLY ANNOUNCE THE DEBUT OF A
SHOW-BIZ & LITERARY SALON
WITH THE SAME NAME AS THAT OF THE BOOK YOU'RE READING:

CELEBRIY &
THE IRONIES OF FAME

YOU'RE INVITED!

Blood Moon Productions, from its headquarters at **Magnolia House** on Staten Island, proudly announces the debut of a unique series of **LITERARY and SHOW-BIZ SALONS**, each open to the public, four afternoons a week beginning at 3:30PM.

Marketed by, and developed in collaboration with, **AIRBNB EXPERIENCES**, it's formatted as a 90-minute tea party, with running commentary about Magnolia House's contribution to America's arts, letters, and obsession with celebrities. Developed and delivered by **Danforth Prince**, it evokes a postmodern literary salon with an emphasis on American entertainment, publishing, celebrities, and pop culture.

According to Prince, "I'm always looking to resurrect an art form **(CONVERSATION)** that's at risk of disappearing. So when the 'Experiences' team at AirBnb approached me with the idea of opening Magnolia House for conversations and lectures, I said YES with the understanding that AirBnb would handle the reservations, scheduling, and publicity."

**WANNA KNOW MORE ABOUT
CELEBRITY STUDIES
LIKE YOU'VE SEEN IN THIS BOOK?**

Come by an AirBnb "Experience," and for some unusual insights into The American Century. Memories of celebrities passed are eager to meet you!

For more information (access, scheduling, pricing, and logistics), click on https://www.airbnb.com/experiences/359275

Be Welcome! Be Happy! Be Blessed!
And know in advance how welcome you are at any of our afternoon conversations about

*CELEBRITY &
THE IRONIES OF FAME*

photos courtesy Isabel McGowan

At Historic Magnolia House:
CELEBRITY & THE IRONIES OF FAME

Scheduled four afternoons a week at 3:30pm,
these Conversations about Pop Culture, Celebrity, and Fame
were conceived as a
NEW & CREATIVE WAY TO SPEND QUALITY TIME IN NYC
by Danforth Prince and the AirBnB Experiences Team

https://www.airbnb.com/experiences/359275

POSTSCRIPT FROM THE EDGE—WOMEN WE LOVE

MEDIA BUZZ

Magnolia House Proudly Presents Wellness Advisor, Gerontologist, Magazine Publisher, Radio Guru, & Grande Dame

ANITA FINLEY

The Guiding Light Behind
Boomer Times & Senior Life Magazine

> "You are the salt of the earth. You have borne the pain and joy of motherhood and have earned every beautiful wrinkle and laugh line…so keep smiling and make time for your children and other children. Everyone needs a mother, but especially a grandmother, if you have reached that glorious age. Don't regret it… salivate it."
>
> —**Anita Finley**, addressing mothers everywhere

WHO IS ANITA FINLEY, AND WHAT IS MEDIA BUZZ?

She was an early fan of Darwin Porter. She heard about him during the publicity generated by the long-ago publication of his seminal overviews of Bogart (*The Secret Life of Humphrey Bogart*; 2003) and Hepburn (*Katharine the Great*; 2004).

She's also one of the South's leading gerontologists, a modern-day Amazon, and a Renaissance woman seemingly capable of thriving wherever she happens to land. She's a woman of influence, shaping public opinion and spreading wide her message of tolerance and love.

It's as a radio host that Anita commands her largest audience. Darwin regularly appears on her show.

He also writes MEDIA BUZZ, an artfully gossipy monthly column crafted at Magnolia House and distributed through *Boomer Times* as a regular supplement of *The Miami Herald*. For more information about it, and the **Boomer Expo Events** she choreographs, click on *www.BoomerTimesFL.com*.

Anita Finley is one of the best educated, best informed and most charming of the many guests who have passed through my life and through Magnolia House. She's also a qualified and sought-after public speaker, promoting her personal conviction that it's never too late to learn or to try something new She also organizes and choreographs an annual symposium about wellness and health, the C.U.R.E. Symposiums.

Blood Moon extends recognition and gratitude to Anita, a woman we love. She will always be welcome at Magnolia House

> **Danforth Prince**
> Publisher
> Blood Moon Productions, Ltd.

LISTEN TO ANITA EVERY SATURDAY FROM 5-8AM ON WSBR 740AM WHICH BROADCASTS IN AND AROUND PALM BEACH, BROWARD, AND DADE COUNTIES.

FROM ANYWHERE IN THE WORLD CLICK ON WWW.WSBRRADIO.COM AND/OR WWW.WWNNRADIO.COM

BoomerTimes RADIO

WHAT IS DARWIN PORTER'S MEDIA BUZZ?

It's newsy, it's gossipy, it's fun, it's produced inside Magnolia House, and it tends to generate headlines. Four reprints of Media Buzz appear within the pages that follow.

Headlines inspired by *Media Buzz* appeared within several major international newspapers AFTER their revelations first appeared in *Boomer Times*. Here are some pithy examples:

THE XXX-RATED LIFE OF PETER O'TOOLE

*

THEN-MARRIED VIVIEN LEIGH BEDDED GUYS—AND GALS!

*

PAUL NEWMAN & STEVE McQUEEN WERE LOVERS

*

JUNE ALLYSON SLEPT WITH TWO PRESIDENTS

*

HOW LIZ TAYLOR BEDDED TINSELTOWN

*

BILL CLINTON TRIED TO SEDUCE JACKIE KENNEDY IN A WRESTLING MATCH IN HER NEW YORK APARTMENT.

Media Buzz Excerpt #1 of 4
By Darwin Porter
As it appeared in the January 2017 edition of
Boomer Times Magazine

KIRK DOUGLAS

A Century of Conquests

At last, a decades-long question can be answered. Which big movie star from Hollywood's Golden Age would survive all others? Certainly not Clark Gable, Gary Cooper, Tyrone Power, Errol Flynn, or Robert Taylor. These matinee idols died relatively young.

The answer is Kirk Douglas, the first anti-hero superstar of the postwar era. The owner of the screen's most celebrated cleft chin was born Issur Danielovitch on December 6, 1918, in Amsterdam, New York. Survivor of a serious stroke, he lived to celebrate his 100th birthday in December of 2016, and was met with such headlines as "LEGENDARY HOLLYWOOD HORNDOG TURNS 100."

The longest-lived Golden Age female star was Luise Rainer, who died in London at the age of 104. She was the first actress to win two consecutive Oscars, each of them back to back—*The Great Ziegfeld* (1936) and *The Good Earth* ('37).

Douglas immortalized himself in film after film, but had a rough go of it: He was beaten up in *The Champion* ('49); stabbed in the stomach in *Ace in the Hole* ('51); lost a finger in *The Big Sky* ('52); rolled in barbed wire in *Man Without a Star* ('55); cut off his ear as Vincent van Gogh in *Lust for Life* ('56), had his eye put out in *The Vikings* ('58), was crucified in *Spartacus* ('60), and was whipped by his servant in *The Way West* ('67).

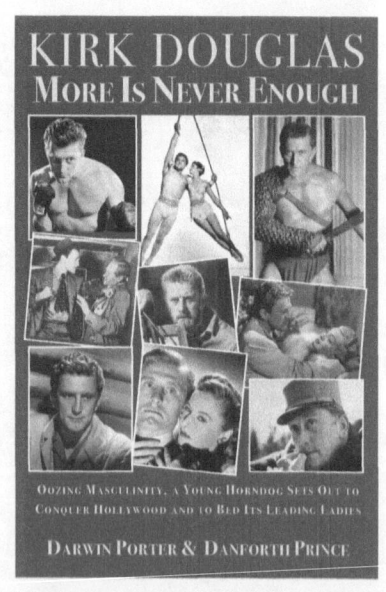

OOZING MASCULINITY, A YOUNG HORNDOG SETS OUT TO CONQUER HOLLYWOOD AND TO BED ITS LEADING LADIES

DARWIN PORTER & DANFORTH PRINCE

Throughout his career, when he was on talk shows hawking his latest film, interviewers wanted him to reveal the secrets of his love life. Talk show host Dick Cavett didn't want to talk about *A Gunfight* ('71). Instead, he wanted the dish on his leading ladies. "What About Faye Dunaway in *The Arrangement* ('69), or Kim Novak in *Strangers When We Meet* ('60)?" he asked.

Douglas was furious.

But by the time he turned 71, his tongue had loosened during the composition of his autobiography, *The Ragman's Son*. He had been married twice, once to actress Diana Dill, with whom he became the father of the future mega-star, Michael Douglas. After their divorce, he married Anne Buydens, a film publicist.

At fourteen, he lost his virginity to his English teacher. His first movie star seduction was on a rooftop in Greenwich Village with a sultry teenage blonde model, Betty Bacall. Later, she went to Hollywood, changed her name to Lauren, and married Bogie. Although for years, each of them denied her "deflowering," near the end of her life, she said, "Of course he did. Don't be a fool!"

In a nutshell, here are some tantalizing insights into how Douglas bedded the screen goddesses of yesterday:

Joan Crawford: "She was the aggressor, ripping off her dress in the foyer, too eager to go upstairs. I was nearly overcome with the fumes of her bad breath."

Rita Hayworth: "I went to bed with my fantasy of *Gilda* (her most famous film '46). I woke up to find a sweet, unsophisticated girl whose likeness had been stamped on the first atomic bomb dropped on Hiroshima."

Evelyn Keyes: "Scarlett O'Hara's Younger Sister wrote in a memoir that I was parlor-sized."

Marlene Dietrich: "She preferred fellatio and had sex without preference for gender."

Marilyn Monroe: "She kept me waiting for two hours. I practically had to put things on ice, I was so eager."

Marilyn Maxwell: "She was no lady, telling me she preferred Frank Sinatra."

Ann Sothern: "She played my wife in *A Letter to Three Wives* ('49). We rehearsed our husband-and-wife scenes in my bed."

Ava Gardner: "She turned to me when Sinatra kicked her out of his house."

Patricia Neal: "She cried during the whole thing, claiming she was cheating on the man she loved—the much-married Gary Cooper."

Gene Tierney: "She was a good kisser once you got beyond the overbite."

Lana Turner: "She was my co-star in her most memorable movie: *The Bad and the Beautiful* ('53). She told me I was twice as good as Ronnie Reagan and ten times better than Senator John F. Kennedy."

Pier Angeli: "She wanted to marry me when not in the beds of James Dean, Clark Gable, or the singer, Vic Damone. (He actually married her.)"

Mae West: Early in his career, she auditioned Douglas for her stage show. She insisted he wear skimpy briefs for her inspection. He did not make the grade.

His most bizarre seduction occurred one summer when he worked as a bellboy at a resort in New York State. It was owned by a vicious anti-Semite woman who didn't know he was Jewish. "Before I left that summer, she seduced me. At the point of her glorious climax, I screamed in her ear, 'I'm a Jew!'"

*****

Media Buzz Media Excerpt #2 of 4
By Darwin Porter
As it appeared in the December 2017 edition of
Boomer Times Magazine

THE CASTING COUCH

Yesterday & Today

Journalists are evaluating Blood Moon's latest biography, *Rock Hudson Erotic Fire*, for salacious information about how the casting couch operated during the dying days of Golden Age Hollywood.

Its November release coincided with an avalanche of charges of sexual harassment currently being splashed across the tabloids, many of them dominating television's 24-hour news cycle.

Perhaps beginning with Bill Cosby and in time embroiling producer Harvey Weinstein, accusations against sexually harassing "gropers" have engulfed an astonishingly wide range of men, everyone from Dustin Hoffman to the Rev. Jesse Jackson; Alabama's senatorial candidate Roy Moore; even such unlikely malfeasants as the late ex-Prez, George H.W. Bush, who admitted, "I once liked to pat women's rears and was known as David Cop-a-Feel."

During Rock's heyday, the term "sexual harassment" didn't exist, entering the public lexicon as late as 1977. Many young men and women arrived in Hollywood during the post-war years, expecting to extend their sexual favors as the vehicle that would help them break into show-business. Rock Hudson, it's revealed, played the game very well, indeed.

After service in the Navy, in the Philippines, during World War II, Rock—handsome, strapping, charming, and hunky—arrived in Hollywood at around the same time as another hopeful, Marilyn Monroe.

They met after she'd been been fired from Columbia, and appeared on the Universal lot (Rock's "home studio") looking for a job. He had ten dollars in his pocket, and she had nothing. Their affair began when he bought her breakfast. It was intense but brief. She advised that if they ever wanted to become movie stars, they each needed to spend lots of time as cooperative hopefuls on as many casting couches as possible.

Her advice played out well—not only for herself, but for him, too. The head of Universal, Ed Muhl, despite his status as a married man and the father of three, fell under Rock's spell. At three o'clock every afternoon, Rock was summoned into Muhl's office, and the door was firmly locked with them alone together in the room. Muhl's rising young star left about an hour later, and within months, he was awarded with a string of starring roles.

Men of various sexual persuasions were not alone in their emphasis on casting couches. Many powerful leading ladies of the day, including Joan Crawford, Marlene Dietrich, and Bette Davis, maneuvered sexual favors from whomever was awarded laurels as their leading men.

This brings us, of course, back to Rock Hudson: In a series of romantic encounters that hugely influenced his career, Oscar winner Jane Wyman (ex-wife of Ronald Reagan) developed a crush on him and insisted that he be cast as her leading man in the 1954 remake of *Magnificent Obsession*. *[An earlier version of this "four-hanky weeper" had been released in 1935.]* The picture helped morph Hudson into a superstar, leading to his Oscar-nominated performance in Edna Ferber's sprawling saga of Texas, *Giant* (1956).

Rock spent many a night at Wyman's home during the making of *Magnificent Obsession*. Her affair with Rock ended abruptly when Rock, Wyman, and her husband, bandleader Fred Karger, flew to Manhattan to attend the premiere of the film.

To her horror, after returning unexpectedly to her suite at the Plaza, she found Karger in bed with Rock. Although she continued her professional relationship with Rock, she divorced her errant young husband shortly thereafter, remarrying him in 1961, and then divorcing him again in 1965. Rock, in contrast, emerged as the world's Number One box office attraction for an undisputed seven years in a row.

Since his widely publicized death from AIDS, most of the public erroneously assumes that Rock was gay when, in fact, he was a rampaging bisexual, especially during his younger days. He seduced obsessively, and without gender preference, everyone from Elizabeth Taylor to James Dean, from Lana Turner to the inevitable Miss Crawford, even such bizarre couplings as Tallulah Bankhead and Liberace. He fathered a son, and became sought-after in some of the upper-tier society circuits of Europe, even enjoying sexual intimacies with three royal princesses: Margaret Rose of Kensington Palace; Princess Grace of Monaco; and Princess Soraya, the former queen of Iran.

Researched over a period of decades, *Erotic Fire* reveals details—for the first time—about the often tragic life of this astonishingly successful fallen idol. He was the first mega-celebrity stricken with AIDS, and became, in 1985, the first famous person to succumb to a black death that, in time, killed millions of men, women, and children, especially in the sub-Sahara.

On Rock's deathbed, he told Elizabeth Taylor, "If my dying calls world attention to this plague, and people will raise money to try to find a cure, then this will be my shining hour."

Beautiful Elizabeth took up the banner and became the chief fundraiser for AIDS. The rest is history.

***

In the dying days of Hollywood's Golden Age, Rock Hudson became the most celebrated phallic symbol and lust object in America. Darwin Porter's biography tells how he did it. EROTIC FIRE. Another example of Blood Moon's Award-winning Entertainment About How America Interprets its Celebrities.

*****

Media Buzz Excerpt #3 of 4
By Darwin Porter
As it appeared in the May 2016 edition of
Boomer Times Magazine

JAMES DEAN

THE "OTHER" (AFTER MARILYN MONROE AND JFK) MOST ENDURING ICON OF "THE AMERICAN CENTURY"

Fame is the most fickle of addictions. She's capricious when, with her magic wand, she bestows her recognition on just a select few.

During their respective eras, many people achieve greatness and a kind of short-term recognition, but in the long course of history, most are forgotten. Only a handful emerge, generations later, to re-capture the imagination of the world.

Cleopatra was not the greatest of the ancient pharaohs—her reign over Egypt was a disaster. But she immortalized herself through (highly politicized) affairs with both Julius Caesar and Marc Antony, then committed suicide with the poisonous bite of an asp as her empire crumbled around her. The drama, purported romance, and epic scope of her story prolonged the life of her legend.

Moving forward to the mid-20th Century: Despite the huge numbers of household names that emerged, only three of them became enduring pop culture icons: John F. Kennedy, Marilyn Monroe, and James Dean.

As most historians agree, JFK was not the greatest of presidents. Had he lived, he'd have become soiled by the quagmire of Vietnam and his sexual indiscretions, his reputation permanently tarnished.

Marilyn did not have a particularly distinguished career, either. Most of her early films are still unknown to the general public. But as a pop icon, she's remembered and in many cases, celebrated by each new generation. Her affairs with the Kennedy brothers, her controversial death, and perhaps her status as "the ultimate blonde" made her a legend.

Each of these three luminaries from "The American Century's" middle years—JFK, Marilyn, and Jimmy Dean—had one element in common: Each of them died young and violently, and each is forever associated with the implicitly tragic motto "Live fast, die young."

Had she lived, Marilyn might have evolved into an aging, blowsy showgirl, desperately clinging to her elusive glory and fast-fading sexual charms. As her last director, George Cukor said, with pointed irony, "Marilyn was not meant for old age."

In contrast, as the youngest of the three (he died when he was 24), Jimmy might have gone on to make some of the greatest movies in Hollywood. At the time of his death, he could have had virtually any role he wanted in Hollywood. He was big, and growing bigger by the day.

Through Blood Moon Productions, in honor of the 60th anniversary of James Dean's death (September 30, 1955), we just released the most complete overview of his unfulfilled life ever told. During the fifty years spent researching it, hundreds of witnesses, friends, "frenemies," and enemies, emerged with testimonials—many of them soaked with scandal—that have never been published before.

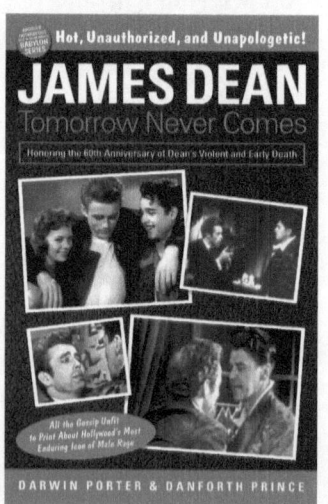

"I was fortunate to have known and worked in television with many of the key figures of his life, each with a story to tell," I related to my co-author, Danforth. "During the course of its compilation (I actually began it back in 1970), I managed to obtain at least three prolonged "deathbed" confessions from mentors who loved and/or nurtured him, and who no longer had careers to protect. Some of the greatest stars, both male and female, seduced him; others detested him. Whereas Marlene Dietrich held him in contempt; Gary Cooper treated him like a son. As actress Geraldine Page told me, 'No one ever knew the real James Dean because he only shared one small part of his life with each person, hugging the rest close to his breast.'"

Intense, handsome, vulnerable, and highly original, he mesmerized moviegoers and still does to this day. Each new generation reads into his legend their spin on what he symbolizes. Marlon Brando, to whom Jimmy was often compared, said, "Nothing fascinates the public as much as an unfinished life. All of us speculate what might have been in our own lives had we taken a different path."

*****

 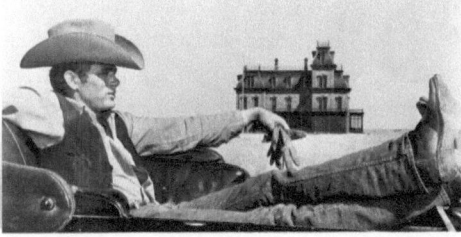

Publicity stills for James Dean with Elizabeth Taylor in *GIANT* (1956)

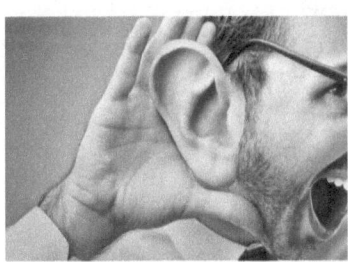

Media Buzz by Darwin Porter
Excerpt #4 of 4
As it appeared in the January 2018 edition of
Boomer Times Magazine

HEDY LAMARR
THE MOTHER OF THE CELLPHONE

The sultry, enigmatic brunette, Hedy Lamarr, during the dark days of World War II, was hailed as "the world's most beautiful woman."

What is far less known about her fabled life is that she was a world-class inventor, conjuring up an invention that helped revolutionize modern communications, earning her the label of "The Mother of the Cellphone." In 2014, she was posthumously inducted into the National Inventors Hall of Fame.

At last, her remarkable, almost unbelievable story is the subject of a movie, *Bombshell: The Hedy Lamarr Story*, playing in theaters across America this winter.

The review of the movie in *The New York Times* was headlined: "A Hollywood Beauty Who Helped Change the World."

Her story began in Vienna in 1914 when she was born on the eve of World War I, whose aftermath included the collapse of the Austro-Hungarian Empire. She had always wanted to be an actress, and by 1933, she appeared in Gustav Machaty's notorious film, *Ecstasy*, in which she was seen running nude in the woods. In that controversial, avant-garde film, she was also depicted in the throes of orgasm. (Machaty achieved the desired effect by sticking a pin into her).

She abandoned her career when she married Fritz Mandl, an Austrian arms merchant selling munitions to fuel the Nazi war machine. Ironically, both the sadistic Mandl and Hedy were Jewish.

During that loveless marriage, she entertained, and was entertained by, the elite hierarchies of the Fascist world. She found Hitler "an arrogant, dangerous *poseur*," and Mussolini "a pompous ass."

On a hunt for new talent in Europe, Louis B. Mayer discovered the divorced actress and signed her to an MGM contract, hoping to replace Greta Garbo, who would soon retire.

She became an overnight sensation after the release of *Algiers* (1938), starring Charles Boyer. Luminous, she was forever after associated with praise for her porcelain skin, her large, marbly eyes, her lilting Viennese accent, her Mona Lisa smile, and her aura of mystery. Throughout the course of the 1940s (the heyday of her film career), she seemed more like a celluloid mannequin than a natural woman.

Some of the era's most famous movie stars seduced her, including Errol Flynn, Charlie Chaplin, James Stewart, Robert Taylor, Stewart Granger, Victor Mature, William Powell, and John Garfield.

Along the way, she picked up five more husbands and had an affair with a young naval hero who had recently returned from the war in the Pacific. "John F. Kenney was charming, handsome, charismatic, and a real heartbreaker," she said.

As the century moved on, the U.S. government began to pay attention to her ground-breaking invention, which she'd created with the intent of doing something for the war effort. She had her own laboratory for inventions. Her lover, aviator Howard Hughes, lent her some of his top scientists. In return, she counseled him on plane design.

Her greatest achievement, with help from her friend, the *avant-garde* composer George Antheil, was a radio-controlled torpedo whose navigation systems could not be jammed.

Hedy's invention, which she patented in 1942, foiled attempts to sabotage its trajectory based on rapidly switching frequencies. The system it used for that incorporated "spread spectrums" which, years later, became the foundation for cellular phones and other wireless devices.

In the early 1960s, around the time of the U.S./Cuban missile confrontation, an updated version of Hedy's World War II invention was incorporated into all U.S. naval vessels.

As the years wore on, Hedy tried, unsuccessfully, to rescue her fading beauty with cosmetic surgeries. She and I had signed with the same literary agent, and to some degree, we shared the same circle of friends, and, as such, I visited her often during her retirement in Florida.

Often dazed and confused, she became involved in two shoplifting incidents. The first was in June of 1961 at the May Company Department Store in Los Angeles, where she walked out with gold slippers and various sundries. At the time, her purse contained $14,000 of undeposited checks.

The second shoplifting incident transpired in August of 1991 in Casselberry, Florida. Once again, she walked out with unpaid merchandise—in this case, $21.48 worth of laxative tablets and eyedrops. Eventually, both charges were dropped.

I found her a dear, tormented soul, obsessively sharing memories of a fabled life.

She died on January 19, 2000, age 85, in Altamonte Springs, Florida. Her son, Anthony Loder, flew with her ashes to Austria and tossed them into the winds rustling through the Vienna Woods. She left a $3.5 million estate.

Today, anywhere you go in America, you can see people with cellphones, yet except for Baby Boomers, most of these people have never heard of the mother of that remarkable invention.

As Hedy once told me, "A woman can be beautiful and still have a brain."

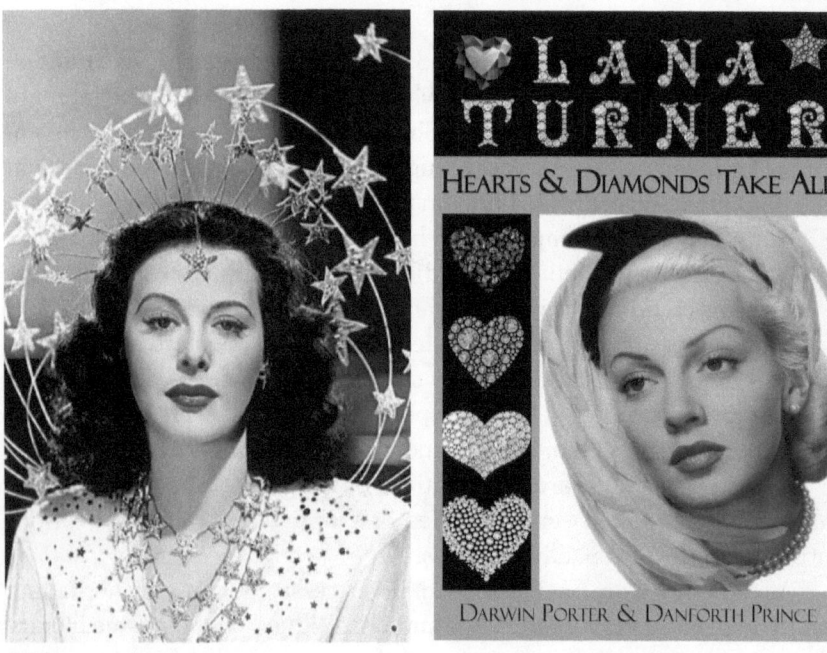

HEDY

LANA

HEDY LAMARR...Rivaled only by **LANA TURNER**, whose biography Darwin wrote and which Blood Moon published in 2017, she was
THE ULTIMATE MOVIE STAR.

Postscript from the Edge

In Honor of the Author of

Catch a Falling Star: Untold Tales of Celebrity Secrets

JOHN COHAN

A friend of Blood Moon and a noted celebrity psychic, John Cohan has contributed greatly to our biographies of the stars.

In Hollywood, he was known as "The Celebrity Psychic to the Stars," and his predictions appear annually in Cindy Adams' column in *The New York Post*.

Over the years, many in show-biz have turned to him for insights during some crisis they might be having and for guidance for their futures. Some of his most famous clients have included Elvis Presley, Elizabeth Taylor, along with the likes of Merv Griffin, Burt Reynolds, Lana Turner, Rock Hudson, and *Playboy's* Hugh Hefner. Cohan played a special role in the life of Sandra Dee, whom he defines as having been "The Love of My Life."

Even the indomitable Joan Crawford was John's client for many years.

John Cohan is a friend of Magnolia House

"John is a great man to know during one's darkest hours," said Danforth Prince. "He's kind, he's generous, he's deeply spiritual, he has valuable insights into the agonies of 'the celebrity experience,' and he's an emotionally intelligent and very positive guiding force for anyone barging a path through the insecurities and doubts of a career in show-biz."

In a memoir, Cohan once wrote: "My gift is something that has been with me since I was born. Most of my adolescence, I spent time and energy ignoring or suppressing my psychic ability, because I didn't know what it was that possessed me. Finally, I did grasp hold of it and actually embraced my talent."

Many of Cohan's insights and revelations have been published in *Catch a Falling Star,* an overview of his life as a psychic. It's filled with startling revelations.

As a close friend of Nicole Brown Simpson, he reveals the compelling truth about who really killed her. He also offers insights about the last moments in the troubled life of Natalie Wood, who drowned under mysterious circumstances off the coast of Catalina Island.

He also writes eloquently about the secrets of both John F. Kennedy, Jr., and Burt Reynolds, who died in 2018 amid a mass of humiliations and self-recriminations at the age of 82 in Florida.

Cohan warns clients to expect possible disappointment but not disillusionment in marriage or love relationships. "I've been disappointed but never pessimistic. True love is the one infallible shield against all the ugly and harsh things in the world. Once you find it, hold onto it and cherish it carefully, forever."

John has been a most welcome guest at Magnolia House.

AUTHORS OF THIS BOOK & CARETAKERS
OF THIS HOUSE INCLUDE:

DARWIN PORTER

As an intense nine-year-old, **Darwin Porter** began meeting movie stars, TV personalities, politicians, and singers through his vivacious and attractive mother, Hazel, an eccentric but charismatic Southern girl who had lost her husband in World War II. Migrating from the Depression-ravaged valleys of western North Carolina to Miami Beach during its most ebullient heyday, Hazel became a stylist, wardrobe mistress, and personal assistant to the vaudeville *comedienne* **Sophie Tucker**, the bawdy and irrepressible "Last of the Red Hot Mamas."

Virtually every show-biz celebrity who visited Miami Beach paid a call on "Miss Sophie," and Darwin, as a pre-teen loosely and indulgently supervised by his mother, was regularly dazzled by the likes of **Judy Garland, Dinah Shore,** and **Frank Sinatra.**

It was at Miss Sophie's that he met his first political figure, who was actually an actor at the time. Between marriages, **Ronald Reagan** came to call on Ms. Sophie, who was his favorite singer. He was accompanied by a young blonde starlet, **Marilyn Monroe.**

At the University of Miami, Darwin edited the school newspaper. He first met and interviewed **Eleanor Roosevelt** at the Fontainebleau Hotel on Miami Beach and invited her to spend a day at the university. She accepted, much to his delight.

After graduation, he became the Bureau Chief of *The Miami Herald* in Key West, Florida, where he got to take early morning walks with the former U.S. president **Harry S Truman**, discussing his presidency and the events that had shaped it.

Through Truman, Darwin was introduced and later joined the staff of **Senator George Smathers** of Florida. His best friend was a young senator, **John F. Kennedy.** Through "Gorgeous George," as Smathers was known in the Senate, Darwin got to meet Jack and Jacqueline in Palm Beach. He later wrote two books about them—*The Kennedys, All the Gossip Unfit to Print,* and one of his all-time bestsellers, *Jacqueline Kennedy Onassis—A Life Beyond Her Wildest Dreams.*

For about a decade in New York, Darwin worked in television journalism and advertising with his long-time partner, the journalist, art director, and arts-industry socialite **Stanley Mills Haggart**.

Stanley (as an art director) and Darwin (as a writer and assistant), worked as freelance agents in television. Jointly, they helped produce TV commercials that included testimonials from **Joan Crawford** (then feverishly promoting Pepsi-Cola); **Ronald Reagan** (General Electric); and **Debbie Reynolds** (Singer sewing machines). Other personalities appearing and delivering televised sales pitches included **Louis Armstrong, Lena Horne,** and **Arlene Dahl,** each of them hawking a commercial product.

Beginning in the early 1960s, Darwin joined forces with the then-fledgling **Arthur Frommer** organization, playing a key role in researching and writing more than 50 titles and defining the style and values that later emerged as the world's leading travel guidebooks, *The Frommer Guides,* with particular emphasis on Europe, New England, and the Caribbean. Between the creation and updating of hundreds of editions of detailed travel guides to England, France, Italy, Spain, Portugal, Austria, Hungary, Germany, Switzerland, the Caribbean, and California, he continued to interview and discuss the triumphs, feuds, and frustrations of celebrities, many by then reclusive, whom he either sought out or encountered randomly as part of his extensive travels. **Ava Gardner, Debbie Reynolds,** and **Lana Turner** were particularly insightful.

It was while living in New York that Darwin became fascinated by the career of a rising real estate mogul changing the skyline of Manhattan. He later, of course, became the "gambling czar" of Atlantic City and a star of reality TV.

Darwin began collecting an astonishing amount of data on Donald Trump, squirreling it away in boxes, hoping one day to write a biography of this charismatic, controversial figure.

Before doing that, he penned more than thirty-five uncensored, unvarnished, and unauthorized biographies on subjects that included **Playboy's Hugh Hefner, Debbie Reynolds and Carrie Fisher, Donald Trump, Bill and Hillary Clinton, Ronald Reagan and Nancy Davis, Jane Wyman, Jacqueline Kennedy, John F. Kennedy, Lana Turner, Peter O'Toole, James Dean, Marlon Brando, Merv Griffin, Katharine Hepburn, Howard Hughes, Humphrey Bogart, Michael Jackson, Paul Newman, Steve McQueen, Marilyn Monroe, Elizabeth Taylor, Rock Hudson, Frank Sinatra, Vivien Leigh, Laurence Olivier, the notorious porn star Linda Lovelace, Zsa Zsa Gabor and her sisters, Eva and Magda, Tennessee Williams, Gore Vidal,** and **Truman Capote.**

As a departure from his usual repertoire, Darwin also wrote the controversial *J. Edgar Hoover & Clyde Tolson: Investigating the Sexual Secrets of America's Most Famous Men and Women,* a book about celebrity, voyeurism, political and sexual repression, and blackmail within the highest circles of the U.S. government.

Porter's biographies, over the years, have won thirty first prize or "runner-up to first prize" awards at literary festivals in cities or states which include New England, New York, Los Angeles, Hollywood, San Francisco, Florida, California, and Paris.

Darwin can be heard at regular intervals as a radio and television commentator, "dishing" celebrities, pop culture, politics, and scandal.

A resident of New York City, Darwin's latest work is on a startling new biography of Kirk Douglas: *More Is Never Enough.*

DANFORTH PRINCE

Danforth Prince is president and founder of Blood Moon Productions, a publishing venture that's devoted to salvaging, compiling, and marketing the oral histories of America's entertainment industry.

Prince launched his career in journalism in the 1970s at the Paris Bureau of *The New York Times*. In the early '80s, he joined Darwin Porter in developing first editions of many of the titles within *The Frommer Guides*. Together, they reviewed and articulated the travel scenes of more than 50 nations, most of them within Europe and The Caribbean. Authoritative and comprehensive, they became best-selling "travel bibles" for millions of readers.

Prince, in collaboration with Porter, is also the co-author of several award-winning celebrity biographies, each configured as a title within **Blood Moon's Babylon series.** These have included *Hollywood Babylon—It's Back!; Hollywood Babylon Strikes Again; The Kennedys: All the Gossip Unfit to Print; Frank Sinatra, The Boudoir Singer, Elizabeth Taylor: There Is Nothing Like a Dame; Pink Triangle: The Feuds and Private Lives of Tennessee Williams, Gore Vidal, Truman Capote, and Members of their Entourages*; and *Jacqueline Kennedy Onassis: A Life Beyond Her Wildest Dreams.* More recent efforts include *Lana Turner, Hearts and Diamonds Take All; Peter O'Toole—Hellraiser, Sexual Outlaw, Irish Rebel; Bill & Hillary—So This Is That Thing Called Love; James Dean, Tomorrow Never Comes; Rock Hudson Erotic Fire; Carrie Fisher and Debbie Reynolds, Princess Leia & Unsinkable Tammy in Hell*, and *Playboy's Hugh Hefner, Empire of Skin*.

One of his recent projects, co-authored with Darwin Porter, is *Donald Trump, The Man Who Would Be King*. Configured for release directly into the frenzy of the 2016 presidential elections, and winner of at least three literary awards at book festivals in New York, California, and Florida. It's a celebrity *exposé* of the decades of pre-presidential scandals—personal, political, and dynastic—associated with **Donald Trump** during the rambunctious decades when no one ever thought he'd actually get elected.

Prince is also the co-author of four books on film criticism, three of which won honors at regional bookfests in Los Angeles and San Francisco.

Prince, a graduate of Hamilton College and a native of Easton and Bethlehem, Pennsylvania, is the president and founder of the Georgia Literary Association (1996), and of the Porter and Prince Corporation (1983) which has produced dozens of titles for Simon & Schuster, Prentice Hall, and John Wiley & Sons. In 2011, he was named "Publisher of the Year" by a consortium of literary critics and marketers spearheaded by the J.M. Northern Media Group.

He has electronically documented some of the controversies associated with his stewardship of Blood Moon in at least 50 documentaries, book trailers, public speeches, and TV or radio interviews. Most of these are available on **YouTube.com** and **Facebook** *(keyword: "Danforth Prince")*; on **Twitter** *(#BloodyandLunar);* or by clicking on **BloodMoonProductions.com**.

His latest bio is devoted to the last remaining male icon of Hollywood's Golden Age, **Kirk Douglas**.

Do you want to meet him up close, personal, and at home? Prince is also an innkeeper, running a historic bed & breakfast in New York City, **Magnolia House (www.MagnoliaHouseSaintGeorge.com)**. Affiliated with AirBnb, and increasingly sought out by filmmakers as an evocative locale for moviemaking, it lies in the fast-gentrified neighborhood of St. George, at the northern tip of Staten Island, a district that's historically associated with Henry James, Theodore Dreiser, the Vanderbilts, and key moments in America's colonial history.

Set in a large, elaborately terraced garden, and boasting a history of visits from literary and show-biz stars who have included Tennessee Williams, Gloria Swanson, Jolie Gabor, Ruth Warwick, Greta Keller, Lucille Lortel, and many of the luminaries of Broadway, the inn is within a ten-minute walk to the ferries sailing at 20- to 30-minute intervals to Lower Manhattan.

Publicized as "a reasonably priced celebrity-centric retreat with links to the book trades," and the beneficiary of rave ("superhost") reviews from hundreds of previous clients, **Magnolia House** is loaded with furniture and memorabilia that Prince collected during his decades as a travel journalist for the Frommer Guides.

Stay with Us! Learn more about "Celebrity-Centric Sleepovers" at Blood Moon's **Magnolia House**, a historic and moderately priced "Airbnb" in New York City.

For more information about the hospitality that's waiting for you in NYC at the Bed and Breakfast affiliate of Blood Moon Productions, click on
MagnoliaHouseSaintGeorge.com

*If You Want to Meet the Authors of this Book,
Consider a Sleepover at their Headquarters in New York City.*

Magnolia House

Our publishing operation lies immediately upstairs from a reasonably priced, widely reviewed "AirBnB" in New York City. Elegant, historic, well-furnished, comfortable, and loaded with memorabilia from years in the book trades, it's an architectural and literary landmark in St. George, Staten Island, a ten-minute walk from the departure point of the famous ferryboats to Manhattan.

As stated by its co-owner and resident manager, **Danforth Prince**, "Magnolia House results from my 30-year role as co-author of many titles, and many editions, of *The Frommer Guides*, each of which included evaluations of the bed and breakfast inns of Europe. Whereas I'm still writing travel articles and celebrity *exposés* from the upper floors of this building, most of it now operates as a celebrity-centric AirBnb with links to the early days of the Frommer Guides, 'the Golden Age of Travel,' and Blood Moon's associations with Broadway, Hollywood, and the Entertainment Industry. The next time you visit New York City, say hello and COME STAY WITH US!"

Edgy media associations have always been part of the Magnolia House experience. Previous guests have included **Tennessee Williams** (*"Magnolia House reminds me of Blanche DuBois' lost plantation, Bellereve!"*); golden age film personality **Joan Blondell** (a close friend of celebrity biographer and co-owner, **Darwin Porter**); **Lucille Lortel** (the philanthropic but very temperamental Queen of Off-Broadway); the very outspoken **Jolie Gabor** (mother of the three "Bombshells from Budapest," **Zsa Zsa, Eva, and Magda**); and a host of other stars, *starlettes, demi-mondains* and hellraisers of all descriptions and persuasions.

For photographs, testimonials from previous guests, and more information , click on
www.MagnoliaHouseSaintGeorge.com.

 Magnolia House is the historic landmark in NYC where Blood Moon researches, writes, & publishes its award-winning entertainment about how America interprets its celebrities.

It's a mixture of the Old South with film noir and European hospitality, and it collaborates with AirBnB. It's New York City's only Magnolia-scented Bed & Breakfast.
MagnoliaHouseSaintGeorge.com
Come for the night and stay for breakfast! It's show-biz, dahling...

COMING SOON FROM BLOOD MOON PRODUCTIONS
AT MAGNOLIA HOUSE

KIRK DOUGLAS

Of the many male stars of Golden Age Hollywood, Kirk Douglas became the final survivor, the last icon of a fabled, optimistic era that the world will never see again. When he celebrated his birthday in 2016, a headline read— LEGENDARY HOLLYWOOD HORNDOG TURNS 100.

He was both a charismatic actor and a man of uncommon force and vigor. His restless and volcanic spirit is reflected both in his films and through his many sexual conquests.

Douglas was the son of Russian-Jewish immigrants, his father a collector and seller of rags. After service in the Navy during World War II, he hit Hollywood, oozing masculinity and charm. Conquering Tinseltown and bedding its leading ladies, he became the personification of the American dream, moving from obscurity and (literally) rags to riches and major-league fame.

En route to his status as a myth and legend, his performances reflected both his personal pain and the brutalization of the characters he played. In *Champion* (1949), he was beaten to a fatal bloody pulp. As the sleazy, heartless reporter in *Ace in the Hole* (1951), he was stabbed with a knife in his gut. As Van Gogh in *Lust for Life* (1956), he writhed in emotional agony and unrequited love before slicing off his ear with a razor. His World War I movie, *Paths of Glory* (1957) grows more profound over the years. He lost an eye in *The Vikings* (1958), and, as the Thracian slave leading a revolt against Roman legions in *Spartacus* (1960), he was crucified.

All of this is brought out, with photos, in this remarkable testimonial to the last hero of Hollywood's cinematic and swashbuckling Golden Age, an inspiring testimonial to the values and core beliefs of an America that's Gone With the Wind, yet lovingly remembered as a time when it, in many ways, was truly great.

KIRK DOUGLAS: More Is Never Enough

By Darwin Porter and Danforth Prince

Biography/Entertainment & Performing Arts
624 pages, 150 B/W photos. 6x9, $34.95
978-1-936003-61-7
Available everywhere, worldwide, in APRIL 2019

www.BloodMoonProductions.com

SCARLETT O'HARA,

Desperately in Love with Heathcliff,

Together on the Road to Hell

Here, for the first time, is a biography that raises the curtain on the secret lives of **Lord Laurence Olivier**, often cited as the finest actor in the history of England, and **Vivien Leigh,** who immortalized herself with her Oscar-winning portrayals of Scarlett O'Hara in *Gone With the Wind,* and as Blanche DuBois in Tennessee Williams' *A Streetcar Named Desire.*

Dashing and "impossibly handsome," Laurence Olivier was pursued by the most dazzling luminaries, male and female, of the movie and theater worlds.

Lord Olivier's beautiful and brilliant but emotionally disturbed wife (Viv to her lovers) led a tumultuous off-the-record life whose paramours ranged from the A-list celebrities to men she selected randomly off the street. But none of the brilliant roles depicted by Lord and Lady Olivier, on stage or on screen, ever matched the power and drama of personal dramas which wavered between Wagnerian opera and Greek tragedy. *Damn You, Scarlett O'Hara* is the definitive and most revelatory portrait ever published of the most talented and tormented actor and actress of the 20th century.

Darwin Porter is the principal author of this seminal work.

"The folks over at TMZ would have had a field day tracking Laurence Olivier and Vivien Leigh with flip cameras in hand. **Damn You, Scarlett O'Hara** *can be a dazzling read, the prose unmannered and instantly digestible. The authors' ability to pile scandal atop scandal, seduction after seduction, can be impossible to resist."*

—THE WASHINGTON TIMES

DAMN YOU, SCARLETT O'HARA
The Private Lifes of Laurence Olivier and Vivien Leigh

Darwin Porter and Roy Moseley

Winner of four distinguished literary awards, this is the best biography of Vivien Leigh and Laurence Olivier ever published, with hundreds of insights into the London Theatre, the role of the Oliviers in the politics of World War II, and the passion, fury, and frustration of their lives together as actors in the West End, on Broadway, and in Hollywood.

ISBN 978-1-936003-15-0   Hardcover, 708 pages, with about a hundred photos.

PINK TRIANGLE

The Feuds and Private Lives of
TENNESSEE WILLIAMS, GORE VIDAL, & TRUMAN CAPOTE

Darwin Porter & Danforth Prince

This book, the only one of its kind, reveals the backlot intrigues associated with the literary and script-writing *enfants terribles* of America's entertainment community during the mid-20th century.

It exposes their bitchfests, their slugfests, and their relationships with the *glitterati*—Marilyn Monroe, Brando, the Oliviers, the Paleys, U.S. Presidents, a gaggle of other movie stars, millionaires, and international *débauchés*.

This is for anyone who's interested in the formerly concealed scandals of Hollywood and Broadway, and the values and pretentions of both the literary community and the entertainment industry.

"A banquet... If PINK TRIANGLE had not been written for us, we would have had to research and type it all up for ourselves...Pink Triangle is nearly seven hundred pages of the most entertaining histrionics ever sliced, spiced, heated, and serviced up to the reading public. Everything that Blood Moon has done before pales in comparison.
Given the fact that the subjects of the book themselves were nearly delusional on the subject of themselves (to say nothing of each other) it is hard to find fault. Add to this the intertwined jungle that was the relationship among Williams, Capote, and Vidal, of the times they vied for things they loved most—especially attention—and the times they enthralled each other and the world, [Pink Triangle is] the perfect antidote to the Polar Vortex."

—**Vinton McCabe in the NY JOURNAL OF BOOKS**

"Full disclosure: I have been a friend and follower of Blood Moon Productions' tomes for years, and always marveled at the amount of information in their books—it's staggering. The index alone to Pink Triangle runs to 21 pages—and the scale of names in it runs like a Who's Who of American social, cultural and political life through much of the 20th century."

—**Perry Brass in THE HUFFINGTON POST**

"We Brits are not spared the Porter/Prince silken lash either. PINK TRIANGLE's research is, quite frankly, breathtaking. PINK TRIANGLE will fascinate you for many weeks to come. Once you have made the initial titillating dip, the day will seem dull without it."

—**Jeffery Tayor in THE SUNDAY EXPRESS (UK)**

PINK TRIANGLE—*The Feuds and Private Lives of Tennessee Williams, Gore Vidal, Truman Capote, and Famous Members of their Entourages*
Darwin Porter & Danforth Prince
Softcover, 700 pages, with photos   ISBN 978-1-936003-37-2   Also Available for E-Readers

ROCK HUDSON EROTIC FIRE

Another tragic, myth-shattering, & uncensored tale about America's obsession with celebrities, from Blood Moon Productions.

In the dying days of Hollywood's Golden Age, Rock Hudson was the most celebrated phallic symbol and lust object in America. This book describes his rise and fall, and the Entertainment Industry that created him.

Rock Hudson charmed every casting director in Hollywood (and movie-goers throughout America) as the mega-star they most wanted to share PILLOW TALK with. This book describes his rise and fall, and how he handled himself as a closeted but promiscuous bisexual during an age when EVERYBODY tried to throw him onto a casting couch.

Based on dozens of face-to-face interviews with the actor's friends, co-conspirators, and enemies, and researched over a period of a half century, this biography reveals the shame, agonies, and irony of Rock Hudson's complete, never-before-told story.

In 2017, the year of its release, it was designated as winner ("BEST BIOGRAPHY") at two of the Golden State's most prestigious literary competitions, the Northern California and the Southern California Book Festivals.

It was also favorably reviewed by the *Midwestern Book Review, California Book Watch, KNEWS RADIO,* the *New York Journal of Books,* and the editors at the most popular Seniors' magazine in Florida, *BOOMER TIMES.*

Rock Hudson Erotic Fire

Darwin Porter & Danforth Prince
Another Outrageous Title in Blood Moon's Babylon Series

ROCK HUDSON EROTIC FIRE
By Darwin Porter & Danforth Prince
Softcover, 624 pages, with dozens of photos, 6" x 9"
ISBN 978-1-936003-55-6

> NEW FROM BLOOD MOON: THE COMPREHEN-
> SIVE, UNAUTHORIZED EXPOSÉ EVERY PLAYBOY
> AND EVERY PLAYMATE WILL WANT TO READ

Hugh Hefner, the most iconic Playboy in human history, was a visionary, an empire-builder, and a pajama-clad pipe-smoker with a pre-coital grin.

In 1953, he published his first edition of *Playboy* with money borrowed from his puritanical, Nebraska-born mother. Marilyn Monroe appeared on the cover, with her nude calendar inside.

Rebelling against his strict upbringing, he lost his virginity at the age of 22.

Playboy, punctuated with nudes and studded with articles by major literary figures, reached its zenith at eight million readers. As a "tasteful pornographer," Hef became a cultural warrior, fighting government censorship all the way to the U.S. Supreme Court. As the years and his notoriety progressed, he became an advocate of abortion, LGBT equality, and the legalization of pot. Eventually, he engaged in "pubic wars" with Bob Guccione, the flamboyant founder of *Penthouse*, which cut into Hef's sales.

Lauded by millions of avid readers, he was denounced as "the father of sex addiction," "a huckster," "a lecherous low-brow feeder of our vices," "a misogynist," and, near the end of his life, "a symbol of priapic senility."

During his heyday, some of the biggest male stars in Hollywood, including Warren Beatty, Sammy Davis, Jr., Mick Jagger, and Jack Nicholson, came to frolic behind Hef's guarded walls, stripping nude in the hot tub grotto before sampling the rotating beds upstairs. Even a future U.S. president came to call. "Donald Trump had an appreciation of Bunny tail," Hef said.

Hefner's last Viagra-fueled marriage was to a beautiful blonde, Crystal Harris, 60 years his junior. "There's nothing wrong in a man marrying a girl who could be his great-granddaughter," he was famously quoted as saying.

This ground-breaking biography, the latest in Blood Moon's string of outrageously unvarnished mythbusters, will be the first published since Hefner's death at the age of 91 in 2017. It's a provocative saga, rich in tantalizing, often shocking detail. Not recommended for the sanctimonious or the faint of heart, it's available for sale everywhere, now.

> *PLAYBOY'S HUGH HEFNER, EMPIRE OF SKIN,*
> by Darwin Porter and Danforth Prince, 978-1-936003-59-4